PART THREE
* THE *
NEW-ENGLAND
TRAGEDIES

DRAMATIS PERSONÆ.

JOHN ENDICOTT . . . . Governor.
JOHN ENDICOTT . . . . His son.
RICHARD BELLINGHAM . . . . Deputy Governor.
JOHN NORTON . . . . Minister of the Gospel.
EDWARD BUTTER . . . . Treasurer.
WALTER MERRY . . . . Tithing-man.
NICHOLAS UPSALL . . . . An old citizen.
SAMUEL COLE . . . . Landlord of the Three Mariners.
SIMON KEMPTHORN }
RALPH GOLDSMITH } . . . . Sea-captains.
WENLOCK CHRISTISON }
EDITH, *his daughter* } . . . . Quakers.
EDWARD WHARTON }

Assistants, Halberdiers, Marshal, etc.

The Scene is in Boston in the year 1665.

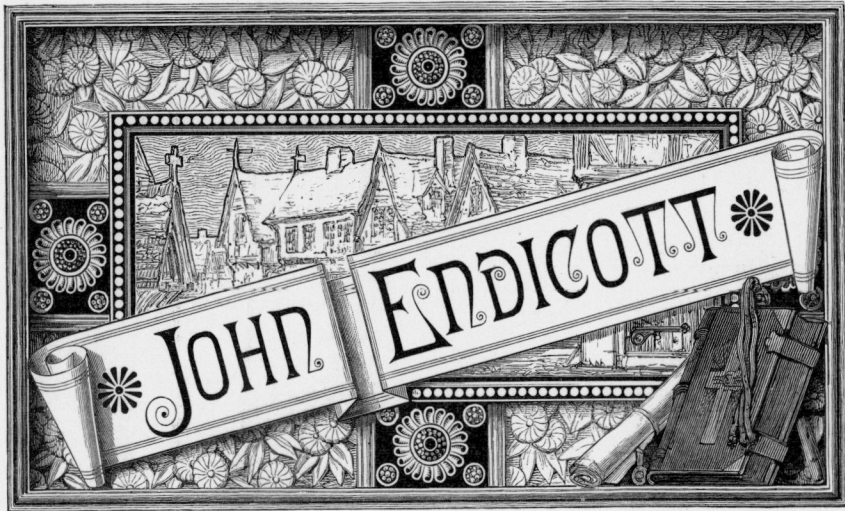

PROLOGUE.

To-night we strive to read, as we may best,
This city, like an ancient palimpsest;
And bring to light, upon the blotted page,
The mournful record of an earlier age,
That, pale and half effaced, lies hidden away
Beneath the fresher writing of to-day.

Rise, then, O buried city that hast been;
Rise up, rebuilded in the painted scene,
And let our curious eyes behold once more
The pointed gable and the pent-house door,
The Meeting-house with leaden-latticed panes,
The narrow thoroughfares, the crooked lanes!

Rise, too, ye shapes and shadows of the
        Past,
Rise from your long-forgotten graves at last;
Let us behold your faces, let us hear
The words ye uttered in those days of fear!
Revisit your familiar haunts again, —
The scenes of triumph, and the scenes of pain,
And leave the footprints of your bleeding feet
Once more upon the pavement of the street!

Nor let the Historian blame the Poet here,
If he perchance misdate the day or year,
And group events together, by his art,
That in the Chronicles lie far apart;
For as the double stars, though sundered far,

Seem to the naked eye a single star,
So facts of history, at a distance seen,
Into one common point of light convene.

"Why touch upon such themes?" perhaps
        some friend
May ask, incredulous; "and to what good end?
Why drag again into the light of day
The errors of an age long passed away?"
I answer: "For the lesson that they teach;
The tolerance of opinion and of speech.
Hope, Faith, and Charity remain, — these
        three;
And greatest of them all is Charity."

Let us remember, if these words be true,
That unto all men Charity is due;
Give what we ask; and pity, while we blame,
Lest we become copartners in the shame,
Lest we condemn, and yet ourselves partake,
And persecute the dead for conscience' sake.

Therefore it is the author seeks and strives
To represent the dead as in their lives,
And lets at times his characters unfold
Their thoughts in their own language, strong
        and bold;
He only asks of you to do the like;
To hear him first, and, if you will, then strike.

ACT I.

SCENE I. — *Sunday afternoon. The interior of the Meeting-house. On the pulpit, an hour-glass; below, a box for contributions.* JOHN NORTON *in the pulpit.* GOVERNOR ENDICOTT *in a canopied seat, attended by four halberdiers. The congregation singing.*

> THE LORD descended from above,
>   And bowed the heavens high;
> And underneath his feet He cast
>   The darkness of the sky.
>
> On Cherubim and Seraphim
>   Right royally He rode,
> And on the wings of mighty winds
>   Came flying all abroad.

NORTON (*rising and turning the hour-glass on the pulpit*).

I heard a great voice from the temple saying
Unto the Seven Angels, Go your ways;
Pour out the vials of the wrath of God
Upon the earth. And the First Angel went
And poured his vial on the earth; and straight
There fell a noisome and a grievous sore
On them which had the birth-mark of the
        Beast,
And them which worshipped and adored his
        image.
On us hath fallen this grievous pestilence.
There is a sense of terror in the air;
And apparitions of things horrible
Are seen by many. From the sky above us
The stars fall; and beneath us the earth
        quakes!
The sound of drums at midnight from afar,
The sound of horsemen riding to and fro,
As if the gates of the invisible world
Were opened, and the dead came forth to warn
        us, —
All these are omens of some dire disaster
Impending over us, and soon to fall.
Moreover, in the language of the Prophet,
Death is again come up into our windows,
To cut off little children from without,
And young men from the streets. And in the
        midst
Of all these supernatural threats and warnings
Doth Heresy uplift its horrid head;
A vision of Sin more awful and appalling
Than any phantasm, ghost, or apparition,

As arguing and portending some enlargement
Of the mysterious Power of Darkness!

EDITH, *barefooted, and clad in sackcloth, with her hair hanging loose upon her shoulders, walks slowly up the aisle, followed by* WHARTON *and other Quakers. The congregation starts up in confusion.*

EDITH (*to* NORTON, *raising her hand*).

                                        Peace!

NORTON.

Anathema maranatha! The Lord cometh!

EDITH.

Yea, verily He cometh, and shall judge
The shepherds of Israel, who do feed them-
    selves,
And leave their flocks to eat what they have
    trodden
Beneath their feet.

NORTON.

                Be silent, babbling woman!
St. Paul commands all women to keep silence
Within the churches.

EDITH.

                Yet the women prayed
And prophesied at Corinth in his day;
And, among those on whom the fiery tongues
Of Pentecost descended, some were women!

NORTON.

The Elders of the Churches, by our law,
Alone have power to open the doors of speech
And silence in the Assembly. I command you!

EDITH.

The law of God is greater than your laws!
Ye build your church with blood, your town
    with crime;
The heads thereof give judgment for reward;
The priests thereof teach only for their hire;
Your laws condemn the innocent to death;
And against this I bear my testimony!

NORTON.

What testimony?

EDITH.

                That of the Holy Spirit,
Which, as your Calvin says, surpasseth reason.

NORTON.

The laborer is worthy of his hire.

EDITH.

Yet our great Master did not teach for hire,
And the Apostles without purse or scrip
Went forth to do his work. Behold this box
Beneath thy pulpit. Is it for the poor?
Thou canst not answer. It is for the Priest;
And against this I bear my testimony.

NORTON.

Away with all these Heretics and Quakers!
Quakers, forsooth! Because a quaking fell
On Daniel, at beholding of the Vision,
Must ye needs shake and quake? Because
    Isaiah
Went stripped and barefoot, must ye wail and
    howl?
Must ye go stripped and naked? must ye make
A wailing like the dragons, and a mourning
As of the owls? Ye verify the adage
That Satan is God's ape! Away with them!

Tumult. The Quakers are driven out with violence, EDITH
following slowly. The congregation retires in confu-
sion.

Thus freely do the Reprobates commit
Such measure of iniquity as fits them
For the intended measure of God's wrath,
And even in violating God's commands
Are they fulfilling the divine decree!
The will of man is but an instrument
Disposed and predetermined to its action
According unto the decree of God,
Being as much subordinate thereto
As is the axe unto the hewer's hand!

He descends from the pulpit, and joins GOVERNOR ENDI-
COTT, *who comes forward to meet him.*

The omens and the wonders of the time,
Famine, and fire, and shipwreck, and disease,
The blast of corn, the death of our young men,
Our sufferings in all precious, pleasant things,
Are manifestations of the wrath divine,
Signs of God's controversy with New Eng-
    land.
These emissaries of the Evil One,
These servants and ambassadors of Satan,
Are but commissioned executioners
Of God's vindictive and deserved displeasure.
We must receive them as the Roman Bishop
Once received Attila, saying, I rejoice
You have come safe, whom I esteem to be
The scourge of God, sent to chastise his
    people.
This very heresy, perchance, may serve
The purposes of God to some good end.
With you I leave it; but do not neglect
The holy tactics of the civil sword.

ENDICOTT.

And what more can be done?

NORTON.

                    The hand that cut
The Red Cross from the colors of the king
Can cut the red heart from this heresy.
Fear not. All blasphemies immediate
And heresies turbulent must be suppressed
By civil power.

ENDICOTT.

    But in what way suppressed?

NORTON.

The Book of Deuteronomy declares
That if thy son, thy daughter, or thy wife,
Ay, or the friend which is as thine own soul,
Entice thee secretly, and say to thee,
Let us serve other gods, then shall thine eye
Not pity him, but thou shalt surely kill him,
And thine own hand shall be the first upon him
To slay him.

ENDICOTT.

        Four already have been slain ;
And others banished upon pain of death.
But they come back again to meet their
    doom,
Bringing the linen for their winding-sheets.
We must not go too far. In truth, I shrink
From shedding of more blood. The people
    murmur
At our severity.

NORTON.

            Then let them murmur !
Truth is relentless ; justice never wavers ;
The greatest firmness is the greatest mercy ;
The noble order of the Magistracy
Cometh immediately from God, and yet
This noble order of the Magistracy
Is by these Heretics despised and out-
    raged.

ENDICOTT.

To-night they sleep in prison. If they die,
They cannot say that we have caused their
    death.
We do but guard the passage, with the sword
Pointed towards them; if they dash upon it,
Their blood will be on their own heads, not
    ours.

NORTON.

Enough. I ask no more. My predecessor
Coped only with the milder heresies
Of Antinomians and of Anabaptists.
He was not born to wrestle with these fiends.
Chrysostom in his pulpit; Augustine
In disputation; Timothy in his house!
The lantern of St. Botolph's ceased to burn
When from the portals of that church he came
To be a burning and a shining light
Here in the wilderness. And, as he lay
On his death-bed, he saw me in a vision
Ride on a snow-white horse into this town.
His vision was prophetic; thus I came,
A terror to the impenitent, and Death
On the pale horse of the Apocalypse
To all the accursed race of Heretics!

                                    [*Exeunt.*

SCENE II. — *A street. On one side,* NICHOLAS UPSALL'S
    house; on the other, WALTER MERRY'S, *with a flock
    of pigeons on the roof.* UPSALL *seated in the porch of
    his house.*

UPSALL.

O DAY of rest! How beautiful, how fair,
How welcome to the weary and the old!
Day of the Lord! and truce to earthly cares!
Day of the Lord, as all our days should be!
Ah, why will man by his austerities
Shut out the blessed sunshine and the light,
And make of thee a dungeon of despair!

WALTER MERRY (*entering, and looking round him*).

All silent as a graveyard! No one stirring;
No footfall in the street, no sound of voices!
By righteous punishment and perseverance,
And perseverance in that punishment,
At last I 've brought this contumacious town
To strict observance of the Sabbath day.
Those wanton gospellers, the pigeons yonder,
Are now the only Sabbath-breakers left.

I cannot put them down. As if to taunt
    me,
They gather every Sabbath afternoon
In noisy congregation on my roof,
Billing and cooing. Whir! take that, ye
    Quakers.
        Throws a stone at the pigeons. Sees UPSALL.
Ah! Master Nicholas!

UPSALL.

                    Good afternoon,
Dear neighbor Walter.

MERRY.

                    Master Nicholas,
You have to-day withdrawn yourself from
    meeting.

UPSALL.

Yea, I have chosen rather to worship God
Sitting in silence here at my own door.

MERRY.

Worship the Devil! You this day have
    broken
Three of our strictest laws. First, by ab-
    staining
From public worship. Secondly, by walking
Profanely on the Sabbath.

UPSALL.

                    Not one step.
I have been sitting still here, seeing the
    pigeons
Feed in the street and fly about the roofs.

MERRY.

You have been in the street with other intent
Than going to and from the Meeting-house.
And, thirdly, you are harboring Quakers here.
I am amazed!

UPSALL.

            Men sometimes, it is said,
Entertain angels unawares.

MERRY.

                    Nice angels!
Angels in broad-brimmed hats and russet
    cloaks,

The color of the Devil's nutting-bag! They
    came
Into the Meeting-house this afternoon
More in the shape of devils than of angels.
The women screamed and fainted ; and the
    boys
Made such an uproar in the gallery
I could not keep them quiet.

UPSALL.

             Neighbor Walter,
Your persecution is of no avail.

MERRY.

'T is prosecution, as the Governor says,
Not persecution.

UPSALL.

           Well, your prosecution ;
Your hangings do no good.

MERRY.

               The reason is,
We do not hang enough. But, mark my
    words,
We 'll scour them ; yea, I warrant ye, we 'll
    scour them !
And now go in and entertain your angels,
And don't be seen here in the street again
Till after sundown ! — There they are again !

Exit UPSALL.   MERRY *throws another stone at the pigeons,
    and then goes into his house.*

SCENE III. — *A room in* UPSALL'S *house. Night.* EDITH,
    WHARTON, *and other Quakers seated at a table.* UP-
    SALL *seated near them. Several books on the table.*

WHARTON.

WILLIAM and Marmaduke, our martyred
    brothers,
Sleep in untimely graves, if aught untimely
Can find place in the providence of God,
Where nothing comes too early or too late.
I saw their noble death. They to the scaf-
    fold
Walked hand in hand. Two hundred armed
    men
And many horsemen guarded them, for fear
Of rescue by the crowd, whose hearts were
    stirred.

EDITH.

O holy martyrs !

WHARTON.

          When they tried to speak,
Their voices by the roll of drums were
    drowned.
When they were dead they still looked fresh
    and fair,
The terror of death was not upon their faces.
Our sister Mary, likewise, the meek woman,
Has passed through martyrdom to her re-
    ward ;
Exclaiming, as they led her to her death,
" These many days I 've been in Paradise."
And, when she died, Priest Wilson threw
    the hangman
His handkerchief, to cover the pale face
He dared not look upon.

EDITH.

              As persecuted,
Yet not forsaken ; as unknown, yet known ;
As dying, and behold we are alive ;
As sorrowful, and yet rejoicing alway ;
As having nothing, yet possessing all !

WHARTON.

And Leddra, too, is dead. But from his
    prison,
The day before his death, he sent these
    words
Unto the little flock of Christ : " What-
    ever
May come upon the followers of the Light, —
Distress, affliction, famine, nakedness,
Or perils in the city or the sea,
Or persecution, or even death itself, —
I am persuaded that God's armor of Light,
As it is loved and lived in, will preserve
    you.
Yea, death itself ; through which you will
    find entrance
Into the pleasant pastures of the fold,
Where you shall feed forever as the herds
That roam at large in the low valleys of
    Achor.
And as the flowing of the ocean fills
Each creek and branch thereof, and then
    retires,

Leaving behind a sweet and wholesome savor;
So doth the virtue and the life of God
Flow evermore into the hearts of those
Whom He hath made partakers of his na-
    ture;
And, when it but withdraws itself a little,
Leaves a sweet savor after it, that many
Can say they are made clean by every word
That He hath spoken to them in their si-
    lence."

EDITH (*rising, and breaking into a kind of chant*).

Truly we do but grope here in the dark,
Near the partition-wall of Life and Death,
At every moment dreading or desiring
To lay our hands upon the unseen door!
Let us, then, labor for an inward stillness, —
An inward stillness and an inward healing;
That perfect silence where the lips and heart

Are still, and we no longer entertain
Our own imperfect thoughts and vain opin-
    ions,
But God alone speaks in us, and we wait
In singleness of heart, that we may know
His will, and in the silence of our spirits,
That we may do His will, and do that only!

*A long pause, interrupted by the sound of a drum ap-
    proaching; then shouts in the street, and a loud knock-
    ing at the door.*

MARSHAL.

Within there! Open the door!

MERRY.

Will no one answer?

MARSHAL.

In the King's name! Within there!

MERRY.

Open the door!

UPSALL (*from the window*).

It is not barred. Come in. Nothing pre-
    vents you.
The poor man's door is ever on the latch.
He needs no bolt nor bar to shut out
    thieves;
He fears no enemies, and has no friends
Importunate enough to need a key.

Enter JOHN ENDICOTT, *the* MARSHAL, MERRY, *and a
    crowd. Seeing the Quakers silent and unmoved, they
    pause, awe-struck.* ENDICOTT *opposite* EDITH.

MARSHAL.

In the King's name do I arrest you all!
Away with them to prison. Master Upsall,
You are again discovered harboring here
These ranters and disturbers of the peace.
You know the law.

UPSALL.

I know it, and am ready
To suffer yet again its penalties.

EDITH (*to* ENDICOTT).

Why dost thou persecute me, Saul of
    Tarsus?

ACT II.

SCENE I. — JOHN ENDICOTT'S *room. Early morning.*

JOHN ENDICOTT.

" WHY dost thou persecute me, Saul of Tar-
    sus? "
All night these words were ringing in mine
    ears!
A sorrowful sweet face; a look that pierced
    me
With meek reproach; a voice of resigna-
    tion
That had a life of suffering in its tone;
And that was all! And yet I could not
    sleep,
Or, when I slept, I dreamed that awful
    dream!
I stood beneath the elm-tree on the Com-
    mon
On which the Quakers have been hanged,
    and heard
A voice, not hers, that cried amid the dark-
    ness,
" This is Aceldama, the field of blood!
I will have mercy, and not sacrifice!"
    Opens the window, and looks out.
The sun is up already; and my heart
Sickens and sinks within me when I think
How many tragedies will be enacted
Before his setting. As the earth rolls round,
It seems to me a huge Ixion's wheel,
Upon whose whirling spokes we are bound
    fast,

And must go with it! Ah, how bright the sun
Strikes on the sea and on the masts of ves-
    sels,
That are uplifted in the morning air,
Like crosses of some peaceable crusade!
It makes me long to sail for lands unknown,
No matter whither! Under me, in shadow,
Gloomy and narrow lies the little town,
Still sleeping, but to wake and toil awhile,
Then sleep again. How dismal looks the
    prison,
How grim and sombre in the sunless
    street, —
The prison where she sleeps, or wakes and
    waits
For what I dare not think of, — death, per-
    haps!
A word that has been said may be unsaid:
It is but air. But when a deed is done
It cannot be undone, nor can our thoughts
Reach out to all the mischiefs that may
    follow.
'T is time for morning prayers. I will go
    down.
My father, though severe, is kind and just;
And when his heart is tender with devo-
    tion, —
When from his lips have fallen the words,
    "Forgive us
As we forgive," — then will I intercede
For these poor people, and perhaps may
    save them.   [*Exit.*

SCENE II. — *Dock Square. On one side, the tavern of the Three Mariners. In the background, a quaint building with gables; and, beyond it, wharves and shipping.* CAPTAIN KEMPTHORN *and others seated at a table before the door.* SAMUEL COLE *standing near them.*

KEMPTHORN.

COME, drink about! Remember Parson Melham,
And bless the man who first invented flip!
They drink.

COLE.

Pray, Master Kempthorn, where were you last night?

KEMPTHORN.

On board the Swallow, Simon Kempthorn, master,
Up for Barbadoes, and the Windward Islands.

COLE.

The town was in a tumult.

KEMPTHORN.

And for what?

COLE.

Your Quakers were arrested.

KEMPTHORN.

How my Quakers?

COLE.

Those you brought in your vessel from Barbadoes.
They made an uproar in the Meeting-house
Yesterday, and they're now in prison for it.
I owe you little thanks for bringing them
To the Three Mariners.

KEMPTHORN.

They have not harmed you.
I tell you, Goodman Cole, that Quaker girl
Is precious as a sea-bream's eye. I tell you
It was a lucky day when first she set

Her little foot upon the Swallow's deck,
Bringing good luck, fair winds, and pleasant
    weather.

COLE.

I am a law-abiding citizen;
I have a seat in the new Meeting-house,
A cow-right on the Common; and, besides,
Am corporal in the Great Artillery.
I rid me of the vagabonds at once.

KEMPTHORN.

Why should you not have Quakers at your
    tavern
If you have fiddlers?

COLE.

          Never! never! never!
If you want fiddling you must go elsewhere,
To the Green Dragon and the Admiral Vernon,
And other such disreputable places.
But the Three Mariners is an orderly house,
Most orderly, quiet, and respectable.
Lord Leigh said he could be as quiet here
As at the Governor's. And have I not
King Charles's Twelve Good Rules, all framed
    and glazed,
Hanging in my best parlor?

KEMPTHORN.

          Here's a health
To good King Charles. Will you not drink
    the King?
Then drink confusion to old Parson Palmer.

COLE.

And who is Parson Palmer? I don't know
    him.

KEMPTHORN.

He had his cellar underneath his pulpit,
And so preached o'er his liquor, just as you
    do.

A drum within.

COLE.

Here comes the Marshal.

MERRY (*within*).

Make room for the Marshal.

KEMPTHORN.

How pompous and imposing he appears!
His great buff doublet bellying like a
    mainsail,
And all his streamers fluttering in the
    wind.
What holds he in his hand?

COLE.

          A Proclamation.

Enter the MARSHAL, *with a proclamation; and* MERRY,
   with a halberd. They are preceded by a drummer, and
   followed by the hangman, with an armful of books, and
   a crowd of people, among whom are UPSALL *and*
   JOHN ENDICOTT. *A pile is made of the books.*

MERRY.

Silence, the drum! Good citizens, attend
To the new laws enacted by the Court.

MARSHAL (*reads*).

"Whereas a cursed sect of Heretics
Has lately risen, commonly called Quakers,
Who take upon themselves to be commis-
    sioned
Immediately of God, and furthermore
Infallibly assisted by the Spirit
To write and utter blasphemous opinions,
Despising Government and the order of
    God
In Church and Commonwealth, and speak-
    ing evil
Of Dignities, reproaching and reviling
The Magistrates and Ministers, and seeking
To turn the people from their faith, and
    thus
Gain proselytes to their pernicious ways; —
This Court, considering the premises,
And to prevent like mischief as is wrought
By their means in our land, doth hereby
    order,
That whatsoever master or commander
Of any ship, bark, pink, or catch shall
    bring
To any roadstead, harbor, creek, or cove
Within this Jurisdiction any Quakers,
Or other blasphemous Heretics, shall pay
Unto the Treasurer of the Commonwealth
One hundred pounds, and for default
    thereof

Be put in prison, and continue there
Till the said sum be satisfied and paid."

COLE.

Now, Simon Kempthorn, what say you to
that?

KEMPTHORN.

I pray you, Cole, lend me a hundred pounds!

MARSHAL (*reads*).

"If any one within this Jurisdiction
Shall henceforth entertain, or shall conceal
Quakers, or other blasphemous Heretics,

Knowing them so to be, every such person
Shall forfeit to the country forty shillings
For each hour's entertainment or conceal-
ment,
And shall be sent to prison, as aforesaid,
Until the forfeiture be wholly paid."

Murmurs in the crowd.

KEMPTHORN.

Now, Goodman Cole, I think your turn
has come!

COLE.

Knowing them so to be!

KEMPTHORN.

At forty shillings
The hour, your fine will be some forty
pounds!

COLE.

Knowing them so to be! That is the law.

MARSHAL (*reads*).

" And it is further ordered and enacted,
If any Quaker or Quakers shall presume
To come henceforth into this Jurisdiction,
Every male Quaker for the first offence
Shall have one ear cut off; and shall be
    kept
At labor in the Workhouse, till such time
As he be sent away at his own charge.
And for the repetition of the offence
Shall have his other ear cut off, and then
Be branded in the palm of his right hand.
And every woman Quaker shall be whipt
Severely in three towns; and every Quaker,
Or he or she, that shall for a third time
Herein again offend, shall have their
    tongues
Bored through with a hot iron, and shall
    be
Sentenced to Banishment on pain of Death."
Loud murmurs. The voice of CHRISTISON *in the crowd.*

O patience of the Lord! How long, how
    long,
Ere thou avenge the blood of Thine Elect?

MERRY.

Silence, there, silence! Do not break the
    peace!

MARSHAL (*reads*).

" Every inhabitant of this Jurisdiction
Who shall defend the horrible opinions
Of Quakers, by denying due respect
To equals and superiors, and withdrawing
From Church Assemblies, and thereby ap-
    proving
The abusive and destructive practices
Of this accursed sect, in opposition
To all the orthodox received opinions
Of godly men, shall be forthwith com-
    mitted
Unto close prison for one month; and
    then
Refusing to retract and to reform
The opinions as aforesaid, he shall be
Sentenced to Banishment on pain of Death.
By the Court. Edward Rawson, Secretary."
Now, hangman, do your duty. Burn those
    books.
Loud murmurs in the crowd. The pile of books is lighted.

UPSALL.

I testify against these cruel laws!
Forerunners are they of some judgment on us;
And, in the love and tenderness I bear
Unto this town and people, I beseech you,
O Magistrates, take heed, lest ye be found
As fighters against God!

JOHN ENDICOTT (*taking* UPSALL'S *hand*).

Upsall, I thank you
For speaking words such as some younger
    man,
I or another, should have said before you.
Such laws as these are cruel and oppressive;
A blot on this fair town, and a disgrace
To any Christian people.

MERRY (*aside, listening behind them*).

Here's sedition!
I never thought that any good would come
Of this young popinjay, with his long hair
And his great boots, fit only for the Russians
Or barbarous Indians, as his father says!

THE VOICE.

Woe to the bloody town! And rightfully
Men call it the Lost Town! The blood of
    Abel
Cries from the ground, and at the final judg-
    ment
The Lord will say, "Cain, Cain! where is thy
    brother?"

MERRY.

Silence there in the crowd!

UPSALL (*aside*).

'T is Christison!

THE VOICE.

O foolish people, ye that think to burn
And to consume the truth of God, I tell you
That every flame is a loud tongue of fire
To publish it abroad to all the world
Louder than tongues of men!

KEMPTHORN (*springing to his feet*).

Well said, my hearty!
There's a brave fellow! There's a man of
    pluck!

A man who's not afraid to say his say,
Though a whole town's against him. Rain,
    rain, rain,
Bones of St. Botolph, and put out this fire!

The drum beats. Exeunt all but MERRY, KEMPTHORN,
and COLE.

MERRY.

And now that matter's ended, Goodman Cole,
Fetch me a mug of ale, your strongest ale.

KEMPTHORN (*sitting down*).

And me another mug of flip; and put
Two gills of brandy in it.

                    [*Exit* COLE.

MERRY.

            No; no more.
Not a drop more, I say. You've had enough.

KEMPTHORN.

And who are you, sir?

MERRY.

            I'm a Tithing-man,
And Merry is my name.

KEMPTHORN.

            A merry name!
I like it; and I'll drink your merry health
Till all is blue.

MERRY.

        And then you will be clapped
Into the stocks, with the red letter D
Hung round about your neck for drunkenness.
You're a free-drinker, — yes, and a free-
    thinker!

KEMPTHORN.

And you are Andrew Merry, or Merry An-
    drew.

MERRY.

My name is Walter Merry, and not Andrew.

KEMPTHORN.

Andrew or Walter, you 're a merry fellow;
I 'll swear to that.

MERRY.

No swearing, let me tell you.
The other day one Shorthose had his tongue
Put into a cleft stick for profane swearing.
COLE *brings the ale.*

KEMPTHORN.

Well, where 's my flip? As sure as my name's
Kempthorn —

MERRY.

Is your name Kempthorn?

KEMPTHORN.

That 's the name I go by.

MERRY.

What, Captain Simon Kempthorn of the Swallow?

KEMPTHORN.

No other.

MERRY (*touching him on the shoulder*).

Then you 're wanted. I arrest you
In the King's name.

KEMPTHORN.

And where 's your warrant?

MERRY (*unfolding a paper, and reading*).

Here.
Listen to me. "Hereby you are required,
In the King's name, to apprehend the body
Of Simon Kempthorn, mariner, and him
Safely to bring before me, there to an-
swer
All such objections as are laid to him,
Touching the Quakers." Signed, John Endi-
cott.

KEMPTHORN.

Has it the Governor's seal?

MERRY.

Ay, here it is.

KEMPTHORN.

Death's head and cross-bones. That 's a pi-
rate's flag!

MERRY.

Beware how you revile the Magistrates;
You may be whipped for that.

KEMPTHORN.

Then mum 's the word.
Exeunt MERRY *and* KEMPTHORN.

COLE.

There 's mischief brewing! Sure, there 's mischief brewing!
I feel like Master Josselyn when he found
The hornet's nest, and thought it some strange
fruit,
Until the seeds came out, and then he dropped
it.   [*Exit.*

SCENE III. — *A room in the Governor's house.   Enter*
GOVERNOR ENDICOTT *and* MERRY.

ENDICOTT.

MY son, you say?

MERRY.

Your Worship's eldest son.

ENDICOTT.

Speaking against the laws?

MERRY.

Ay, worshipful sir.

ENDICOTT.

And in the public market-place?

MERRY.

I saw him
With my own eyes, heard him with my own
ears.

ENDICOTT.

Impossible!

MERRY.

He stood there in the crowd
With Nicholas Upsall, when the laws were read

To-day against the Quakers, and I heard
    him
Denounce and vilipend them as unjust,
And cruel, wicked, and abominable.

ENDICOTT.

Ungrateful son! O God! thou layest upon
    me
A burden heavier than I can bear!
Surely the power of Satan must be great
Upon the earth, if even the elect
Are thus deceived and fall away from grace!

MERRY.

Worshipful sir! I meant no harm —

ENDICOTT.

              'T is well.
You 've done your duty, though you 've done
    it roughly,

And every word you 've uttered since you
    came
Has stabbed me to the heart!

MERRY.

               I do beseech
Your Worship's pardon!

ENDICOTT.

           He whom I have nurtured
And brought up in the reverence of the
    Lord!
The child of all my hopes and my affec-
    tions!
He upon whom I leaned as a sure staff
For my old age! It is God's chastisement
For leaning upon any arm but His!

MERRY.

Your Worship! —

ENDICOTT.

        And this comes from holding parley
With the delusions and deceits of Satan.
At once, forever, must they be crushed out,
Or all the land will reek with heresy!
Pray, have you any children?

MERRY.

               No, not any.

ENDICOTT.

Thank God for that. He has delivered you
From a great care. Enough; my private
    griefs
Too long have kept me from the public ser-
    vice.

Exit MERRY. ENDICOTT *seats himself at the table and
arranges his papers.*

The hour has come; and I am eager now
To sit in judgment on these Heretics.
    (*A knock.*)
Come in. Who is it? (*Not looking up.*)

JOHN ENDICOTT.

             It is I.

ENDICOTT (*restraining himself*).

               Sit down!

JOHN ENDICOTT (*sitting down*).

I come to intercede for these poor people
Who are in prison, and await their trial.

ENDICOTT.

It is of them I wish to speak with you.
I have been angry with you, but 't is
    passed.
For when I hear your footsteps come or go,
See in your features your dead mother's
    face,
And in your voice detect some tone of
    hers,
All anger vanishes, and I remember
The days that are no more, and come no
    more,
When as a child you sat upon my knee,
And prattled of your playthings, and the
    games
You played among the pear trees in the
    orchard!

JOHN ENDICOTT.

Oh, let the memory of my noble mother
Plead with you to be mild and merciful!
For mercy more becomes a Magistrate
Than the vindictive wrath which men call
    justice!

ENDICOTT.

The sin of heresy is a deadly sin.
'T is like the falling of the snow, whose
    crystals
The traveller plays with, thoughtless of
    his danger,
Until he sees the air so full of light
That it is dark; and blindly staggering
    onward,
Lost, and bewildered, he sits down to
    rest;
There falls a pleasant drowsiness upon
    him,
And what he thinks is sleep, alas! is
    death.

JOHN ENDICOTT.

And yet who is there that has never
    doubted?
And doubting and believing, has not said,
" Lord, I believe; help thou my unbelief " ?

ENDICOTT.

In the same way we trifle with our doubts,
Whose shining shapes are like the stars de-
    scending;
Until at last, bewildered and dismayed,
Blinded by that which seemed to give us
    light,
We sink to sleep, and find that it is death,
    (*Rising.*)
Death to the soul through all eternity!
Alas that I should see you growing up
To man's estate, and in the admonition
And nurture of the Law, to find you now
Pleading for Heretics!

JOHN ENDICOTT (*rising*).

           In the sight of God,
Perhaps all men are Heretics. Who dares
To say that he alone has found the truth?
We cannot always feel and think and act
As those who go before us. Had you done
    so,
You would not now be here.

ENDICOTT.

           Have you forgotten
The doom of Heretics, and the fate of
    those
Who aid and comfort them? Have you for-
    gotten
That in the market-place this very day
You trampled on the laws? What right have
    you,
An inexperienced and untravelled youth,
To sit in judgment here upon the acts
Of older men and wiser than yourself,
Thus stirring up sedition in the streets,
And making me a byword and a jest?

JOHN ENDICOTT.

Words of an inexperienced youth like me
Were powerless if the acts of older men
Went not before them. 'T is these laws
    themselves
Stir up sedition, not my judgment of them.

ENDICOTT.

Take heed, lest I be called, as Brutus
    was
To be the judge of my own son! Begone!

When you are tired of feeding upon husks,
Return again to duty and submission,
But not till then.

JOHN ENDICOTT.

I hear and I obey!

[*Exit.*

ENDICOTT.

Oh happy, happy they who have no children!
He 's gone! I hear the hall door shut behind
    him.

It sends a dismal echo through my heart,
As if forever it had closed between us,
And I should look upon his face no more!
Oh, this will drag me down into my grave, —
To that eternal resting-place wherein
Man lieth down, and riseth not again!
Till the heavens be no more he shall not
    wake,
Nor be roused from his sleep; for Thou dost
    change
His countenance, and sendest him away!

[*Exit.*

ACT III.

SCENE I. — *The Court of Assistants.* ENDICOTT, BEL-
    LINGHAM, ATHERTON, *and other magistrates.*
    KEMPTHORN, MERRY, *and constables.* *Afterwards*
    WHARTON, EDITH, *and* CHRISTISON.

ENDICOTT.

CALL Captain Simon Kempthorn.

MERRY.

        Simon Kempthorn.
Come to the bar!

KEMPTHORN *comes forward.*

ENDICOTT.

    You are accused of bringing
Into this Jurisdiction, from Barbadoes,
Some persons of that sort and sect of people
Known by the name of Quakers, and main-
    taining
Most dangerous and heretical opinions;
Purposely coming here to propagate
Their heresies and errors; bringing with them
And spreading sundry books here, which con-
    tain
Their doctrines most corrupt and blasphemous,
And contrary to the truth professed among us.
What say you to this charge?

KEMPTHORN.

        I do acknowledge,
Among the passengers on board the Swallow
Were certain persons saying Thee and Thou.
They seemed a harmless people, mostways si-
    lent,
Particularly when they said their prayers.

ENDICOTT.

Harmless and silent as the pestilence!
You 'd better have brought the fever or the
    plague
Among us in your ship! Therefore, this Court,
For preservation of the Peace and Truth,
Hereby commands you speedily to transport,
Or cause to be transported speedily,
The aforesaid persons hence unto Barbadoes,
From whence they came; you paying all the
    charges
Of their imprisonment.

KEMPTHORN.

        Worshipful sir,
No ship e'er prospered that has carried Quak-
    ers
Against their will! I knew a vessel once —

ENDICOTT.

And for the more effectual performance
Hereof you are to give security
In bonds amounting to one hundred pounds.
On your refusal, you will be committed
To prison till you do it.

KEMPTHORN.

        But you see
I cannot do it. The law, sir, of Barbadoes
Forbids the landing Quakers on the island.

ENDICOTT.

Then you will be committed. Who comes
    next?

MERRY.

There is another charge against the Captain.

ENDICOTT.

What is it?

MERRY.

Profane swearing, please your Worship.
He cursed and swore from Dock Square to
the Court-house.

ENDICOTT.

Then let him stand in the pillory for one hour.
[*Exit* KEMPTHORN *with constable.*
Who 's next?

MERRY.

The Quakers.

ENDICOTT.

Call them.

MERRY.

Edward Wharton,
Come to the bar!

WHARTON.

Yea, even to the bench.

ENDICOTT.

Take off your hat.

WHARTON.

My hat offendeth not.
If it offendeth any, let him take it;
For I shall not resist.

ENDICOTT.

Take off his hat.
Let him be fined ten shillings for contempt.
MERRY *takes off* WHARTON'S *hat.*

WHARTON.

What evil have I done?

ENDICOTT.

Your hair 's too long;
And in not putting off your hat to us
You 've disobeyed and broken that command-
ment

Which sayeth "Honor thy father and thy
mother."

WHARTON.

John Endicott, thou art become too proud;
And lovest him who putteth off the hat,
And honoreth thee by bowing of the body,
And sayeth "Worshipful sir!" 'Tis time for
thee
To give such follies over, for thou mayest
Be drawing very near unto thy grave.

ENDICOTT.

Now, sirrah, leave your canting. Take the
oath.

WHARTON.

Nay, sirrah me no sirrahs!

ENDICOTT.

Will you swear?

WHARTON.

Nay, I will not.

ENDICOTT.

You made a great disturbance,
And uproar yesterday in the Meeting-house,
Having your hat on.

WHARTON.

I made no disturbance;
For peacefully I stood, like other people.
I spake no words; moved against none my
hand;
But by the hair they haled me out, and
dashed
Their books into my face.

ENDICOTT.

You, Edward Wharton,
On pain of death, depart this Jurisdiction
Within ten days. Such is your sentence. Go.

WHARTON.

John Endicott, it had been well for thee
If this day's doings thou hadst left undone.
But, banish me as far as thou hast power,
Beyond the guard and presence of my God
Thou canst not banish me!

ENDICOTT.

               Depart the Court;
We have no time to listen to your babble.
Who's next ?   [*Exit* WHARTON.

MERRY.

      This woman, for the same offence.
      EDITH *comes forward.*

ENDICOTT.

What is your name ?

EDITH.

          'T is to the world unknown,
But written in the Book of Life.

ENDICOTT.

                 Take heed
It be not written in the Book of Death !
What is it ?

EDITH.

      Edith Christison.

ENDICOTT (*with eagerness*).

                The daughter
Of Wenlock Christison ?

EDITH.

          I am his daughter.

ENDICOTT.

Your father hath given us trouble many times.
A bold man and a violent, who sets
At naught the authority of our Church and
        State,
And is in banishment on pain of death.
Where are you living ?

EDITH.

      In the Lord.

ENDICOTT.

                Make answer
Without evasion. Where?

EDITH.

                My outward being
Is in Barbadoes.

ENDICOTT.

      Then why come you here?

EDITH.

I come upon an errand of the Lord.

ENDICOTT.

'T is not the business of the Lord you 're do-
    ing;
It is the Devil's. Will you take the oath?
Give her the Book.
        MERRY *offers the book.*

EDITH.

        You offer me this Book
To swear on; and it saith, " Swear not at all,
Neither by heaven, because it is God's Throne,
Nor by the earth, because it is his footstool! "
I dare not swear.

ENDICOTT.

      You dare not? Yet you Quakers
Deny this Book of Holy Writ, the Bible,
To be the Word of God.

EDITH (*reverentially*).

          Christ is the Word,
The everlasting oath of God. I dare not.

ENDICOTT.

You own yourself a Quaker, — do you not?

EDITH.

I own that in derision and reproach
I am so called.

ENDICOTT.

      Then you deny the Scripture
To be the rule of life.

EDITH.

        Yea, I believe

The Inner Light, and not the Written
    Word,
To be the rule of life.

ENDICOTT.

        And you deny
That the Lord's Day is holy.

EDITH.

           Every day
Is the Lord's Day. It runs through all
    our lives,
As through the pages of the Holy Bible
" Thus saith the Lord."

ENDICOTT.

        You are accused of making
An horrible disturbance, and affrighting
The people in the Meeting-house on Sunday.
What answer make you?

EDITH.

          I do not deny
That I was present in your Steeple-house
On the First Day; but I made no disturb-
    ance.

ENDICOTT.

Why came you there?

EDITH.

      Because the Lord commanded.
His word was in my heart, a burning fire
Shut up within me and consuming me,
And I was very weary with forbearing;
I could not stay.

ENDICOTT.

  'T was not the Lord that sent you;
As an incarnate devil did you come!

EDITH.

On the First Day, when, seated in my
    chamber,
I heard the bells toll, calling you together,
The sound struck at my life, as once at
    his,
The holy man, our Founder, when he heard
The far-off bells toll in the Vale of Beavor.
It sounded like a market bell to call

The folk together, that the Priest might set
His wares to sale. And the Lord said
    within me,
" Thou must go cry aloud against that Idol,
And all the worshippers thereof." I went
Barefooted, clad in sackcloth, and I stood
And listened at the threshold ; and I heard
The praying and the singing and the preach-
    ing,
Which were but outward forms, and with-
    out power.
Then rose a cry within me, and my heart
Was filled with admonitions and reproofs.
Remembering how the Prophets and Apos-
    tles
Denounced the covetous hirelings and di-
    viners,
I entered in, and spake the words the
    Lord
Commanded me to speak. I could no less.

ENDICOTT.

Are you a Prophetess ?

EDITH.

                    Is it not written,
" Upon my handmaidens will I pour out
My spirit, and they shall prophesy " ?

ENDICOTT.

                            Enough ;
For out of your own mouth are you con-
    demned !
Need we hear further ?

THE JUDGES.

            We are satisfied.

ENDICOTT.

It is sufficient. Edith Christison,
The sentence of the Court is, that you be
Scourged in three towns, with forty stripes
    save one,
Then banished upon pain of death !

EDITH.

            Your sentence
Is truly no more terrible to me
Than had you blown a feather into the
    air,

And, as it fell upon me, you had said,
" Take heed it hurt thee not ! " God's will
    be done !

WENLOCK CHRISTISON (unseen in the crowd).

Woe to the city of blood ! The stone shall
    cry
Out of the wall ; the beam from out the
    timber
Shall answer it ! Woe unto him that build-
    eth
A town with blood, and stablisheth a city
By his iniquity !

ENDICOTT.

            Who is it makes
Such outcry here ?

CHRISTISON (coming forward).

            I, Wenlock Christison !

ENDICOTT.

Banished on pain of death, why come you
  here?

CHRISTISON.

I come to warn you that you shed no
  more
The blood of innocent men! It cries aloud
For vengeance to the Lord!

ENDICOTT.

              Your life is forfeit
Unto the law; and you shall surely die,
And shall not live.

CHRISTISON.

        Like unto Eleazer,
Maintaining the excellence of ancient years
And the honor of his gray head, I stand
        before you;
Like him disdaining all hypocrisy,
Lest, through desire to live a little longer,
I get a stain to my old age and name!

ENDICOTT.

Being in banishment, on pain of death,
You come now in among us in rebellion.

CHRISTISON.

I come not in among you in rebellion,
But in obedience to the Lord of Heaven.
Not in contempt to any Magistrate,
But only in the love I bear your souls,
As ye shall know hereafter, when all men
Give an account of deeds done in the body!
God's righteous judgments ye cannot escape.

ONE OF THE JUDGES.

Those who have gone before you said the
  same,
And yet no judgment of the Lord hath fallen
Upon us.

CHRISTISON.

          He but waiteth till the measure
Of your iniquities shall be filled up,
And ye have run your race. Then will his
  wrath
Descend upon you to the uttermost!
For thy part, Humphrey Atherton, it hangs

Over thy head already. It shall come
Suddenly, as a thief doth in the night,
And in the hour when least thou thinkest
  of it!

ENDICOTT.

We have a law, and by that law you die.

CHRISTISON.

I, a free man of England and freeborn,
Appeal unto the laws of mine own nation!

ENDICOTT.

There's no appeal to England from this
  Court!
What! do you think our statutes are but
  paper?
Are but dead leaves that rustle in the wind?
Or litter to be trampled under foot?
What say ye, Judges of the Court, — what
  say ye?
Shall this man suffer death? Speak your
  opinions.

ARTIST: F. T. MERRILL.

"And ye shall be accursed forevermore."

John Endicott.

ONE OF THE JUDGES.

I am a mortal man, and die I must,
And that erelong; and I must then appear
Before the awful judgment-seat of Christ,
To give account of deeds done in the body.
My greatest glory on that day will be,
That I have given my vote against this man.

CHRISTISON.

If, Thomas Danforth, thou hast nothing more
To glory in upon that dreadful day
Than blood of innocent people, then thy
glory
Will be turned into shame! The Lord hath
said it!

ANOTHER JUDGE.

I cannot give consent, while other men
Who have been banished upon pain of death
Are now in their own houses here among us.

ENDICOTT.

Ye that will not consent, make record of it.
I thank my God that I am not afraid
To give my judgment. Wenlock Christison,
You must be taken back from hence to prison,
Thence to the place of public execution,
There to be hanged till you be dead — dead
— dead!

CHRISTISON.

If ye have power to take my life from me, —
Which I do question, — God hath power to
raise
The principle of life in other men,
And send them here among you. There
shall be
No peace unto the wicked, saith my God.
Listen, ye Magistrates, for the Lord hath
said it!
The day ye put his servitors to death,
That day the Day of your own Visitation,
The Day of Wrath, shall pass above your
heads,
And ye shall be accursed forevermore!
        (*To* EDITH, *embracing her.*)
Cheer up, dear heart! they have not power
to harm us.

[*Exeunt* CHRISTISON *and* EDITH *guarded. The Scene
closes.*
88

SCENE II. — *A Street.* Enter JOHN ENDICOTT *and*
UPSALL.

JOHN ENDICOTT.

SCOURGED in three towns! and yet the busy
people
Go up and down the streets on their af-
fairs
Of business or of pleasure, as if nothing
Had happened to disturb them or their
thoughts!
When bloody tragedies like this are acted
The pulses of a nation should stand still;
The town should be in mourning, and the
people
Speak only in low whispers to each other.

UPSALL.

I know this people; and that underneath
A cold outside there burns a secret fire
That will find vent, and will not be put out,
Till every remnant of these barbarous laws
Shall be to ashes burned, and blown away.

JOHN ENDICOTT.

Scourged in three towns! It is incredible
Such things can be! I feel the blood within
me
Fast mounting in rebellion, since in vain
Have I implored compassion of my father!

UPSALL.

You know your father only as a father;
I know him better as a Magistrate.
He is a man both loving and severe;
A tender heart; a will inflexible.
None ever loved him more than I have loved
him.
He is an upright man and a just man
In all things save the treatment of the Quak-
ers.

JOHN ENDICOTT.

Yet I have found him cruel and unjust
Even as a father. He has driven me forth
Into the street; has shut his door upon
me,
With words of bitterness. I am as home-
less
As these poor Quakers are.

UPSALL.

Then come with me.
You shall be welcome for your father's
    sake,
And the old friendship that has been between
    us.

He will relent erelong. A father's anger
Is like a sword without a handle, piercing
Both ways alike, and wounding him that
    wields it
No less than him that it is pointed at.

[*Exeunt.*

SCENE III. — *The prison. Night.* EDITH *reading the
    Bible by a lamp.*

EDITH.

" BLESSED are ye when men shall persecute
        you,
    And shall revile you, and shall say against
        you
    All manner of evil falsely for my sake !

Rejoice, and be exceeding glad, for great
Is your reward in heaven. For so the
        prophets,
Which were before you, have been perse-
        cuted."

Enter JOHN ENDICOTT.

JOHN ENDICOTT.

Edith !

EDITH.

Who is it speaketh?

JOHN ENDICOTT.

      Saul of Tarsus;
As thou didst call me once.

EDITH (*coming forward*).

      Yea, I remember.
Thou art the Governor's son.

JOHN ENDICOTT.

      I am ashamed
Thou shouldst remember me.

EDITH.

      Why comest thou
Into this dark guest-chamber in the night?
What seekest thou?

JOHN ENDICOTT.

Forgiveness!

EDITH.

      I forgive
All who have injured me. What hast thou
  done?

JOHN ENDICOTT.

I have betrayed thee, thinking that in this
I did God service. Now, in deep contrition,
I come to rescue thee.

EDITH.

      From what?

JOHN ENDICOTT.

      From prison.

EDITH.

I am safe here within these gloomy walls.

JOHN ENDICOTT.

From scourging in the streets, and in three
  towns!

EDITH.

Remembering who was scourged for me I
  shrink not
Nor shudder at the forty stripes save one.

JOHN ENDICOTT.

Perhaps from death itself!

EDITH.

      I fear not death,
Knowing who died for me.

JOHN ENDICOTT (*aside*).

      Sure some divine
Ambassador is speaking through those lips
And looking through those eyes! I cannot
  answer!

EDITH.

If all these prison doors stood opened wide
I would not cross the threshold, — not one
  step.
There are invisible bars I cannot break;
There are invisible doors that shut me in,
And keep me ever steadfast to my pur-
  pose.

JOHN ENDICOTT.

Thou hast the patience and the faith of
  Saints!

EDITH.

Thy Priest hath been with me this day to
  save me,
Not only from the death that comes to all,
But from the second death!

JOHN ENDICOTT.

      The Pharisee!
My heart revolts against him and his creed!
Alas! the coat that was without a seam
Is rent asunder by contending sects;
Each bears away a portion of the garment,
Blindly believing that he has the whole!

EDITH.

When Death, the Healer, shall have touched
  our eyes
With moist clay of the grave, then shall we
  see
The truth as we have never yet beheld it.
But he that overcometh shall not be
Hurt of the second death. Has he forgot-
  ten
The many mansions in our father's house?

JOHN ENDICOTT.

There is no pity in his iron heart!
The hands that now bear stamped upon their
     palms
The burning sign of Heresy, hereafter
Shall be uplifted against such accusers,
And then the imprinted letter and its meaning
Will not be Heresy, but Holiness!

EDITH.

Remember, thou condemnest thine own father!

JOHN ENDICOTT.

I have no father! He has cast me off.
I am as homeless as the wind that moans
And wanders through the streets. Oh, come
     with me!
Do not delay. Thy God shall be my God,
And where thou goest I will go.

EDITH.

            I cannot.
Yet will I not deny it, nor conceal it;
From the first moment I beheld thy face
I felt a tenderness in my soul towards thee.
My mind has since been inward to the
     Lord,
Waiting his word. It has not yet been spoken.

JOHN ENDICOTT.

I cannot wait. Trust me. Oh, come with me!

EDITH.

In the next room, my father, an old man,

Sitteth imprisoned and condemned to death,
Willing to prove his faith by martyrdom;
And thinkest thou his daughter would do less?

JOHN ENDICOTT.

Oh, life is sweet, and death is terrible!

EDITH.

I have too long walked hand in hand with
     death
To shudder at that pale familiar face.
But leave me now. I wish to be alone.

JOHN ENDICOTT.

Not yet. Oh, let me stay.

EDITH.

            Urge me no more.

JOHN ENDICOTT.

Alas! good night. I will not say good-by!

EDITH.

Put this temptation underneath thy feet.
To him that overcometh shall be given
The white stone with the new name written
     on it,
That no man knows save him that doth re-
     ceive it,
And I will give thee a new name, and call
     thee
Paul of Damascus and not Saul of Tarsus.

[*Exit* ENDICOTT. EDITH *sits down again to read the
     Bible.*

ACT IV.

SCENE I. — *King Street, in front of the town-house.* KEMP-
THORN *in the pillory.* MERRY, *and a crowd of
lookers-on.*

KEMPTHORN (*sings*).

THE world is full of care,
  Much like unto a bubble;
Women and care, and care and women,
  And women and care and trouble.

Good Master Merry, may I say confound?

KEMPTHORN.

Ay, that you may.

KEMPTHORN.

     Well, then, with your permission,
Confound the Pillory!

MERRY.

        That 's the very thing
The joiner said who made the Shrewsbury
    stocks.
He said, Confound the stocks, because they put
    him
Into his own. He was the first man in them.

KEMPTHORN.

For swearing, was it?

MERRY.

       No, it was for charging;
He charged the town too much; and so the
    town,
To make things square, set him in his own
    stocks,
And fined him five pound sterling, — just
    enough
To settle his own bill.

KEMPTHORN.

       And served him right;
But, Master Merry, is it not eight bells?

MERRY.

Not quite.

KEMPTHORN.

For, do you see? I 'm getting tired

Of being perched aloft here in this cro' nest
Like the first mate of a whaler, or a Middy
Mast-headed, looking out for land! Sail ho!
Here comes a heavy-laden merchantman
With the lee clews eased off, and running
    free
Before the wind. A solid man of Boston.
A comfortable man, with dividends,
And the first salmon, and the first green peas.
    A gentleman passes.
He does not even turn his head to look.
He 's gone without a word. Here comes an-
    other,
A different kind of craft on a taut bow-
    line, —
Deacon Giles Firmin the apothecary,
A pious and a ponderous citizen,
Looking as rubicund and round and splendid
As the great bottle in his own shop window!
    DEACON FIRMIN *passes.*
And here 's my host of the Three Mariners,
My creditor and trusty taverner,
My corporal in the Great Artillery!
He 's not a man to pass me without speak-
    ing.
    COLE *looks away and passes.*
Don't yaw so; keep your luff, old hypo-
    crite!
Respectable, ah yes, respectable,
You, with your seat in the new Meeting-
    house,
Your cow-right on the Common! But who 's
    this?
I did not know the Mary Ann was in!
And yet this is my old friend, Captain Gold-
    smith,
As sure as I stand in the bilboes here.
Why, Ralph, my boy!
    Enter RALPH GOLDSMITH.

GOLDSMITH.

       Why, Simon, is it you?
Set in the bilboes?

KEMPTHORN.

       Chock-a-block, you see,
And without chafing-gear.

GOLDSMITH.

And what's it for?

KEMPTHORN.

Ask that starbowline with the boat-hook there,
That handsome man.

MERRY (*bowing*).

For swearing.

KEMPTHORN.

In this town
They put sea-captains in the stocks for swear-
ing,
And Quakers for not swearing. So look out.

GOLDSMITH.

I pray you set him free; he meant no harm;
'T is an old habit he picked up afloat.

MERRY.

Well, as your time is out, you may come
down.

The law allows you now to go at large
Like Elder Oliver's horse upon the Common.

KEMPTHORN.

Now, hearties, bear a hand! Let go and haul.

KEMPTHORN *is set free, and comes forward, shaking*
GOLDSMITH'S *hand.*

KEMPTHORN.

Give me your hand, Ralph. Ah, how good
it feels!
The hand of an old friend.

GOLDSMITH.

God bless you, Simon!

KEMPTHORN.

Now let us make a straight wake for the tavern
Of the Three Mariners, Samuel Cole com-
mander;
Where we can take our ease, and see the
shipping,
And talk about old times.

GOLDSMITH.

First I must pay
My duty to the Governor, and take him
His letters and despatches. Come with me.

KEMPTHORN.

I 'd rather not. I saw him yesterday.

GOLDSMITH.

Then wait for me at the Three Nuns and
Comb.

KEMPTHORN.

I thank you. That 's too near to the town
pump.
I will go with you to the Governor's,
And wait outside there, sailing off and on;
If I am wanted, you can hoist a signal.

MERRY.

Shall I go with you and point out the way?

GOLDSMITH.

Oh no, I thank you. I am not a stranger
Here in your crooked little town.

MERRY.

How now, sir?
Do you abuse our town?   [*Exit.*

GOLDSMITH.

Oh, no offence.

KEMPTHORN.

Ralph, I am under bonds for a hundred pound.

GOLDSMITH.

Hard lines. What for?

KEMPTHORN.

To take some Quakers back
I brought here from Barbadoes in the Swallow.
And how to do it I don't clearly see,
For one of them is banished, and another
Is sentenced to be hanged! What shall I do?

GOLDSMITH.

Just slip your hawser on some cloudy night;
Sheer off, and pay it with the topsail,
Simon!   [*Exeunt.*

SCENE II. — *Street in front of the prison. In the background a gateway and several flights of steps leading up terraces to the* GOVERNOR'S *house. A pump on one side of the street.* JOHN ENDICOTT, MERRY, UPSALL, *and others. A drum beats.*

JOHN ENDICOTT.

OH shame, shame, shame!

MERRY.

Yes, it would be a shame
But for the damnable sin of Heresy!

JOHN ENDICOTT.

A woman scourged and dragged about our
streets!

MERRY.

Well, Roxbury and Dorchester must take
Their share of shame. She will be whipped
in each!
Three towns, and Forty Stripes save one;
that makes
Thirteen in each.

JOHN ENDICOTT.

And are we Jews or Christians?
See where she comes, amid a gaping crowd!
And she a child. Oh, pitiful! pitiful!
There 's blood upon her clothes, her hands,
her feet!

Enter MARSHAL *and a drummer,* EDITH, *stripped to the waist, followed by the hangman with a scourge, and a noisy crowd.*

EDITH.

Here let me rest one moment. I am tired.
Will some one give me water?

MERRY.

At his peril.

UPSALL.

Alas! that I should live to see this day!

A WOMAN.

Did I forsake my father and my mother
And come here to New England to see this?

EDITH.

I am athirst. Will no one give me water?

JOHN ENDICOTT

(*making his way through the crowd with water*).

In the Lord's name!

EDITH (*drinking*).

        In his name I receive it!
Sweet as the water of Samaria's well
This water tastes. I thank thee. Is it thou?
I was afraid thou hadst deserted me.

JOHN ENDICOTT.

Never will I desert thee, nor deny thee.
Be comforted.

MERRY.

        O Master Endicott,
Be careful what you say.

JOHN ENDICOTT.

        Peace, idle babbler!

MERRY.

You 'll rue these words!

JOHN ENDICOTT.

        Art thou not better now?

EDITH.

They 've struck me as with roses.

JOHN ENDICOTT.

        Ah, these wounds!
These bloody garments!

EDITH.

        It is granted me
To seal my testimony with my blood.

JOHN ENDICOTT.

O blood-red seal of man's vindictive wrath!
O roses of the garden of the Lord!
I, of the household of Iscariot,
I have betrayed in thee my Lord and Master!

WENLOCK CHRISTISON *appears above, at the window of the prison, stretching out his hands through the bars.*

CHRISTISON.

Be of good courage, O my child! my child!
Blessed art thou when men shall persecute
    thee!

Fear not their faces, saith the Lord, fear not,
For I am with thee to deliver thee.

A CITIZEN.

Who is it crying from the prison yonder!

MERRY.

It is old Wenlock Christison.

CHRISTISON.

           Remember
Him who was scourged, and mocked, and cru-
    cified!
I see his messengers attending thee.
Be steadfast, oh, be steadfast to the end!

EDITH (*with exultation*).

I cannot reach thee with these arms, O
    father!
But closely in my soul do I embrace thee
And hold thee. In thy dungeon and thy death
I will be with thee, and will comfort thee!

MARSHAL.

Come, put an end to this. Let the drum
    beat.

The drum beats. Exeunt all but JOHN ENDICOTT, UPSALL, *and* MERRY.

CHRISTISON.

Dear child, farewell! Never shall I behold
Thy face again with these bleared eyes of
    flesh;
And never wast thou fairer, lovelier, dearer
Than now, when scourged and bleeding, and
    insulted
For the truth's sake. O pitiless, pitiless town!
The wrath of God hangs over thee; and the
    day
Is near at hand when thou shalt be abandoned
To desolation and the breeding of nettles.
The bittern and the cormorant shall lodge
Upon thine upper lintels, and their voice
Sing in thy windows. Yea, thus saith the
    Lord!

JOHN ENDICOTT.

Awake! awake! ye sleepers, ere too late,
And wipe these bloody statutes from your
    books!   [*Exit.*

MERRY.

Take heed; the walls have ears!

UPSALL.

At last, the heart
Of every honest man must speak or break!
Enter GOVERNOR ENDICOTT *with his halberdiers.*

ENDICOTT.

What is this stir and tumult in the street?

MERRY.

Worshipful sir, the whipping of a girl,
And her old father howling from the prison.

ENDICOTT (*to his halberdiers*).

Go on.

CHRISTISON.

Antiochus! Antiochus!
O thou that slayest the Maccabees! The Lord
Shall smite thee with incurable disease,
And no man shall endure to carry thee!

MERRY.

Peace, old blasphemer!

CHRISTISON.

I both feel and see
The presence and the waft of death go forth
Against thee, and already thou dost look
Like one that's dead!

MERRY (*pointing*).

And there is your own son,
Worshipful sir, abetting the sedition.

ENDICOTT.

Arrest him. Do not spare him.

MERRY (*aside*).

His own child!
There is some special providence takes care
That none shall be too happy in this world!
His own first-born!

ENDICOTT.

O Absalom, my son!

[*Exeunt; the* GOVERNOR *with his halberdiers ascending
the steps of his house.*
89

SCENE III. — *The Governor's private room. Papers upon
the table.* ENDICOTT *and* BELLINGHAM.

ENDICOTT.

THERE is a ship from England has come in,
Bringing despatches and much news from
home.
His Majesty was at the Abbey crowned;
And when the coronation was complete
There passed a mighty tempest o'er the city,
Portentous with great thunderings and
lightnings.

BELLINGHAM.

After his father's, if I well remember,
There was an earthquake, that foreboded
evil.

ENDICOTT.

Ten of the Regicides have been put to
death!
The bodies of Cromwell, Ireton, and Brad-
shaw
Have been dragged from their graves, and
publicly
Hanged in their shrouds at Tyburn.

BELLINGHAM.

Horrible!

ENDICOTT.

Thus the old tyranny revives again!
Its arm is long enough to reach us here,
As you will see. For, more insulting still
Than flaunting in our faces dead men's
shrouds,
Here is the King's Mandamus, taking from
us,
From this day forth, all power to punish
Quakers.

BELLINGHAM.

That takes from us all power; we are but
puppets,
And can no longer execute our laws.

ENDICOTT.

His Majesty begins with pleasant words,
" Trusty and well-beloved, we greet you
well; "

Then with a ruthless hand he strips from me
All that which makes me what I am; as if
From some old general in the field, grown
    gray
In service, scarred with many wounds,
Just at the hour of victory, he should strip
His badge of office and his well-gained honors,
And thrust him back into the ranks again.

Opens the Mandamus, and hands it to BELLINGHAM; *and,*
* while he is reading,* ENDICOTT *walks up and down the*
* room.*

Here read it for yourself; you see his words
Are pleasant words — considerate — not re-
    proachful —
Nothing could be more gentle — or more
    royal;
But then the meaning underneath the words,
Mark that. He says all people known as
    Quakers
Among us, now condemned to suffer death
Or any corporal punishment whatever,
Who are imprisoned, or may be obnoxious
To the like condemnation, shall be sent
Forthwith to England, to be dealt with there
In such wise as shall be agreeable
Unto the English law and their demerits.
Is it not so?

BELLINGHAM (*returning the paper*).

    Ay, so the paper says.

ENDICOTT.

It means we shall no longer rule the Prov-
    ince;
It means farewell to law and liberty,
Authority, respect for Magistrates,
The peace and welfare of the Common-
    wealth.
If all the knaves upon this continent
Can make appeal to England, and so thwart
The ends of truth and justice by delay,
Our power is gone forever. We are noth-
    ing
But ciphers, valueless save when we follow
Some unit; and our unit is the King!
'T is he that gives us value.

BELLINGHAM.

    I confess
Such seems to be the meaning of this paper,

But being the King's Mandamus, signed and
    sealed,
We must obey, or we are in rebellion.

ENDICOTT.

I tell you, Richard Bellingham, — I tell you,
That this is the beginning of a struggle
Of which no mortal can foresee the end.
I shall not live to fight the battle for you,
I am a man disgraced in every way;
This order takes from me my self-respect
And the respect of others. 'T is my doom,
Yes, my death-warrant, but must be obeyed!
Take it, and see that it is executed
So far as this, that all be set at large;
But see that none of them be sent to Eng-
    land
To bear false witness, and to spread reports
That might be prejudicial to ourselves.

    [*Exit* BELLINGHAM.

There's a dull pain keeps knocking at my
    heart,
Dolefully saying, "Set thy house in order,
For thou shalt surely die, and shalt not
    live!"
For me the shadow on the dial-plate
Goeth not back, but on into the dark!

    [*Exit.*

SCENE IV. — *The street. A crowd, reading a placard on*
* the door of the Meeting-house.* NICHOLAS UPSALL
* among them. Enter* JOHN NORTON.

NORTON.

WHAT is this gathering here?

UPSALL.

    One William Brand,
An old man like ourselves, and weak in body,
Has been so cruelly tortured in his prison,
The people are excited, and they threaten
To tear the prison down.

NORTON.

    What has been done?

UPSALL.

He has been put in irons, with his neck
And heels tied close together, and so left
From five in the morning until nine at night.

NORTON.

What more was done?

UPSALL.

He has been kept five days
In prison without food, and cruelly beaten,
So that his limbs were cold, his senses stopped.

NORTON.

What more?

UPSALL.

And is this not enough?

NORTON.

Now hear me.
This William Brand of yours has tried to
    beat
Our Gospel Ordinances black and blue ;
And, if he has been beaten in like man-
    ner,
It is but justice, and I will appear

In his behalf that did so. I suppose
That he refused to work.

UPSALL.

He was too weak.
How could an old man work, when he was
    starving ?

NORTON.

And what is this placard?

UPSALL.

The Magistrates,
To appease the people and prevent a tumult,
Have put up these placards throughout the
    town,
Declaring that the jailer shall be dealt with
Impartially and sternly by the Court.

NORTON (*tearing down the placard*).

Down with this weak and cowardly conces-
    sion,

This flag of truce with Satan and with Sin!
I fling it in his face! I trample it
Under my feet! It is his cunning craft,
The masterpiece of his diplomacy,
To cry and plead for boundless toleration.
But toleration is the first-born child
Of all abominations and deceits.
There is no room in Christ's triumphant army
For tolerationists. And if an Angel
Preach any other gospel unto you
Than that ye have received, God's malediction
Descend upon him! Let him be accursed,

[*Exit.*

UPSALL.

Now, go thy ways, John Norton! go thy ways,
Thou Orthodox Evangelist, as men call thee!
But even now there cometh out of England,
Like an o'ertaking and accusing conscience,
An outraged man, to call thee to account
For the unrighteous murder of his son!

[*Exit.*

SCENE V. — *The Wilderness. Enter* EDITH.

EDITH.

How beautiful are these autumnal woods!
The wilderness doth blossom like the rose,

And change into a garden of the Lord!
How silent everywhere! Alone and lost
Here in the forest, there comes over me
An inward awfulness. I recall the words
Of the Apostle Paul: " In journeyings often,
Often in perils in the wilderness,
In weariness, in painfulness, in watchings,
In hunger and thirst, in cold and nakedness; "
And I forget my weariness and pain,

My watchings, and my hunger and my thirst.
The Lord hath said that He will seek his flock
In cloudy and dark days, and they shall dwell
Securely in the wilderness, and sleep
Safe in the woods! Whichever way I turn,
I come back with my face towards the town.

Dimly I see it, and the sea beyond it.
O cruel town! I know what waits me there,
And yet I must go back; for ever louder
I hear the inward calling of the Spirit,
And must obey the voice. O woods, that
    wear
Your golden crown of martyrdom, blood-
    stained,
From you I learn a lesson of submission,
And am obedient even unto death,
If God so wills it.   [*Exit.*

JOHN ENDICOTT (*within*).

      Edith! Edith! Edith!
        He enters.

It is in vain! I call, she answers not;
I follow, but I find no trace of her!
Blood! blood! The leaves above me and
    around me
Are red with blood! The pathways of the
    forest,

The clouds that canopy the setting sun,
And even the little river in the meadows
Are stained with it! Where'er I look, I
    see it!
Away, thou horrible vision! Leave me!
    leave me!
Alas! yon winding stream, that gropes its
    way
Through mist and shadow, doubling on itself,
At length will find, by the unerring law
Of nature, what it seeks. O soul of man,
Groping through mist and shadow, and re-
    coiling
Back on thyself, are, too, thy devious ways
Subject to law? and when thou seemest to
    wander
The farthest from thy goal, art thou still
    drawing
Nearer and nearer to it, till at length
Thou findest, like the river, what thou seek-
    est?   [*Exit.*

ACT V.

SCENE I. — *Daybreak. Street in front of* UPSALL'S *house.
A light in the window. Enter* JOHN ENDICOTT.

JOHN ENDICOTT.

O SILENT, sombre, and deserted streets,
To me ye 're peopled with a sad procession,
And echo only to the voice of sorrow!
O houses full of peacefulness and sleep,
Far better were it to awake no more
Than wake to look upon such scenes again!
There is a light in Master Upsall's window.
The good man is already risen, for sleep
Deserts the couches of the old.
    Knocks at UPSALL'S *door.*

UPSALL (*at the window*).

          Who 's there?

JOHN ENDICOTT.

Am I so changed you do not know my
    voice?

UPSALL.

I know you. Have you heard what things
    have happened?

JOHN ENDICOTT.

I have heard nothing.

UPSALL.

Stay; I will come down.

JOHN ENDICOTT.

I am afraid some dreadful news awaits me!
I do not dare to ask, yet am impatient
To know the worst. Oh, I am very weary
With waiting and with watching and pursu-
    ing!

Enter UPSALL.

UPSALL.

Thank God, you have come back! I 've much
    to tell you.
Where have you been?

JOHN ENDICOTT.

You know that I was seized,
Fined, and released again. You know that
    Edith,
After her scourging in three towns, was ban-
    ished
Into the wilderness, into the land
That is not sown; and there I followed
    her,
But found her not. Where is she?

UPSALL.

She is here.

JOHN ENDICOTT.

Oh, do not speak that word, for it means
    death!

UPSALL.

No, it means life. She sleeps in yonder
    chamber.
Listen to me. When news of Leddra's death
Reached England, Edward Burroughs, having
    boldly
Got access to the presence of the King,
Told him there was a vein of innocent blood
Opened in his dominions here, which threat-
    ened
  To overrun them all. The King replied,
"But I will stop that vein!" and he forth-
    with

Sent his Mandamus to our Magistrates,
That they proceed no further in this busi-
    ness.
So all are pardoned, and all set at large.

JOHN ENDICOTT.

Thank God! This is a victory for truth!
Our thoughts are free. They cannot be
    shut up
In prison walls, nor put to death on scaf-
    folds!

UPSALL.

Come in; the morning air blows sharp and
    cold
Through the damp streets.

JOHN ENDICOTT.

It is the dawn of day
That chases the old darkness from our
    sky,
And fills the land with liberty and light.
                     [*Exeunt.*

SCENE II. — *The parlor of the Three Mariners.*
    Enter KEMPTHORN.

KEMPTHORN.

A DULL life this, — a dull life anyway!
Ready for sea; the cargo all aboard,
Cleared for Barbadoes, and a fair wind
    blowing
From nor'-nor'-west; and I, an idle lub-
    ber,
Laid neck and heels by that confounded
    bond!
I said to Ralph, says I, "What 's to be
    done?"
Says he: "Just slip your hawser in the
    night;
Sheer off, and pay it with the topsail, Si-
    mon."
But that won't do; because, you see, the
    owners
Somehow or other are mixed up with it.
Here are King Charles's Twelve Good Rules,
    that Cole
Thinks as important as the Rule of Three.
    (*Reads.*)

" Make no comparisons; make no long meals."

Those are good rules and golden for a land-
　　lord
To hang in his best parlor, framed and
　　glazed !
" Maintain no ill opinions; urge no healths."
I drink the King's, whatever he may say,
And, as to ill opinions, that depends.
Now of Ralph Goldsmith I 've a good
　　opinion,
And of the bilboes I 've an ill opinion ;
And both of these opinions I 'll maintain
As long as there 's a shot left in the locker.

Enter EDWARD BUTTER *with an ear-trumpet.*

BUTTER.

Good morning, Captain Kempthorn.

KEMPTHORN.

　　　　　　Sir, to you.
You 've the advantage of me. I don't
　　know you.
What may I call your name ?

BUTTER.

　　That 's not your name ?

KEMPTHORN.

Yes, that 's my name. What 's yours ?

BUTTER.

　　　　　My name is Butter.
I am the treasurer of the Commonwealth.

KEMPTHORN.

Will you be seated ?

BUTTER.

　　What say ? Who 's conceited ?

KEMPTHORN.

Will you sit down ?

BUTTER.

　　Oh, thank you.

KEMPTHORN.

　　　　　　Spread yourself
Upon this chair, sweet Butter.

BUTTER (*sitting down*).

　　　　A fine morning.

KEMPTHORN.

Nothing's the matter with it that I know of.
I have seen better, and I have seen worse.
The wind 's nor'west. That 's fair for them
 that sail.

BUTTER.

You need not speak so loud; I understand
 you.
You sail to-day.

KEMPTHORN.

 No, I don't sail to-day.
So, be it fair or foul, it matters not.
Say, will you smoke? There 's choice tobacco
 here.

BUTTER.

No, thank you. It 's against the law to
 smoke.

KEMPTHORN.

Then, will you drink? There 's good ale at
 this inn.

BUTTER.

No, thank you. It 's against the law to
 drink.

KEMPTHORN.

Well, almost everything 's against the law
In this good town. Give a wide berth to one
 thing,
You 're sure to fetch up soon on something
 else.

BUTTER.

And so you sail to-day for dear Old Eng-
 land.
I am not one of those who think a sup
Of this New England air is better worth
Than a whole draught of our Old England's
 ale.

KEMPTHORN.

Nor I. Give me the ale and keep the air.
But, as I said, I do not sail to-day.

BUTTER.

Ah yes; you sail to-day.

KEMPTHORN.

 I 'm under bonds
To take some Quakers back to the Barbadoes;
And one of them is banished, and another
Is sentenced to be hanged.

BUTTER.

 No, all are pardoned,
All are set free, by order of the Court;
But some of them would fain return to Eng-
 land.
You must not take them. Upon that condi-
 tion
Your bond is cancelled.

KEMPTHORN.

 Ah, the wind has shifted!
I pray you, do you speak officially!

BUTTER.

I always speak officially. To prove it,
Here is the bond.
  Rising and giving a paper.

KEMPTHORN.

 And here 's my hand upon it.
And, look you, when I say I 'll do a thing
The thing is done. Am I now free to go?

BUTTER.

What say?

KEMPTHORN.

 I say, confound the tedious man
With his strange speaking-trumpet! Can I
 go?

BUTTER.

You 're free to go, by order of the Court.
Your servant, sir.   [*Exit.*

KEMPTHORN (*shouting from the window*).

 Swallow, ahoy! Hallo!
If ever a man was happy to leave Boston,
That man is Simon Kempthorn of the Swal-
 low!
  Reënter BUTTER.

BUTTER.

Pray, did you call?

KEMPTHORN.

Call? Yes, I hailed the Swallow.

BUTTER.

That's not my name. My name is Edward
Butter.
You need not speak so loud.

KEMPTHORN (*shaking hands*).

Good by! Good by!

BUTTER.

Your servant, sir.

KEMPTHORN.

And yours a thousand times!

[*Exeunt.*

SCENE III. — GOVERNOR ENDICOTT's *private room. An
open window.* ENDICOTT *seated in an arm-chair.*
BELLINGHAM *standing near.*

ENDICOTT.

O LOST, O loved! wilt thou return no more?
O loved and lost, and loved the more when
lost!
How many men are dragged into their graves
By their rebellious children! I now feel
The agony of a father's breaking heart
In David's cry, "O Absalom, my son!"

90

BELLINGHAM.

Can you not turn your thoughts a little
while
To public matters? There are papers here
That need attention.

ENDICOTT.

Trouble me no more!
My business now is with another world.
Ah, Richard Bellingham! I greatly fear
That in my righteous zeal I have been
led

To doing many things which, left undone,
My mind would now be easier. Did I dream
          it,
Or has some person told me, that John Norton
Is dead?

BELLINGHAM.

          You have not dreamed it. He is dead,
And gone to his reward. It was no dream.

ENDICOTT.

Then it was very sudden; for I saw him
Standing where you now stand, not long ago.

BELLINGHAM.

By his own fireside, in the afternoon,
A faintness and a giddiness came o'er him;
And, leaning on the chimney-piece, he cried,
" The hand of God is on me ! " and fell
          dead.

ENDICOTT.

And did not some one say, or have I
          dreamed it,
That Humphrey Atherton is dead?

BELLINGHAM.

                                   Alas !
He too is gone, and by a death as sudden.
Returning home one evening, at the place
Where usually the Quakers have been
          scourged,
His horse took fright, and threw him to
          the ground,
So that his brains were dashed about the
          street.

ENDICOTT.

I am not superstitious, Bellingham,
And yet I tremble lest it may have been
A judgment on him.

BELLINGHAM.
                    So the people think.
They say his horse saw standing in the way
The ghost of William Leddra, and was fright-
            ened.
And furthermore, brave Richard Davenport,
The captain of the Castle, in the storm
Has been struck dead by lightning.

ENDICOTT.
                        Speak no more.
For as I listen to your voice it seems
As if the Seven Thunders uttered their voices,
And the dead bodies lay about the streets
Of the disconsolate city! Bellingham,
I did not put those wretched men to death.
I did but guard the passage with the sword
Pointed towards them, and they rushed upon
            it!
Yet now I would that I had taken no part
In all that bloody work.

BELLINGHAM.
                    The guilt of it
Be on their heads, not ours.

ENDICOTT.
                        Are all set free?

BELLINGHAM.
All are at large.

ENDICOTT.
                    And none have been sent back
To England to malign us with the King?

BELLINGHAM.
The ship that brought them sails this very hour,
But carries no one back.
                    A distant cannon.

ENDICOTT.
                        What is that gun?

BELLINGHAM.
Her parting signal. Through the window
            there,

Look, you can see her sails, above the roofs,
Dropping below the Castle, outward bound.

ENDICOTT.

O white, white, white! Would that my soul
    had wings
As spotless as those shining sails to fly with!
Now lay this cushion straight. I thank you.
    Hark!
I thought I heard the hall door open and
    shut!
I thought I heard the footsteps of my boy!

BELLINGHAM.

It was the wind. There 's no one in the pas-
    sage.

ENDICOTT.

O Absalom, my son! I feel the world
Sinking beneath me, sinking, sinking, sinking!
Death knocks! I go to meet him! Welcome,
    Death!

*Rises, and sinks back dead; his head falling aside upon
his shoulder.*

BELLINGHAM.

O ghastly sight! Like one who has been
    hanged!
Endicott! Endicott! He makes no answer!
    Raises ENDICOTT'S *head.*
He breathes no more! How bright this signet-
    ring
Glitters upon his hand, where he has worn
    it
Through such long years of trouble, as if
    Death
Had given him this memento of affection,
And whispered in his ear, "Remember me!"
How placid and how quiet is his face,
Now that the struggle and the strife are
    ended!
Only the acrid spirit of the times
Corroded this true steel. Oh, rest in peace,
Courageous heart! Forever rest in peace!

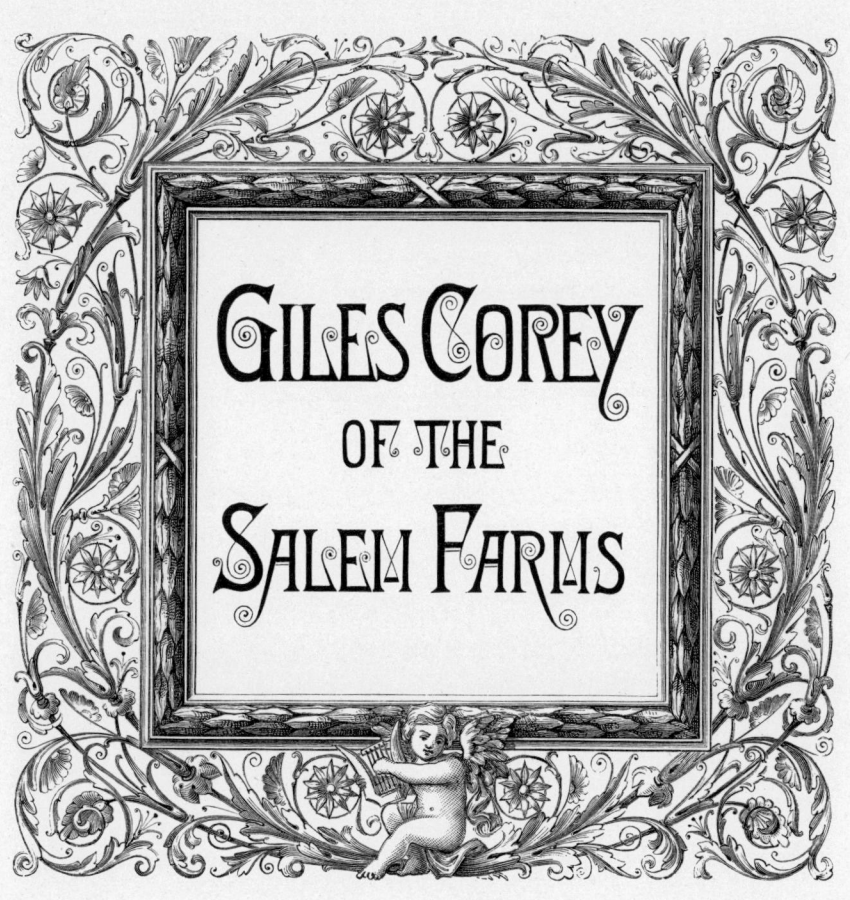

GILES COREY
OF THE
SALEM FARMS

DRAMATIS PERSONÆ.

GILES COREY .	*Farmer.*
JOHN HATHORNE	*Magistrate.*
COTTON MATHER	*Minister of the Gospel.*
JONATHAN WALCOT	*A youth.*
RICHARD GARDNER	*Sea-captain.*
JOHN GLOYD	*Corey's hired man.*
MARTHA .	*Wife of Giles Corey.*
TITUBA	*An Indian woman.*
MARY WALCOT	*One of the Afflicted.*

The Scene is in Salem in the year 1692.

ARTIST: A. F. BELLOWS.

PLEASANT STREET, SALEM.

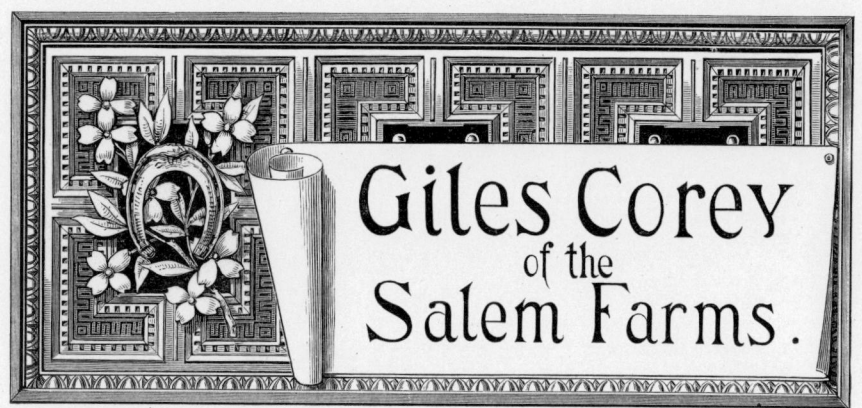

PROLOGUE.

DELUSIONS of the days that once have been,
Witchcraft and wonders of the world unseen,
Phantoms of air, and necromantic arts
That crushed the weak and awed the stoutest
    hearts, —
These are our theme to-night; and vaguely
    here,
Through the dim mists that crowd the at-
    mosphere,
We draw the outlines of weird figures cast
In shadow on the background of the Past.

Who would believe that in the quiet town
Of Salem, and amid the woods that crown
The neighboring hillsides, and the sunny
    farms
That fold it safe in their paternal arms, —
Who would believe that in those peaceful
    streets,
Where the great elms shut out the summer
    heats,
Where quiet reigns, and breathes through
    brain and breast
The benediction of unbroken rest, —
Who would believe such deeds could find a
    place
As these whose tragic history we retrace?

'T was but a village then: the goodman
    ploughed
His ample acres under sun or cloud;

The goodwife at her doorstep sat and spun,
And gossiped with her neighbors in the sun:
The only men of dignity and state
Were then the Minister and the Magistrate,
Who ruled their little realm with iron rod,
Less in the love than in the fear of God;
And who believed devoutly in the Powers
Of Darkness, working in this world of ours,
In spells of Witchcraft, incantations dread,
And shrouded apparitions of the dead.

Upon this simple folk " with fire and flame,"
Saith the old Chronicle "the Devil came;
Scattering his firebrands and his poisonous
    darts,
To set on fire of Hell all tongues and hearts!
And 't is no wonder; for, with all his host,
There most he rages where he hateth most,
And is most hated; so on us he brings
All these stupendous and portentous things!"

Something of this our scene to-night will
    show:
And ye who listen to the Tale of Woe,
Be not too swift in casting the first stone,
Nor think New England bears the guilt alone.
This sudden burst of wickedness and crime
Was but the common madness of the time,
When in all lands, that lie within the sound
Of Sabbath bells, a Witch was burned or
    drowned.

ACT I.

SCENE I. — *The woods near Salem Village. Enter* TITUBA, *with a basket of herbs.*

TITUBA.

HERE 's monk's-hood, that breeds fever in the
    blood ;
And deadly nightshade, that makes men see
    ghosts ;
And henbane, that will shake them with con-
    vulsions ;
And meadow-saffron and black hellebore,
That rack the nerves, and puff the skin with
    dropsy ;
And bitter-sweet, and briony, and eye-bright,
That cause eruptions, nosebleed, rheumatisms ;
I know them, and the places where they hide
In field and meadow ; and I know their
    secrets,
And gather them because they give me power
Over all men and women. Armed with these,
I, Tituba, an Indian and a slave,
Am stronger than the captain with his sword,
Am richer than the merchant with his money,
Am wiser than the scholar with his books,
Mightier than Ministers and Magistrates,
With all the fear and reverence that attend
    them !
For I can fill their bones with aches and
    pains,
Can make them cough with asthma, shake
    with palsy,

Can make their daughters see and talk with
    ghosts,
Or fall into delirium and convulsions.
I have the Evil Eye, the Evil Hand ;
A touch from me, and they are weak with
    pain,
A look from me, and they consume and die.
The death of cattle and the blight of corn,
The shipwreck, the tornado, and the fire, —
These are my doings, and they know it not.
Thus I work vengeance on mine enemies,
Who, while they call me slave, are slaves to
    me !

Exit TITUBA.   *Enter* MATHER, *booted and spurred, with
a riding-whip in his hand.*

MATHER.

Methinks that I have come by paths un-
    known
Into the land and atmosphere of Witches ;
For, meditating as I journeyed on,
Lo ! I have lost my way ! If I remember
Rightly, it is Scribonius the learned
That tells the story of a man who, praying
For one that was possessed by Evil Spirits,
Was struck by Evil Spirits in the face ;
I, journeying to circumvent the Witches,
Surely by Witches have been led astray.
I am persuaded there are few affairs
In which the Devil doth not interfere.
We cannot undertake a journey even,

But Satan will be there to meddle with it
By hindering or by furthering. He hath led
    me
Into this thicket, struck me in the face
With branches of the trees, and so entangled
The fetlocks of my horse with vines and
    brambles,
That I must needs dismount, and search on
    foot
For the lost pathway leading to the village.
        Reënter TITUBA.
What shape is this? What monstrous ap-
    parition,
Exceeding fierce, that none may pass that
    way ?
Tell me, good woman, if you are a woman —

        TITUBA.

I am a woman, but I am not good.
I am a Witch !

        MATHER.

      Then tell me, Witch and woman,
For you must know the pathways through
    this wood,
Where lieth Salem Village ?

        TITUBA.

        Reverend sir,
The village is near by. I 'm going there
With these few herbs. I 'll lead you. Follow
    me.

        MATHER.

First say, who are you? I am loath to follow
A stranger in this wilderness, for fear
Of being misled, and left in some morass.
Who are you?

        TITUBA.

      I am Tituba the Witch,
Wife of John Indian.

MATHER.

You are Tituba?
I know you then. You have renounced the
    Devil,
And have become a penitent confessor.
The Lord be praised! Go on, I 'll follow you.
Wait only till I fetch my horse, that stands
Tethered among the trees, not far from here.

TITUBA.

Let me get up behind you, reverend sir.

MATHER.

The Lord forbid! What would the people
    think,
If they should see the Reverend Cotton
    Mather
Ride into Salem with a Witch behind him?
The Lord forbid!

TITUBA.

                I do not need a horse!
I can ride through the air upon a stick,
Above the tree-tops and above the houses,
And no one see me, no one overtake me!
                                [*Exeunt.*

SCENE II. — *A room at* JUSTICE HATHORNE'S. *A clock
    in the corner. Enter* HATHORNE *and* MATHER.

HATHORNE.

YOU are welcome, reverend sir, thrice welcome
    here
Beneath my humble roof.

MATHER.

                I thank your Worship.

HATHORNE.

Pray you be seated. You must be fatigued
With your long ride through unfrequented
    woods.
                They sit down.

MATHER.

You know the purport of my visit here, —
To be advised by you, and counsel with you,
And with the Reverend Clergy of the village,
Touching these witchcrafts that so much af-
    flict you;

And see with mine own eyes the wonders
    told
Of spectres and the shadows of the dead,
That come back from their graves to speak
    with men.

HATHORNE.

Some men there are, I have known such, who
    think
That the two worlds — the seen and the un-
    seen,
The world of matter and the world of spirit —
Are like the hemispheres upon our maps,
And touch each other only at a point.
But these two worlds are not divided thus,
Save for the purposes of common speech.
They form one globe, in which the parted
    seas
All flow together and are intermingled,
While the great continents remain distinct.

MATHER.

I doubt it not. The spiritual world
Lies all about us, and its avenues
Are open to the unseen feet of phantoms
That come and go, and we perceive them not,
Save by their influence, or when at times
A most mysterious Providence permits them
To manifest themselves to mortal eyes.

HATHORNE.

You, who are always welcome here among
    us,
Are doubly welcome now. We need your
    wisdom,
Your learning in these things, to be our
    guide.
The Devil hath come down in wrath upon us,
And ravages the land with all his hosts.

MATHER.

The Unclean Spirit said, " My name is Le-
    gion ! "
Multitudes in the Valley of Destruction!
But when our fervent, well-directed prayers,
Which are the great artillery of Heaven,
Are brought into the field, I see them scat-
    tered
And driven like Autumn leaves before the
    wind.

HATHORNE.

You, as a Minister of God, can meet them
With spiritual weapons; but, alas!
I, as a Magistrate, must combat them
With weapons from the armory of the flesh.

MATHER.

These wonders of the world invisible, —
These spectral shapes that haunt our habita-
    tions, —
The multiplied and manifold afflictions
With which the aged and the dying saints
Have their death prefaced and their age im-
    bittered, —
Are but prophetic trumpets that proclaim
The Second Coming of our Lord on earth.
The evening wolves will be much more
    abroad,
When we are near the evening of the world.

HATHORNE.

When you shall see, as I have hourly seen,
The sorceries and the witchcrafts that tor-
    ment us,

See children tortured by invisible spirits,
And wasted and consumed by powers unseen,
You will confess the half has not been told
    you.

MATHER.

It must be so. The death-pangs of the Devil
Will make him more a Devil than before;
And Nebuchadnezzar's furnace will be heated
Seven times more hot before its putting out.

HATHORNE.

Advise me, reverend sir. I look to you
For counsel and for guidance in this matter.
What further shall we do?

MATHER.

             Remember this,
That as a sparrow falls not to the ground
Without the will of God, so not a Devil
Can come down from the air without his
    leave.
We must inquire.

HATHORNE.

           Dear sir, we have inquired;
Sifted the matter thoroughly through and
    through,
And then resifted it.

MATHER.

          If God permits
These Evil Spirits from the unseen regions
To visit us with surprising informations,
We must inquire what cause there is for
    this,
But not receive the testimony borne
By spectres as conclusive proof of guilt
In the accused.

HATHORNE.

        Upon such evidence
We do not rest our case. The ways are
    many
In which the guilty do betray themselves.

MATHER.

Be careful. Carry the knife with such exact-
    ness,
That on one side no innocent blood be shed

By too excessive zeal, and, on the other
No shelter given to any work of darkness.

HATHORNE.

For one, I do not fear excess of zeal.
What do we gain by parleying with the
    Devil?
You reason, but you hesitate to act!
Ah, reverend sir! believe me, in such cases
The only safety is in acting promptly.
'T is not the part of wisdom to delay
In things where not to do is still to do
A deed more fatal than the deed we shrink
    from.
You are a man of books and meditation,
But I am one who acts.

MATHER.

                    God give us wisdom
In the directing of this thorny business,
And guide us, lest New England should be-
    come
Of an unsavory and sulphurous odor
In the opinion of the world abroad!
            The clock strikes.
I never hear the striking of a clock
Without a warning and an admonition
That time is on the wing, and we must
    quicken
Our tardy pace in journeying Heavenward,
As Israel did in journeying Canaan-ward!
            They rise.

HATHORNE.

Then let us make all haste; and I will show
    you
In what disguises and what fearful shapes
The Unclean Spirits haunt this neighbor-
    hood,
And you will pardon my excess of zeal.

MATHER.

Ah, poor New England! He who hurrica-
    noed
The house of Job is making now on thee
One last assault, more deadly and more
    snarled
With unintelligible circumstances
Than any thou hast hitherto encountered!
            [*Exeunt.*

SCENE III. — *A room in* WALCOT's *house.* MARY WAL-
    COT *seated in an arm-chair.* TITUBA *with a mir-
    ror.*

MARY.

Tell me another story, Tituba.
A drowsiness is stealing over me
Which is not sleep; for, though I close mine
    eyes,
I am awake, and in another world.
Dim faces of the dead and of the absent
Come floating up before me, — floating, fad-
    ing,
And disappearing.

TITUBA.

                Look into this glass.
What see you?

MARY.

                Nothing but a golden vapor.
Yes, something more. An island, with the
    sea
Breaking all round it, like a blooming hedge.
What land is this?

TITUBA.

                It is San Salvador,
Where Tituba was born. What see you now?

MARY.

A man all black and fierce.

TITUBA.

                    That is my father.
He was an Obi man, and taught me magic, —
Taught me the use of herbs and images.
What is he doing?

MARY.

                Holding in his hand
A waxen figure. He is melting it
Slowly before a fire.

TITUBA.

            And now what see you?

MARY.

A woman lying on a bed of leaves,
Wasted and worn away. Ah, she is dy-
    ing!

TITUBA.

That is the way the Obi men destroy
The people they dislike ! That is the way
Some one is wasting and consuming you.

MARY.

You terrify me, Tituba ! Oh, save me
From those who make me pine and waste
    away !
Who are they ? Tell me.

TITUBA.

       That I do not know,
But you will see them. They will come to
    you.

MARY.

No, do not let them come ! I cannot bear it !
I am too weak to bear it ! I am dying ;
    Falls into a trance.

TITUBA.

Hark ! there is some one coming !
   Enter HATHORNE, MATHER, *and* WALCOT.

WALCOT.

        There she lies,
Wasted and worn by devilish incantations !
O my poor sister !

MATHER.

    Is she always thus ?

WALCOT.

Nay, she is sometimes tortured by convul-
    sions.

MATHER.

Poor child ! How thin she is ! How wan
    and wasted !

HATHORNE.

Observe her. She is troubled in her sleep.

MATHER.

Some fearful vision haunts her.

HATHORNE.

           You now see
With your own eyes, and touch with your
    own hands,
The mysteries of this Witchcraft.

MATHER.

                One would need
The hands of Briareus and the eyes of Argus
To see and touch them all.

HATHORNE.

             You now have entered
The realm of ghosts and phantoms, — the
    vast realm
Of the unknown and the invisible,
Through whose wide-open gates there blows
    a wind
From the dark valley of the shadow of Death,
That freezes us with horror.

MARY (*starting*).

              Take her hence!
Take her away from me. I see her there!
She's coming to torment me!

WALCOT (*taking her hand*).

              O my sister!
What frightens you? She neither hears nor
    sees me.
She's in a trance.

MARY.

        Do you not see her there?

TITUBA.

My child, who is it?

MARY.

           Ah, I do not know.
I cannot see her face.

TITUBA.

          How is she clad?

MARY.

She wears a crimson bodice. In her hand
She holds an image, and is pinching it
Between her fingers. Ah, she tortures me!
I see her face now. It is Goodwife Bishop!
Why does she torture me? I never harmed
    her!
And now she strikes me with an iron rod!
Oh, I am beaten!

MATHER.

        This is wonderful!

I can see nothing! Is this apparition
Visibly there, and yet we cannot see it?

HATHORNE.

It is. The spectre is invisible
Unto our grosser senses, but she sees it.

MARY.

Look! look! there is another clad in gray!
She holds a spindle in her hand, and threat-
    ens
To stab me with it! It is Goodwife Corey!
Keep her away! Now she is coming at me!
O mercy! mercy!

WALCOT (*thrusting with his sword*).

        There is nothing there!

MATHER (*to* HATHORNE).

Do you see anything?

HATHORNE.

           The laws that govern
The spiritual world prevent our seeing
Things palpable and visible to her.
These spectres are to us as if they were not.
Mark her; she wakes.
    TITUBA *touches her, and she awakes.*

MARY.

        Who are these gentlemen?

WALCOT.

They are our friends. Dear Mary, are you
    better?

MARY.

Weak, very weak.
    Taking a spindle from her lap, and holding it up.
        How came this spindle here?

TITUBA.

You wrenched it from the hand of Good-
    wife Corey
When she rushed at you.

HATHORNE.

        Mark that, reverend sir!

MATHER.

It is most marvellous, most inexplicable!

TITUBA (*picking up a bit of gray cloth from the floor*).
And here, too, is a bit of her gray dress,
That the sword cut away.

MATHER.

Beholding this,
It were indeed by far more credulous
To be incredulous than to believe.
None but a Sadducee, who doubts of all
Pertaining to the spiritual world,
Could doubt such manifest and damning proofs!

HATHORNE.
Are you convinced?

MATHER (*to Mary*).

Dear child, be comforted!
Only by prayer and fasting can you drive
These Unclean Spirits from you.   An old man
Gives you his blessing. God be with you, Mary!

ACT II.

SCENE I. — GILES COREY'S *farm. Morning. Enter*
COREY, *with a horseshoe and a hammer.*

COREY.

THE LORD hath prospered me. The rising sun
Shines on my Hundred Acres and my woods
As if he loved them. On a morn like this
I can forgive mine enemies, and thank God
For all his goodness unto me and mine.
My orchard groans with russets and pear-mains;
My ripening corn shines golden in the sun;
My barns are crammed with hay, my cattle thrive;
The birds sing blithely on the trees around me!
And blither than the birds my heart within me,
But Satan still goes up and down the earth;
And to protect this house from his assaults,
And keep the powers of darkness from my door,
This horseshoe will I nail upon the threshold.
Nails down the horseshoe.
There, ye night-hags and witches that torment
The neighborhood, ye shall not enter here! —
What is the matter in the field? — John Gloyd!
The cattle are all running to the woods! —
John Gloyd! Where is the man?
Enter JOHN GLOYD.
92

Look there!
What ails the cattle?   Are they all be-witched?
They run like mad.

GLOYD.

They have been overlooked.

COREY.

The Evil Eye is on them sure enough.
Call all the men. Be quick. Go after them!
Exit GLOYD *and enter* MARTHA.

MARTHA.

What is amiss?

COREY.

          The cattle are bewitched.
They are broken loose and making for the
          woods.

MARTHA.

Why will you harbor such delusions, Giles?
Bewitched? Well, then it was John Gloyd
          bewitched them;
I saw him even now take down the bars
And turn them loose! They 're only frolic-
          some.

COREY.

The rascal!

MARTHA.

          I was standing in the road,
Talking with Goodwife Proctor, and I saw
          him.

COREY.

With Proctor's wife? And what says Good-
          wife Proctor?

MARTHA.

Sad things indeed; the saddest you can hear
Of Bridget Bishop. She 's cried out upon!

COREY.

Poor soul! I 've known her forty year or
          more.
She was the widow Wasselby; and then
She married Oliver, and Bishop next.
She 's had three husbands. I remember well
My games of shovel-board at Bishop's tavern
In the old merry days, and she so gay
With her red paragon bodice and her ribbons!
Ah, Bridget Bishop always was a Witch!

MARTHA.

They 'll little help her now, — her caps and
          ribbons,
And her red paragon bodice, and her plumes,
With which she flaunted in the Meeting-house!
When next she goes there, it will be for trial.

COREY.

When will that be?

MARTHA.

          This very day at ten.

COREY.

Then get you ready. We will go and see it.
Come; you shall ride behind me on the pillion.

MARTHA.

Not I. You know I do not like such things.
I wonder you should. I do not believe
In Witches nor in Witchcraft.

COREY.

                    Well, I do.
There 's a strange fascination in it all,
That draws me on and on, I know not why.

MARTHA.

What do we know of spirits good or ill,
Or of their power to help us or to harm us?

COREY.

Surely what 's in the Bible must be true.
Did not an Evil Spirit come on Saul?
Did not the Witch of Endor bring the ghost
Of Samuel from his grave? The Bible says so.

MARTHA.

That happened very long ago.

COREY.

                    With God
There is no long ago.

MARTHA.

          There is with us.

COREY.

And Mary Magdalene had seven devils,
And he who dwelt among the tombs a legion!

MARTHA.

God's power is infinite. I do not doubt it.
If in his providence He once permitted
Such things to be among the Israelites,
It does not follow He permits them now,
And among us who are not Israelites.
But we will not dispute about it, Giles.
Go to the village, if you think it best,
And leave me here ; I 'll go about my work.

[Exit into the house.

COREY.

And I will go and saddle the gray mare.
The last word always. That is woman's
    nature.
If an old man will marry a young wife,
He must make up his mind to many things.
It 's putting new cloth into an old garment,
When the strain comes, it is the old gives way.

Goes to the door.

O Martha ! I forgot to tell you something.
I 've had a letter from a friend of mine,
A certain Richard Gardner of Nantucket,
Master and owner of a whaling-vessel ;

He writes that he is coming down to see us.
I hope you 'll like him.

MARTHA.

            I will do my best.

COREY.

That 's a good woman. Now I will be gone.
I 've not seen Gardner for this twenty year ;
But there is something of the sea about
    him, —
Something so open, generous, large, and strong,
It makes me love him better than a brother.

[Exit.

MARTHA *comes to the door.*

MARTHA.

Oh these old friends and cronies of my husband,
These captains from Nantucket and the Cape,
That come and turn my house into a tavern
With their carousing ! Still, there 's some-
    thing frank
In these seafaring men that makes me like
    them.

Why, here 's a horseshoe nailed upon the
    doorstep !
Giles has done this to keep away the Witches,
I hope this Richard Gardner will bring with
    him
A gale of good sound common-sense, to blow
The fog of these delusions from his brain !

COREY (*within*).

Ho ! Martha ! Martha !
    Enter COREY.
        Have you seen my saddle ?

MARTHA.

I saw it yesterday.

COREY.

       Where did you see it ?

MARTHA.

On a gray mare, that somebody was riding
Along the village road.

COREY.

       Who was it ? Tell me.

MARTHA.

Some one who should have stayed at home.

COREY (*restraining himself*).

                 I see !
Don't vex me, Martha.   Tell me where it is.

MARTHA.

I 've hidden it away.

COREY.

       Go fetch it me.

MARTHA.

Go find it.

COREY.

    No. I 'll ride down to the village
Bare-back ; and when the people stare and
    say,
" Giles Corey, where 's your saddle ? " I will
    answer,
" A Witch has stolen it."   How shall you like
    that ?

MARTHA.

I shall not like it.

COREY.

      Then go fetch the saddle.
                [*Exit* MARTHA.
If an old man will marry a young wife,
Why then — why then — why then — he must
    spell Baker ![1]
Enter MARTHA *with the saddle, which she throws down.*

MARTHA.

There !   There 's the saddle.

COREY.

             Take it up.

MARTHA.

                  I won't !

COREY.

Then let it lie there. I 'll ride to the vil-
    lage,
And say you are a Witch.

MARTHA.

          No, not that, Giles.
    She takes up the saddle.

COREY.

Now come with me, and saddle the gray
    mare
With your own hands ; and you shall see me
    ride
Along the village road as is becoming
Giles Corey of the Salem Farms, your husband !
                [*Exeunt.*

SCENE II. — *The Green in front of the Meeting-house in
    Salem Village. People coming and going. Enter* GILES
    COREY.

COREY.

A MELANCHOLY end !   Who would have
    thought
That Bridget Bishop e'er would come to this ?

---

[1] A local expression for doing anything difficult. In the old
spelling-books, Baker was the first word of two syllables, and
when a child came to it he thought he had a hard task before
him.

Accused, convicted, and condemned to death
For Witchcraft! And so good a woman too!

A FARMER.

Good morrow, neighbor Corey.

COREY (*not hearing him*).

           Who is safe?
How do I know but under my own roof
I too may harbor Witches, and some Devil
Be plotting and contriving against me?

FARMER.

He does not hear. Good morrow, neighbor
    Corey!

COREY.

Good morrow.

FARMER.

    Have you seen John Proctor lately?

COREY.

No, I have not.

FARMER.

    Then do not see him, Corey.

COREY.

Why should I not?

FARMER.

    Because he's angry with you.
So keep out of his way. Avoid a quarrel.

COREY.

Why does he seek to fix a quarrel on me?

FARMER.

He says you burned his house.

COREY.

    I burn his house?

If he says that, John Proctor is a liar!
The night his house was burned I was in
    bed,
And I can prove it! Why, we are old friends!
He could not say that of me.

FARMER.

                 He did say it.
I heard him say it.

COREY.

             Then he shall unsay it.

FARMER.

He said you did it out of spite to him
For taking part against you in the quarrel
You had with your John Gloyd about his
    wages.
He says you murdered Goodell; that you
    trampled
Upon his body till he breathed no more.
And so beware of him; that's my advice!
                        [*Exit.*

COREY.

By Heaven! this is too much! I'll seek him
    out,
And make him eat his words, or strangle him.
I'll not be slandered at a time like this,
When every word is made an accusation,
When every whisper kills, and every man
Walks with a halter round his neck!
        Enter GLOYD *in haste.*
                     What now?

GLOYD.

I came to look for you. The cattle—

COREY.

                    Well,
What of them? Have you found them?

GLOYD.

               They are dead.
I followed them through the woods, across
    the meadows;
Then they all leaped into the Ipswich River,
And swam across, but could not climb the
    bank,
And so were drowned.

COREY.

           You are to blame for this;
For you took down the bars, and let them
    loose.

GLOYD.

That I deny. They broke the fences down.
You know they were bewitched.

COREY.

              Ah, my poor cattle!
The Evil Eye was on them; that is true.
Day of disaster! Most unlucky day!
Why did I leave my ploughing and my reap-
    ing
To plough and reap this Sodom and Go-
    morrah?
Oh, I could drown myself for sheer vexation!
                        [*Exit.*

GLOYD.

He's going for his cattle. He won't find
    them.
By this time they have drifted out to sea.
They will not break his fences any more,
Though they may break his heart. And
    what care I?   [*Exit.*

SCENE III. — COREY'S *kitchen. A table with supper.*
    MARTHA *knitting.*

MARTHA.

HE's come at last. I hear him in the passage.
Something has gone amiss with him to-day;
I know it by his step, and by the sound
The door made as he shut it. He is angry.

Enter COREY *with his riding-whip. As he speaks he
takes off his hat and gloves, and throws them down
violently.*

COREY.

I say if Satan ever entered man
He's in John Proctor!

MARTHA.

           Giles, what is the matter?
You frighten me.

COREY.

           I say if any man

Can have a Devil in him, then that man
Is Proctor, — is John Proctor, and no other !

MARTHA.

Why, what has he been doing?

COREY.

Everything!
What do you think I heard there in the
village?

MARTHA.

I 'm sure I cannot guess. What did you
hear?

COREY.

He says I burned his house !

MARTHA.

Does he say that ?

COREY.

He says I burned his house. I was in bed
And fast asleep that night ; and I can prove
it.

MARTHA.

If he says that, I think the Father of Lies
Is surely in the man.

COREY.

He does say that,
And that I did it to wreak vengeance on
him
For taking sides against me in the quarrel
I had with that John Gloyd about his wages.
And God knows that I never bore him mal-
ice
For that, as I have told him twenty times !

MARTHA.

It is John Gloyd has stirred him up to this.
I do not like that Gloyd. I think him
crafty,
Not to be trusted, sullen, and untruthful.
Come, have your supper. You are tired and
hungry.

COREY.

I 'm angry, and not hungry.

MARTHA.

Do eat something.
You 'll be the better for it.

COREY (*sitting down*).

I 'm not hungry.

MARTHA.

Let not the sun go down upon your wrath.

COREY.

It has gone down upon it, and will rise
To-morrow, and go down again upon it.
They have trumped up against me the old
story
Of causing Goodell's death by trampling on
him.

MARTHA.

Oh, that is false. I know it to be false.

COREY.

He has been dead these fourteen years or
more.
Why can't they let him rest? Why must
they drag him
Out of his grave to give me a bad name !
I did not kill him. In his bed he died,
As most men die, because his hour had come.
I have wronged no man. Why should Proc-
tor say
Such things about me? I will not forgive
him
Till he confesses he has slandered me.
Then, I 've more trouble. All my cattle gone.

MARTHA.

They will come back again.

COREY.

Not in this world.
Did I not tell you they were overlooked?
They ran down through the woods, into the
meadows,
And tried to swim the river, and were
drowned.
It is a heavy loss.

MARTHA.

I 'm sorry for it.

COREY.

All my dear oxen dead. I loved them,
    Martha,
Next to yourself. I liked to look at them,
And watch the breath come out of their
    wide nostrils,
And see their patient eyes. Somehow I
    thought
It gave me strength only to look at them.
And how they strained their necks against
    the yoke
If I but spoke, or touched them with the
    goad !
They were my friends ; and when Gloyd
    came and told me
They were all drowned, I could have
    drowned myself
From sheer vexation ; and I said as much
To Gloyd and others.

MARTHA.

            Do not trust John Gloyd
With anything you would not have re-
    peated.

COREY.

As I came through the woods this after-
    noon,
Impatient at my loss, and much perplexed
With all that I had heard there in the
    village,
The yellow leaves lit up the trees about
    me
Like an enchanted palace, and I wished
I knew enough of magic or of Witchraft
To change them into gold. Then suddenly
A tree shook down some crimson leaves
    upon me,
Like drops of blood, and in the path be-
    fore me
Stood Tituba the Indian, the old crone.

MARTHA.

Were you not frightened ?

COREY.

            No, I do not think
I know the meaning of that word. Why
    frightened ?

I am not one of those who think the Lord
Is waiting till He catches them some day
In the back yard alone! What should I
    fear?
She started from the bushes by the path,
And had a basket full of herbs and roots
For some witch-broth or other, — the old
    hag!

MARTHA.

She has been here to-day.

COREY.

                    With hand outstretched
She said : " Giles Corey, will you sign the
    Book ? "
" Avaunt ! " I cried : " Get thee behind me,
    Satan ! "
At which she laughed and left me. But a
    voice
Was whispering in my ear continually :
" Self-murder is no crime. The life of man
Is his, to keep it or to throw away ! "

MARTHA.

'T was a temptation of the Evil One !
Giles, Giles ! why will you harbor these
    dark thoughts?

COREY (*rising*).

I am too tired to talk. I 'll go to bed.

MARTHA.

First tell me something about Bridget
    Bishop.
How did she look? You saw her? You
    were there ?

COREY.

I 'll tell you that to-morrow, not to-night.
I 'll go to bed.

MARTHA.

                    First let us pray together.

COREY.

I cannot pray to-night.

MARTHA.

                    Say the Lord's Prayer,
And that will comfort you.

COREY.

                    I cannot say,
" As we forgive those that have sinned
    against us,"
When I do not forgive them.

MARTHA (*kneeling on the hearth*).
                    God forgive you !

COREY.

I will not make believe ! I say, to-night
There 's something thwarts me when I
          wish to pray,
And thrusts into my mind, instead of
          prayers,
Hate and revenge, and things that are not
          prayers.

Something of my old self, — my old, bad
          life, —
And the old Adam in me, rises up,
And will not let me pray. I am afraid
The Devil hinders me. You know I say
Just what I think, and nothing more nor
          less,
And, when I pray, my heart is in my prayer.
I cannot say one thing and mean another.
If I can't pray, I will not make believe !
          [*Exit* COREY. MARTHA *continues kneeling.*

ACT III.

SCENE I. — GILES COREY's *kitchen. Morning.* COREY
  and MARTHA *sitting at the breakfast-table.*

COREY (*rising*).
WELL, now I 've told you all I saw and heard
Of Bridget Bishop ; and I must be gone.

MARTHA.

Don't go into the village, Giles, to-day.
Last night you came back tired and out of
          humor.

COREY.

Say, angry ; say, right angry. I was never
In a more devilish temper in my life.
All things went wrong with me.

MARTHA.

                    You were much vexed ;
So don't go to the village.

COREY (*going*).
                    No, I won't.
I won't go near it. We are going to mow
The Ipswich meadows for the aftermath,
The crop of sedge and rowens.

MARTHA.

                    Stay a moment.
I want to tell you what I dreamed last night.
Do you believe in dreams ?

COREY.

                    Why, yes and no.
When they come true, then I believe in them ;

When they come false, I don't believe in them.
But let me hear.   What did you dream about ?

MARTHA.

I dreamed that you and I were both in prison ;
That we had fetters on our hands and feet ;
That we were taken before the Magistrates,
And tried for Witchcraft, and condemned to
          death !
I wished to pray ; they would not let me
          pray ;
You tried to comfort me, and they forbade it.
But the most dreadful thing in all my dream
Was that they made you testify against me !
And then there came a kind of mist between
          us ;
I could not see you ; and I woke in terror.
I never was more thankful in my life
Than when I found you sleeping at my side !

COREY (*with tenderness*).

It was our talk last night that made you
          dream.
I 'm sorry for it. I 'll control myself
Another time, and keep my temper down !
I do not like such dreams. — Remember,
          Martha,
I 'm going to mow the Ipswich River mead-
          ows ;
If Gardner comes, you 'll tell him where to
          find me.   [*Exit.*

MARTHA.

So this delusion grows from bad to worse.
First, a forsaken and forlorn old woman,

Ragged and wretched, and without a friend;
Then something higher. Now it's Bridget
    Bishop;
God only knows whose turn it will be next!
The Magistrates are blind, the people mad!
If they would only seize the Afflicted Chil-
    dren,
And put them in the Workhouse, where they
    should be,
There 'd be an end of all this wickedness.
                     [*Exit.*

SCENE II. — *A street in Salem Village. Enter* MATHER
      and HATHORNE.

MATHER.

YET one thing troubles me.

HATHORNE.

                And what is that?

MATHER.

May not the Devil take the outward shape
Of innocent persons? Are we not in danger,
Perhaps, of punishing some who are not
    guilty?

HATHORNE.

As I have said, we do not trust alone
To spectral evidence.

MATHER.

            And then again,
If any shall be put to death for Witchcraft,
We do but kill the body, not the soul.
The Unclean Spirits that possessed them once
Live still, to enter into other bodies.
What have we gained? Surely, there 's noth-
    ing gained.

HATHORNE.

Doth not the Scripture say, "Thou shalt not
    suffer
A Witch to live?"

MATHER.

The Scripture sayeth it,
But speaketh to the Jews; and we are Christians.
What say the laws of England?

HATHORNE.

They make Witchcraft
Felony without the benefit of Clergy.
Witches are burned in England. You have read —
For you read all things, not a book escapes you —
The famous "Demonology" of King James?

MATHER.

A curious volume. I remember also
The plot of the Two Hundred, with one Fian,
The Registrar of the Devil, at their head,
To drown his Majesty on his return
From Denmark; how they sailed in sieves or riddles
Unto North Berwick Kirk in Lothian,
And, landing there, danced hand in hand, and sang,
"Goodwife, go ye before! goodwife, go ye!
If ye 'll not go before, goodwife, let me!"
While Geilis Duncan played the Witches' Reel
Upon a jews-harp.

HATHORNE.

Then you know full well
The English law, and that in England Witches,
When lawfully convicted and attainted,
Are put to death.

MATHER.

When lawfully convicted;
That is the point.

HATHORNE.

You heard the evidence
Produced before us yesterday at the trial
Of Bridget Bishop.

MATHER.

One of the Afflicted,
I know, bore witness to the apparition
Of ghosts unto the spectre of this Bishop,
Saying, "You murdered us!" of the truth whereof
There was in matter of fact too much suspicion.

HATHORNE.

And when she cast her eyes on the Afflicted,
They were struck down; and this in such a manner
There could be no collusion in the business.
And when the accused but laid her hand upon them,
As they lay in their swoons, they straight revived,
Although they stirred not when the others touched them.

MATHER.

What most convinced me of the woman's guilt
Was finding hidden in her cellar wall
Those poppets made of rags, with headless pins
Stuck into them point outwards, and whereof
She could not give a reasonable account.

HATHORNE.

When you shall read the testimony given
Before the Court in all the other cases,
I am persuaded you will find the proof
No less conclusive than it was in this.
Come, then, with me, and I will tax your patience
With reading of the documents so far
As may convince you that these sorcerers
Are lawfully convicted and attainted.
Like doubting Thomas, you shall lay your hand
Upon these wounds, and you will doubt no more.   [*Exeunt.*

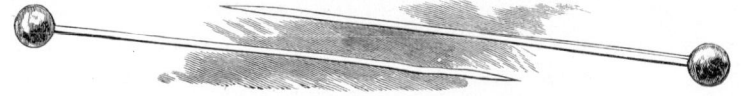

SCENE III. — *A room in* COREY's *house.* MARTHA *and two Deacons of the church.*

MARTHA.

BE seated. I am glad to see you here.
I know what you are come for. You are come
To question me, and learn from my own lips
If I have any dealings with the Devil;
In short, if I 'm a Witch.

DEACON (*sitting down*).

Such is our purpose.
How could you know beforehand why we came?

MARTHA.

'T was only a surmise.

DEACON.

We came to ask you
You being with us in church covenant,
What part you have, if any, in these matters.

MARTHA.

And I make answer, No part whatsoever.
I am a farmer's wife, a working woman;
You see my spinning-wheel, you see my loom,
You know the duties of a farmer's wife,
And are not ignorant that my life among you
Has been without reproach until this day.
Is it not true?

DEACON.

So much we 're bound to own;
And say it frankly, and without reserve.

MARTHA.

I 've heard the idle tales that are abroad;
I 've heard it whispered that I am a Witch;
I cannot help it. I do not believe
In any Witchcraft. It is a delusion.

DEACON.

How can you say that it is a delusion,
When all our learned and good men believe it? —
Our Ministers and worshipful Magistrates?

MARTHA.

Their eyes are blinded, and see not the truth.
Perhaps one day they will be open to it.

DEACON.

You answer boldly. The Afflicted Children
Say you appeared to them.

MARTHA.

And did they say
What clothes I came in?

DEACON.

No, they could not tell.
They said that you foresaw our visit here,
And blinded them, so that they could not see
The clothes you wore.

MARTHA.

The cunning, crafty girls!
I say to you, in all sincerity,
I never have appeared to any one
In my own person. If the Devil takes
My shape to hurt these children, or afflict them,
I am not guilty of it. And I say
It 's all a mere delusion of the senses.

DEACON.

I greatly fear that you will find too late
It is not so.

MARTHA (*rising*).

They do accuse me falsely.
It is delusion, or it is deceit.
There is a story in the ancient Scriptures
Which much I wonder comes not to your minds.
Let me repeat it to you.

DEACON.

We will hear it.

MARTHA.

It came to pass that Naboth had a vineyard
Hard by the palace of the King called Ahab.
And Ahab, King of Israel, spake to Naboth,
And said to him, Give unto me thy vineyard,

That I may have it for a garden of herbs,
And I will give a better vineyard for it,
Or, if it seemeth good to thee, its worth
In money. And then Naboth said to Ahab,
The Lord forbid it me that I should give
The inheritance of my fathers unto thee.
And Ahab came into his house displeased
And heavy at the words which Naboth spake,
And laid him down upon his bed, and turned
His face away; and he would eat no bread.
And Jezebel, the wife of Ahab, came
And said to him, Why is thy spirit sad?
And he said unto her, Because I spake
To Naboth, to the Jezreelite, and said,
Give me thy vineyard; and he answered,
　　saying,
I will not give my vineyard unto thee.
And Jezebel, the wife of Ahab, said,
Dost thou not rule the realm of Israel?
Arise, eat bread, and let thy heart be merry;
I will give Naboth's vineyard unto thee.
So she wrote letters in King Ahab's name,
And sealed them with his seal, and sent the
　　letters
Unto the elders that were in his city
Dwelling with Naboth, and unto the nobles;
And in the letters wrote, Proclaim a fast;
And set this Naboth high among the people,
And set two men, the sons of Belial,
Before him, to bear witness and to say,
Thou didst blaspheme against God and the
　　King;
And carry him out and stone him, that he
　　die!
And the elders and the nobles of the city
Did even as Jezebel, the wife of Ahab,
Had sent to them and written in the let-
　　ters.
And then it came to pass, when Ahab heard
Naboth was dead, that Ahab rose to go
Down unto Naboth's vineyard, and to take
Possession of it. And the word of God
Came to Elijah, saying to him, Arise,
Go down to meet the King of Israel
In Naboth's vineyard, whither he hath gone
To take possession. Thou shalt speak to him,
Saying, Thus saith the Lord! What! hast
　　thou killed
And also taken possession? In the place
Wherein the dogs have licked the blood of
　　Naboth

Shall the dogs lick thy blood, — ay, even thine!
Both of the Deacons start from their seats.
And Ahab then, the King of Israel,
Said, Hast thou found me, O mine enemy?
Elijah the Prophet answered, I have found
　　thee!
So will it be with those who have stirred up
The Sons of Belial here to bear false witness
And swear away the lives of innocent people;
Their enemy will find them out at last,
The Prophet's voice will thunder, I have
　　found thee !　　　　　　[*Exeunt.*

SCENE IV. — *Meadows on Ipswich River.* COREY *and
his men mowing;* COREY *in advance.*

COREY.

WELL done, my men. You see, I lead the
　　field!
I 'm an old man, but I can swing a scythe
Better than most of you, though you be
　　younger.
　　Hangs his scythe upon a tree.

GLOYD (*aside to the others*).

How strong he is! It 's supernatural.
No man so old as he is has such strength.
The Devil helps him!

COREY (*wiping his forehead*).
　　　　　　Now we 'll rest awhile,
And take our nooning. What 's the matter
　　with you?
You are not angry with me, — are you,
　　Gloyd?
Come, come, we will not quarrel. Let 's be
　　friends.
It 's an old story, that the Raven said,
"Read the Third of Colossians and fifteenth."

GLOYD.

You 're handier at the scythe, but I can beat
　　you
At wrestling.

COREY.
　　　　　　Well, perhaps so. I don't know.
I never wrestled with you. Why, you 're
　　vexed!
Come, come, don't bear a grudge.

GLOYD.

You are afraid.

COREY.

What should I be afraid of? All bear witness
The challenge comes from him. Now, then, my man.

They wrestle, and GLOYD *is thrown.*

ONE OF THE MEN.

That's a fair fall.

ANOTHER.

'T was nothing but a foil!

OTHERS.

You've hurt him!

COREY (*helping* GLOYD *rise*).

No; this meadow-land is soft.
You're not hurt, — are you, Gloyd?

GLOYD (*rising*).

No, not much hurt!

COREY.

Well, then, shake hands; and there's an end of it.
How do you like that Cornish hug, my lad?
And now we'll see what's in our basket here.

GLOYD (*aside*).

The Devil and all his imps are in that man!
The clutch of his ten fingers burns like fire!

COREY (*reverentially taking off his hat*).

God bless the food He hath provided for us,
And make us thankful for it, for Christ's sake!

He lifts up a keg of cider, and drinks from it.

GLOYD.

Do you see that? Don't tell me it's not
　　Witchcraft.
Two of us could not lift that cask as he does!

COREY *puts down the keg, and opens a basket. A voice
is heard calling.*

VOICE.

Ho! Corey, Corey!

COREY.

　　　　　What is that? I surely
Heard some one calling me by name!

VOICE.

　　　　　Giles Corey!

Enter a boy, running, and out of breath.

BOY.

Is Master Corey here?

COREY.

　　　　Yes, here I am.

BOY.

O Master Corey!

COREY.

　　Well?

BOY.

　　Your wife — your wife —

COREY.

What's happened to my wife?

BOY.

　　　　She's sent to prison!

COREY.

The dream! the dream! O God, be mer-
　　ciful!

BOY.

She sent me here to tell you.

COREY (*putting on his jacket*).

　　　　　Where's my horse?
Don't stand there staring, fellows. Where's
my horse?　　　　　[*Exit* COREY.

GLOYD.

Under the trees there. Run, old man, run, run!
You've got some one to wrestle with you now
Who'll trip your heels up, with your Cornish
　　hug.
If there's a Devil, he has got you now.
Ah, there he goes! His horse is snorting
　　fire!

ONE OF THE MEN.

John Gloyd, don't talk so! It's a shame to
　　talk so!
He's a good master, though you quarrel with
　　him.

GLOYD.

If hard work and low wages make good
　　masters,
Then he is one. But I think otherwise.
Come, let us have our dinner and be merry,
And talk about the old man and the Witches.
I know some stories that will make you
　　laugh.

They sit down on the grass, and eat.

Now there are Goody Cloyse and Goody Good,
Who have not got a decent tooth between
　　them,
And yet these children — the Afflicted Chil-
　　dren —
Say that they bite them, and show marks of
　　teeth
Upon their arms!

ONE OF THE MEN.

　　　　That makes the wonder greater.
That's Witchcraft. Why, if they had teeth
　　like yours,
'T would be no wonder if the girls were
　　bitten!

GLOYD.

And then those ghosts that come out of their
　　graves
And cry, "You murdered us! you murdered
　　us!"

ONE OF THE MEN.

And all those Apparitions that stick pins
Into the flesh of the Afflicted Children!

GLOYD.

Oh those Afflicted Children! They know
 well
Where the pins come from. I can tell you
 that.
And there's old Corey, he has got a horse-
 shoe
Nailed on his doorstep to keep off the
 Witches,
And all the same his wife has gone to prison.

ONE OF THE MEN.

Oh, she's no Witch. I'll swear that Good-
 wife Corey
Never did harm to any living creature.
She's a good woman, if there ever was one.

GLOYD.

Well, we shall see. As for that Bridget
 Bishop,

She has been tried before; some years ago
A negro testified he saw her shape
Sitting upon the rafters in a barn,
And holding in its hand an egg; and while
He went to fetch his pitchfork, she had van-
 ished.
And now be quiet, will you? I am tired,
And want to sleep here on the grass a little.

They stretch themselves on the grass.

ONE OF THE MEN.

There may be Witches riding through the air
Over our heads on broomsticks at this mo-
 ment,
Bound for some Satan's Sabbath in the
 woods
To be baptized.

GLOYD.

 I wish they'd take you with them,
And hold you under water, head and ears,
Till you were drowned; and that would stop
 your talking,
If nothing else will. Let me sleep, I say.

ACT IV.

SCENE I. — *The Green in front of the village Meeting-house. An excited crowd gathering. Enter* JOHN GLOYD.

A FARMER.

WHO will be tried to-day?

A SECOND.

           I do not know.
Here is John Gloyd. Ask him; he knows.

FARMER.

                 John Gloyd,
Whose turn is it to-day?

GLOYD.

           It 's Goodwife Corey's.

FARMER.

Giles Corey's wife?

GLOYD.

         The same. She is not mine.
It will go hard with her with all her praying.
The hypocrite! She 's always on her knees;
But she prays to the Devil when she prays.
Let us go in.

A trumpet blows.

FARMER.

Here come the Magistrates.

SECOND FARMER.

Who 's the tall man in front?

GLOYD.

         Oh, that is Hathorne,
A Justice of the Court, and Quartermaster
In the Three County Troop. He 'll sift the
     matter.
That 's Corwin with him; and the man in
     black
Is Cotton Mather, Minister of Boston.

Enter HATHORNE *and other Magistrates on horseback, followed by the Sheriff, constables, and attendants on foot. The Magistrates dismount, and enter the Meeting-house, with the rest.*

FARMER.

The Meeting-house is full. I never saw
So great a crowd before.

GLOYD.

           No matter. Come.
We shall find room enough by elbowing
Our way among them. Put your shoulder
     to it.

FARMER.

There were not half so many at the trial
Of Goodwife Bishop.

GLOYD.

          Keep close after me.
I 'll find a place for you. They 'll want me
     there.
I am a friend of Corey's, as you know,
And he can't do without me just at present.
                    [*Exeunt.*

SCENE II. — *Interior of the Meeting-house.* MATHER *and the Magistrates seated in front of the pulpit. Before them a raised platform.* MARTHA *in chains.* COREY *near her.* MARY WALCOT *in a chair. A crowd of spectators, among them* GLOYD. *Confusion and murmurs during the scene.*

HATHORNE.

CALL Martha Corey.

MARTHA.

          I am here.

HATHORNE.

               Come forward.
She ascends the platform.
The Jurors of our Sovereign Lord and Lady
The King and Queen, here present, do accuse
     you
Of having on the tenth of June last past,
And divers other times before and after,
Wickedly used and practised certain arts
Called Witchcrafts, Sorceries, and Incanta-
     tions,
Against one Mary Walcot, single woman,

KILBURN Sc.   J.W.EHNINGER.

Of Salem Village; by which wicked arts
The aforesaid Mary Walcot was tormented,
Tortured, afflicted, pined, consumed, and
    wasted,
Against the peace of our Sovereign Lord and
    Lady
The King and Queen, as well as of the
    Statute
Made and provided in that case. What say
    you?

MARTHA.

Before I answer, give me leave to pray.

HATHORNE.

We have not sent for you, nor are we here,
To hear you pray, but to examine you
In whatsoever is alleged against you.
Why do you hurt this person?

MARTHA.

            I do not.
I am not guilty of the charge against me.

MARY.

Avoid, she-devil! You torment me now!
Avoid, avoid, Witch!

MARTHA.

          I am innocent.
I never had to do with any Witchcraft
Since I was born. I am a gospel woman.

MARY.

You are a gospel Witch!

MARTHA (*clasping her hands*).

            Ah me! ah me!
Oh, give me leave to pray!

MARY (*stretching out her hands*).

She hurts me now.
See, she has pinched my hands!

HATHORNE.

Who made these marks
Upon her hands?

MARTHA.

I do not know. I stand
Apart from her. I did not touch her hands.

HATHORNE.

Who hurt her then?

MARTHA.

I know not.

HATHORNE.

Do you think
She is bewitched?

MARTHA.

Indeed I do not think so.
I am no Witch, and have no faith in
  Witches.

HATHORNE.

Then answer me: When certain persons came
To see you yesterday, how did you know
Beforehand why they came?

MARTHA.

I had had speech
The children said I hurt them, and I thought
These people came to question me about
  it.

HATHORNE.

How did you know the children had been
  told
To note the clothes you wore?

MARTHA.

My husband told me
What others said about it.

HATHORNE.

Goodman Corey,
Say, did you tell her?

COREY.

I must speak the truth;
I did not tell her. It was some one else.

HATHORNE.

Did you not say your husband told you so?
How dare you tell a lie in this assembly?
Who told you of the clothes? Confess the
  truth.
    MARTHA *bites her lips, and is silent.*
You bite your lips, but do not answer me!

MARY.

Ah, she is biting me! Avoid, avoid!

HATHORNE.

You said your husband told you.

MARTHA.

Yes, he told me
The children said I troubled them.

HATHORNE.

Then tell me,
Why do you trouble them?

MARTHA.

I have denied it.

MARY.

She threatened me; stabbed at me with her
  spindle;
And, when my brother thrust her with his
  sword,
He tore her gown, and cut a piece away.
Here are they both, the spindle and the
  cloth.

Shows them.

HATHORNE.

And there are persons here who know the
  truth
Of what has now been said. What answer
  make you?

MARTHA.

I make no answer. Give me leave to pray.

HATHORNE.

Whom would you pray to?

MARTHA.

     To my God and Father.

HATHORNE.

Who is your God and Father?

MARTHA.

     The Almighty!

HATHORNE.

Doth he you pray to say that he is God?
It is the Prince of Darkness, and not God.

MARY.

There is a dark shape whispering in her ear.

HATHORNE.

What does it say to you?

MARTHA.

     I see no shape.

HATHORNE.

Did you not hear it whisper?

MARTHA.

     I heard nothing.

MARY.

What torture! Ah, what agony I suffer!
Falls into a swoon.

HATHORNE.

You see this woman cannot stand before you.
If you would look for mercy, you must look
In God's way, by confession of your guilt.
Why does your spectre haunt and hurt this
    person?

MARTHA.

I do not know. He who appeared of old
In Samuel's shape, a saint and glorified,
May come in whatsoever shape he chooses.
I cannot help it. I am sick at heart!

COREY.

O Martha, Martha! let me hold your hand.

HATHORNE.

No; stand aside, old man.

MARY (*starting up*).

     Look there! Look there!
I see a little bird, a yellow bird,
Perched on her finger; and it pecks at me.
Ah, it will tear mine eyes out!

MARTHA.

     I see nothing.

HATHORNE.

'T is the Familiar Spirit that attends her.

MARY.

Now it has flown away. It sits up there
Upon the rafters. It is gone; is vanished.

MARTHA.

Giles, wipe these tears of anger from mine
    eyes.
Wipe the sweat from my forehead. I am faint.
She leans against the railing.

MARY.

Oh, she is crushing me with all her weight!

.J. W. EHNINGER.

HATHORNE.

Did you not carry once the Devil's Book
To this young woman?

MARTHA.

Never.

HARTHORNE.

Have you signed it,

Or touched it?

MARTHA.

No; I never saw it.

HATHORNE.

Did you not scourge her with an iron rod?

MARTHA.

No, I did not. If any Evil Spirit
Has taken my shape to do these evil deeds,
I cannot help it. I am innocent.

HATHORNE.

Did you not say the Magistrates were blind?
That you would open their eyes?

MARTHA (*with a scornful laugh*).

Yes, I said that;
If you call me a sorceress, you are blind!
If you accuse the innocent, you are blind!
Can the innocent be guilty?

HATHORNE.

Did you not
On one occasion hide your husband's saddle
To hinder him from coming to the Sessions?

MARTHA.

I thought it was a folly in a farmer
To waste his time pursuing such illusions.

HATHORNE.

What was the bird that this young woman saw
Just now upon your hand?

MARTHA.

I know no bird.

HATHORNE.

Have you not dealt with a Familiar Spirit?

MARTHA.

No, never, never!

HATHORNE.

What then was the Book
You showed to this young woman, and be-
sought her
To write in it?

MARTHA.

Where should I have a book?
I showed her none, nor have none.

MARY.

The next Sabbath
Is the Communion Day, but Martha Corey
Will not be there!

MARTHA.

Ah, you are all against me.
What can I do or say?

HATHORNE.

You can confess.

MARTHA.

No, I cannot, for I am innocent.

HATHORNE.

We have the proof of many witnesses
That you are guilty.

MARTHA.

Give me leave to speak.
Will you condemn me on such evidence, —
You who have known me for so many years?
Will you condemn me in this house of God,
Where I so long have worshipped with you all?
Where I have eaten the bread and drunk the
wine
So many times at our Lord's Table with you?
Bear witness, you that hear me; you all know
That I have led a blameless life among you,
That never any whisper of suspicion
Was breathed against me till this accusation.
And shall this count for nothing? Will you
take
My life away from me, because this girl,
Who is distraught, and not in her right mind,
Accuses me of things I blush to name?

HATHORNE.

What! is it not enough? Would you hear
  more?
Giles Corey!

COREY.

I am here.

HATHORNE.

          Come forward, then.
COREY *ascends the platform.*
Is it not true, that on a certain night
You were impeded strangely in your prayers?
That something hindered you? and that you
  left
This woman here, your wife, kneeling alone
Upon the hearth?

COREY.

          Yes; I cannot deny it.

HATHORNE.

Did you not say the Devil hindered you?

COREY.

I think I said some words to that effect.

HATHORNE.

Is it not true, that fourteen head of cattle,
To you belonging, broke from their enclosure
And leaped into the river, and were drowned?

COREY.

It is most true.

HATHORNE.

          And did you not then say
That they were overlooked?

COREY.

          So much I said.
I see; they 're drawing round me closer, closer,
A net I cannot break, cannot escape from!
  (*Aside*).

HATHORNE.

Who did these things?

COREY.

I do not know who did them.

HATHORNE.

Then I will tell you. It is some one near
  you;
You see her now; this woman, your own wife.

COREY.

I call the heavens to witness, it is false!
She never harmed me, never hindered me
In anything but what I should not do.
And I bear witness in the sight of heaven,
And in God's house here, that I never knew
  her
As otherwise than patient, brave, and true,
Faithful, forgiving, full of charity,
A virtuous and industrious and good wife!

HATHORNE.

Tut, tut, man; do not rant so in your speech;
You are a witness, not an advocate!
Here, Sheriff, take this woman back to prison.

MARTHA.

O Giles, this day you 've sworn away my life!

MARY.

Go, go and join the Witches at the door.
Do you not hear the drum? Do you not see
  them?
Go quick. They 're waiting for you. You are
  late.
          [*Exit* MARTHA; COREY *following.*

COREY.

The dream! the dream! the dream!

HATHORNE.

          What does he say?
Giles Corey, go not hence. You are yourself
Accused of Witchcraft and of Sorcery
By many witnesses. Say, are you guilty?

COREY.

I know my death is foreordained by you, —
Mine and my wife's. Therefore I will not
  answer.
During the rest of the scene he remains silent.

HATHORNE.

Do you refuse to plead? — 'T were better for
  you

To make confession, or to plead Not Guilty. —
Do you not hear me? — Answer, are you
    guilty?
Do you not know a heavier doom awaits you,
If you refuse to plead, than if found guilty?
Where is John Gloyd?

GLOYD (*coming forward*).
    Here am I.

HATHORNE.
        Tell the Court;
Have you not seen the supernatural power
Of this old man?   Have you not seen him do
Strange feats of strength?

GLOYD.
    I 've seen him lead the field,
On a hot day, in mowing, and against
Us younger men; and I have wrestled with
    him.

He threw me like a feather.   I have seen him
Lift up a barrel with his single hands,
Which two strong men could hardly lift to-
    gether,
And, holding it above his head, drink from it.

HATHORNE.
That is enough; we need not question further.
What answer do you make to this, Giles
    Corey?

MARY.
See there!   See there!

HATHORNE.
    What is it?   I see nothing.

MARY.
Look! Look!   It is the ghost of Robert
    Goodell,
Whom fifteen years ago this man did murder

By stamping on his body! In his shroud
He comes here to bear witness to the crime!
The crowd shrinks back from COREY *in horror.*

HATHORNE.

Ghosts of the dead and voices of the living
Bear witness to your guilt, and you must die!
It might have been an easier death. Your doom
Will be on your own head, and not on ours.
Twice more will you be questioned of these
  things;

Twice more have room to plead or to con-
  fess.
If you are contumacious to the Court,
And if, when questioned, you refuse to an-
  swer,
Then by the Statute you will be condemned
To the *peine forte et dure!* To have your
  body
Pressed by great weights until you shall be
  dead!
And may the Lord have mercy on your soul!

ACT V.

SCENE I. — COREY'S *farm as in Act II., Scene I.*
Enter RICHARD GARDNER, *looking round him.*

GARDNER.

HERE stands the house as I remember it,
The four tall poplar-trees before the door;
The house, the barn, the orchard, and the
  well,
With its moss-covered bucket and its trough;
The garden, with its hedge of currant-bushes;
The woods, the harvest-fields; and, far be-
  yond,
The pleasant landscape stretching to the sea.
But everything is silent and deserted!
No bleat of flocks, no bellowing of herds,
No sound of flails, that should be beating
  now;
Nor man nor beast astir. What can this
  mean?
   Knocks at the door.
What ho! Giles Corey! Hillo-ho! Giles
  Corey!—
No answer but the echo from the barn,
And the ill-omened cawing of the crow,
That yonder wings his flight across the fields,
As if he scented carrion in the air.
  Enter TITUBA *with a basket.*
What woman's this, that, like an appari-
  tion,
Haunts this deserted homestead in broad day?
Woman, who are you?

TITUBA.

   I am Tituba.
I am John Indian's wife. I am a Witch.

GARDNER.

What are you doing here?

TITUBA.

   I'm gathering herbs,—
Cinquefoil, and saxifrage, and pennyroyal.

GARDNER (*looking at the herbs*).

This is not cinquefoil, it is deadly night-
  shade!
This is not saxifrage, but hellebore!
This is not pennyroyal, it is henbane!
Do you come here to poison these good people?

TITUBA.

I get these for the Doctor in the Village.
Beware of Tituba. I pinch the children;
Make little poppets and stick pins in them,
And then the children cry out they are
  pricked.
The Black Dog came to me, and said, "Serve
  me!"
I was afraid. He made me hurt the children.

GARDNER.

Poor soul! She's crazed, with all these
  Devil's doings.

TITUBA.

Will you, sir, sign the Book?

GARDNER.

   No, I'll not sign it.
Where is Giles Corey? Do you know Giles
  Corey?

95

TITUBA.

He's safe enough.   He's down there in the
    prison.

GARDNER.

Corey in prison?   What is he accused of?

TITUBA.

Giles Corey and Martha Corey are in prison
Down there in Salem Village.   Both are
    Witches.
She came to me and whispered, "Kill the
    children!"
Both signed the Book!

GARDNER.

            Begone, you imp of darkness!
You Devil's dam!

TITUBA.

        Beware of Tituba!

                        [*Exit.*

GARDNER.

How often out at sea on stormy nights,
When the waves thundered round me, and
    the wind
Bellowed, and beat the canvas, and my ship
Clove through the solid darkness, like a
    wedge,
I've thought of him, upon his pleasant farm,
Living in quiet with his thrifty housewife,
And envied him, and wished his fate were
    mine!
And now I find him shipwrecked utterly,
Drifting upon this sea of sorceries,
And lost, perhaps, beyond all aid of man!

                        [*Exit.*

SCENE II. — *The prison.* GILES COREY *at a table on which are some papers.*

COREY.

Now I have done with earth and all its cares;
I give my worldly goods to my dear children;
My body I bequeath to my tormentors.
And my immortal soul to Him who made it.
O God! who in thy wisdom dost afflict me
With an affliction greater than most men
Have ever yet endured or shall endure,
Suffer me not in this last bitter hour
For any pains of death to fall from thee!

MARTHA *is heard singing.*

Arise, O righteous Lord!
  And disappoint my foes;
They are but thine avenging sword,
  Whose wounds are swift to close.

COREY.

Hark, hark! it is her voice! She is not dead!
She lives! I am not utterly forsaken!

MARTHA, *singing.*

By thine abounding grace,
  And mercies multiplied,
I shall awake, and see thy face;
  I shall be satisfied.

COREY *hides his face in his hands. Enter the* JAILER, *followed by* RICHARD GARDNER.

JAILER.

Here's a seafaring man, one Richard Gardner,
A friend of yours, who asks to speak with you.
      COREY *rises. They embrace.*

COREY.

I'm glad to see you, ay, right glad to see you.

GARDNER.

And I most sorely grieved to see you thus.

COREY.

Of all the friends I had in happier days,
You are the first, ay, and the only one,
That comes to seek me out in my disgrace!
And you but come in time to say farewell.
They've dug my grave already in the field.
I thank you. There is something in your presence,

I know not what it is, that gives me strength.
Perhaps it is the bearing of a man
Familiar with all dangers of the deep,
Familiar with the cries of drowning men,
With fire, and wreck, and foundering ships
    at sea!

GARDNER.

Ah, I have never known a wreck like yours!
Would I could save you!

COREY.

                  Do not speak of that.
It is too late. I am resolved to die.

GARDNER.

Why would you die who have so much to live
    for? —
Your daughters, and —

COREY.

                  You cannot say the word.
My daughters have gone from me. They are
    married;
They have their homes, their thoughts, apart
    from me;
I will not say their hearts, — that were too
    cruel.
What would you have me do?

GARDNER.

                  Confess and live.

COREY.

That's what they said who came here yester-
    day
To lay a heavy weight upon my conscience
By telling me that I was driven forth
As an unworthy member of their church.

GARDNER.

It is an awful death.

COREY.

                  'T is but to drown,
And have the weight of all the seas upon
    you.

GARDNER.

Say something; say enough to fend off death
Till this tornado of fanaticism

Blows itself out. Let me come in between
    you
And your severer self, with my plain sense;
Do not be obstinate.

COREY.

             I will not plead.
If I deny, I am condemned already,
In courts where ghosts appear as witnesses,
And swear men's lives away. If I confess,
Then I confess a lie, to buy a life
Which is not life, but only death in life.
I will not bear false witness against any,
Not even against myself, whom I count least.

GARDNER (aside).

Ah, what a noble character is this!

COREY.

I pray you, do not urge me to do that
You would not do yourself. I have already
The bitter taste of death upon my lips;
I feel the pressure of the heavy weight
That will crush out my life within this hour;
But if a word could save me, and that word
Were not the Truth; nay, if it did but swerve
A hair's-breadth from the Truth, I would not
    say it!

GARDNER (aside).

How mean I seem beside a man like this!

COREY.

As for my wife, my Martha and my Martyr, —
Whose virtues, like the stars, unseen by day,
Though numberless, do but await the dark
To manifest themselves unto all eyes, —
She who first won me from my evil ways,
And taught me how to live by her example,
By her example teaches me to die,
And leads me onward to the better life!

SHERIFF. (without).

Giles Corey! Come! The hour has struck!

COREY.

             I come!
Here is my body; ye may torture it,
But the immortal soul ye cannot crush!

                      [Exeunt.

SCENE III. — A street in the Village. Enter GLOYD
             and others.

GLOYD.

Quick, or we shall be late!

A MAN.

           That 's not the way.
Come here; come up this lane.

GLOYD.

             I wonder now
If the old man will die, and will not speak?
He 's obstinate enough and tough enough
For anything on earth.
        A bell tolls.
        Hark! What is that?

A MAN.

The passing bell. He 's dead!

GLOYD.

         We are too late.
            [Exeunt in haste.

SCENE IV. — A field near the graveyard. GILES
COREY lying dead, with a great stone on his breast.
The Sheriff at his head, RICHARD GARDNER at his
feet. A crowd behind. The bell tolling. Enter
HATHORNE and MATHER.

HATHORNE.

THIS is the Potter's Field. Behold the fate
Of those who deal in Witchcrafts, and, when
    questioned,
Refuse to plead their guilt or innocence,
And stubbornly drag death upon themselves.

MATHER.

O sight most horrible! In a land like this,
Spangled with Churches Evangelical,
Inwrapped in our salvations, must we seek
In mouldering statute-books of English Courts
Some old forgotten Law, to do such deeds?
Those who lie buried in the Potter's Field
Will rise again, as surely as ourselves
That sleep in honored graves with epitaphs;
And this poor man, whom we have made a
    victim,
Hereafter will be counted as a martyr!

FINALE
ST. JOHN

SAINT JOHN *wandering over the face of the Earth.*

ST. JOHN.

THE Ages come and go,
The Centuries pass as Years;
My hair is white as the snow,
My feet are weary and slow,
The earth is wet with my tears!
The kingdoms crumble, and fall
Apart, like a ruined wall,

Or a bank that is undermined
By a river's ceaseless flow,
And leave no trace behind!
The world itself is old;
The portals of Time unfold
On hinges of iron, that grate
And groan with the rust and the weight,
Like the hinges of a gate
That hath fallen to decay;
But the evil doth not cease;

There is war instead of peace,
Instead of Love there is hate;
And still I must wander and wait,
Still I must watch and pray,
Not forgetting in whose sight,
A thousand years in their flight
Are as a single day.

The life of man is a gleam
Of light, that comes and goes
Like the course of the Holy Stream,
The cityless river, that flows
From fountains no one knows,
Through the Lake of Galilee,
Through forests and level lands,
Over rocks, and shallows, and sands
Of a wilderness wild and vast,
Till it findeth its rest at last
In the desolate Dead Sea!
But alas! alas for me
Not yet this rest shall be!

What, then! doth Charity fail?
Is Faith of no avail?
Is Hope blown out like a light
By a gust of wind in the night?
The clashing of creeds, and the strife
Of the many beliefs, that in vain
Perplex man's heart and brain,
Are naught but the rustle of leaves,
When the breath of God upheaves
The boughs of the Tree of Life,
And they subside again!
And I remember still
The words, and from whom they came,

Not he that repeateth the name,
But he that doeth the will!

And Him evermore I behold
Walking in Galilee,
Through the cornfield's waving gold,
In hamlet, in wood, and in wold,
By the shores of the Beautiful Sea.
He toucheth the sightless eyes;
Before him the demons flee;
To the dead He sayeth: Arise!
To the living: Follow me!
And that voice still soundeth on
From the centuries that are gone,
To the centuries that shall be!

From all vain pomps and shows,
From the pride that overflows,
And the false conceits of men;
From all the narrow rules
And subtleties of Schools,
And the craft of tongue and pen;
Bewildered in its search,
Bewildered with the cry:
Lo, here! lo, there, the Church!
Poor, sad Humanity
Through all the dust and heat
Turns back with bleeding feet,
By the weary road it came,
Unto the simple thought
By the great Master taught,
And that remaineth still:
Not he that repeateth the name,
But he that doeth the will!

ARTIST: HARRY FENN.

JERUSALEM.

ACT I.

The Citadel of Antiochus at Jerusalem.

Scene I. — Antiochus ; Jason.

Antiochus. O Antioch, my Antioch, my
    city !
Queen of the East ! my solace, my delight !
The dowry of my sister Cleopatra
When she was wed to Ptolemy, and now
Won back and made more wonderful by me !
I love thee, and I long to be once more
Among the players and the dancing women
Within thy gates, and bathe in the Orontes,
Thy river and mine.   O Jason, my High-
    Priest,
For I have made thee so, and thou art mine,
Hast thou seen Antioch the Beautiful ?
    Jason. Never, my Lord.
    Ant.   Then hast thou never seen
The wonder of the world. This city of David
Compared with Antioch is but a village,
And its inhabitants compared with Greeks
Are mannerless boors.
    Jason.   They are barbarians,
And mannerless.
    Ant.   They must be civilized.
They must be made to have more gods than
    one ;
And goddesses besides.
    Jason.   They shall have more.
    Ant. They must have hippodromes, and
    games, and baths,
Stage-plays and festivals, and most of all
The Dionysia.
    Jason.   They shall have them all.
    Ant. By Heracles ! but I should like to see

These Hebrews crowned with ivy, and arrayed
In skins of fawns, with drums and flutes and
    thyrsi,
Revel and riot through the solemn streets
Of their old town. Ha, ha ! It makes me
    merry
Only to think of it ! — Thou dost not laugh.
    Jason. Yea, I laugh inwardly.
    Ant.   The new Greek leaven
Works slowly in this Israelitish dough !
Have I not sacked the Temple, and on the altar
Set up the statue of Olympian Zeus
To Hellenize it ?
    Jason.   Thou hast done all this.
    Ant. As thou wast Joshua once and now
    art Jason,
And from a Hebrew hast become a Greek,
So shall this Hebrew nation be translated,
Their very natures and their names be
    changed,
And all be Hellenized.
    Jason.   It shall be done.
    Ant. Their manners and their laws and way
    of living
Shall all be Greek. They shall unlearn their
    language,
And learn the lovely speech of Antioch.
Where hast thou been to-day ? Thou comest
    late.
    Jason. Playing at discus with the other
    priests
In the Gymnasium.

Ant.   Thou hast done well.
There's nothing better for you lazy priests
Than discus-playing with the common people.
Now tell me, Jason, what these Hebrews call me
When they converse together at their games.
    Jason. Antiochus Epiphanes, my Lord;
Antiochus the Illustrious.
    Ant.   Oh, not that;
That is the public cry; I mean the name
They give me when they talk among them-
        selves,
And think that no one listens; what is that?
    Jason. Antiochus Epimanes, my Lord!
    Ant. Antiochus the Mad! Ay, that is it.
And who hath said it? Who hath set in
        motion
That sorry jest?
    Jason.   The Seven Sons insane
Of a weird woman, like themselves insane.
    Ant. I like their courage, but it shall not
        save them.
They shall be made to eat the flesh of swine
Or they shall die. Where are they?

Jason.   In the dungeons
Beneath this tower.
    Ant.   There let them stay and starve,
Till I am ready to make Greeks of them,
After my fashion.
    Jason.   They shall stay and starve. —
My Lord, the Ambassadors of Samaria
Await thy pleasure.
    Ant.   Why not my displeasure?
Ambassadors are tedious. They are men
Who work for their own ends, and not for
        mine;
There is no furtherance in them. Let them
        go
To Apollonius, my governor
There in Samaria, and not trouble me.
What do they want?
    Jason.   Only the royal sanction
To give a name unto a nameless temple
Upon Mount Gerizim.
    Ant.   Then bid them enter.
This pleases me, and furthers my designs.
The occasion is auspicious. Bid them enter.

SCENE II. — ANTIOCHUS; JASON; *the* SAMARITAN
AMBASSADORS.

Ant. Approach. Come forward; stand not at
  the door
Wagging your long beards, but demean your-
  selves
As doth become Ambassadors.   What seek ye?
An Ambassador. An audience from the
  King.
Ant.   Speak, and be brief.
Waste not the time in useless rhetoric.
Words are not things.
  Ambassador (reading). "To King Anti-
  ochus,
The God, Epiphanes; a Memorial
From the Sidonians, who live at Sichem."
  Ant. Sidonians?
Ambassador.   Ay, my Lord.
  Ant.   Go on, go on!
And do not tire thyself and me with bow-
  ing!
  Ambassador (reading). "We are a colony
  of Medes and Persians."
  Ant. No, ye are Jews from one of the Ten
  Tribes;
Whether Sidonians or Samaritans
Or Jews of Jewry, matters not to me;
Ye are all Israelites, ye are all Jews.
When the Jews prosper, ye claim kindred
  with them;
When the Jews suffer, ye are Medes and
  Persians;
I know that in the days of Alexander
Ye claimed exemption from the annual tribute
In the Sabbatic Year, because, ye said,
Your fields had not been planted in that year.
  Ambassador (reading). "Our fathers, upon
  certain frequent plagues,
And following an ancient superstition,
Were long accustomed to observe that day
Which by the Israelites is called the Sabbath.
And in a temple on Mount Gerizim
Without a name, they offered sacrifice.
Now we, who are Sidonians, beseech thee,
Who art our benefactor and our savior,
Not to confound us with these wicked Jews,
But to give royal order and injunction
To Apollonius in Samaria,
Thy governor, and likewise to Nicanor,
Thy procurator, no more to molest us;

And let our nameless temple now be named
The Temple of Jupiter Hellenius."
  Ant. This shall be done.   Full well it
  pleaseth me
Ye are not Jews, or are no longer Jews,
But Greeks; if not by birth, yet Greeks by
  custom.
Your nameless temple shall receive the name
Of Jupiter Hellenius.   Ye may go!

SCENE III. — ANTIOCHUS; JASON.

  Ant. My task is easier than I dreamed.
  These people
Meet me half-way.   Jason, didst thou take
  note
How these Samaritans of Sichem said
They were not Jews? that they were Medes
  and Persians,
They were Sidonians, anything but Jews?
'T is of good augury.   The rest will follow
Till the whole land is Hellenized.
  Jason.   My Lord,
These are Samaritans.   The tribe of Judah
Is of a different temper, and the task
Will be more difficult.
  Ant.   Dost thou gainsay me?
  Jason. I know the stubborn nature of the
  Jew.
Yesterday, Eleazer, an old man.
Being fourscore years and ten, chose rather
  death
By torture than to eat the flesh of swine.
  Ant. The life is in the blood, and the
  whole nation
Shall bleed to death, or it shall change its
  faith!
  Jason. Hundreds have fled already to the
  mountains
Of Ephraim, where Judas Maccabæus
Hath raised the standard of revolt against
  thee.
  Ant. I will burn down their city, and will
  make it
Waste as a wilderness.   Its thoroughfares
Shall be but furrows in a field of ashes.
It shall be sown with salt as Sodom is!
This hundred and fifty-third Olympiad
Shall have a broad and blood-red seal upon
  it,
Stamped with the awful letters of my name,

Antiochus the God, Epiphanes! —
Where are those Seven Sons?
   Jason.   My Lord, they wait
Thy royal pleasure.
   Ant.   They shall wait no longer!

ACT II.

The Dungeons in the Citadel.

SCENE I. — THE MOTHER *of the* SEVEN SONS
alone, listening.

  The Mother. Be strong, my heart! Break
    not till they are dead.
All, all my Seven Sons; then burst asun-
    der,
And let this tortured and tormented soul
Leap and rush out like water through the
    shards
Of earthen vessels broken at a well.
O my dear children, mine in life and death,
I know not how ye came into my womb;
I neither gave you breath, nor gave you life,
And neither was it I that formed the
    members
Of every one of you. But the Creator,
Who made the world, and made the heavens
    above us,
Who formed the generation of mankind,
And found out the beginning of all things,
He gave you breath and life, and will again
Of his own mercy, as ye now regard
Not your own selves, but his eternal law.
I do not murmur, nay, I thank thee, God,
That I and mine have not been deemed
    unworthy
To suffer for thy sake, and for thy law,
And for the many sins of Israel.
Hark! I can hear within the sound of
    scourges!
I feel them more than ye do, O my sons!
But cannot come to you. I, who was wont
To wake at night at the least cry ye made,
To whom ye ran at every slightest hurt,—
I cannot take you now into my lap
And soothe your pain, but God will take you
    all
Into his pitying arms, and comfort you,
And give you rest.
  A Voice (within). What wouldst thou ask
    of us?

Ready are we to die, but we will never
Transgress the law and customs of our fathers.
  The Mother. It is the voice of my first-
    born! O brave
And noble boy! Thou hast the privilege
Of dying first, as thou wast born the first.
  The same Voice (within). God looketh on
    us, and hath comfort in us;
As Moses in his song of old declared,
He in his servants shall be comforted.
  The Mother. I knew thou wouldst not
    fail! — He speaks no more,
He is beyond all pain!
  Ant. (within).   If thou eat not
Thou shalt be tortured throughout all the
    members
Of thy whole body. Wilt thou eat then?
  Second Voice (within). No.
  The Mother. It is Adaiah's voice. I tremble
    for him.
I know his nature, devious as the wind,
And swift to change, gentle and yielding
    always.
Be steadfast, O my son!

The same Voice (within). Thou, like a fury,
Takest us from this present life, but God,
Who rules the world, shall raise us up again
Into life everlasting.

The Mother. God, I thank thee
That thou hast breathed into that timid heart
Courage to die for thee. O my Adaiah,
Witness of God! if thou for whom I feared
Canst thus encounter death, I need not fear;
The others will not shrink.

Third Voice (within). Behold these hands
Held out to thee, O King Antiochus,
Not to implore thy mercy, but to show
That I despise them. He who gave them to me
Will give them back again.

The Mother. O Avilan,
It is thy voice. For the last time I hear it;
For the last time on earth, but not the last.
To death it bids defiance and to torture.
It sounds to me as from another world,
And makes the petty miseries of this
Seem unto me as naught, and less than
naught.
Farewell, my Avilan; nay, I should say
Welcome, my Avilan; for I am dead
Before thee. I am waiting for the others.
Why do they linger?

Fourth Voice (within). It is good, O King,
Being put to death by men, to look for hope
From God, to be raised up again by him.
But thou — no resurrection shalt thou have
To life hereafter.

The Mother. Four! already four!
Three are still living; nay, they all are
living
Half here, half there. Make haste, Anti-
ochus,
To reunite us; for the sword that cleaves
These miserable bodies makes a door
Through which our souls, impatient of release,
Rush to each other's arms.

Fifth Voice (within). Thou hast the pow-
er;
Thou doest what thou wilt. Abide awhile,
And thou shalt see the power of God, and
how
He will torment thee and thy seed.

The Mother. O hasten;
Why dost thou pause? Thou who hast slain
already

So many Hebrew women, and hast hung
Their murdered infants round their necks,
slay me,
For I too am a woman, and these boys
Are mine. Make haste to slay us all,
And hang my lifeless babes about my neck.

Sixth Voice (within). Think not, Anti-
ochus, that takest in hand
To strive against the God of Israel,
Thou shalt escape unpunished, for his wrath
Shall overtake thee and thy bloody house.

The Mother. One more, my Sirion, and then
all is ended.
Having put all to bed, then in my turn
I will lie down and sleep as sound as they.
My Sirion, my youngest, best beloved!
And those bright golden locks, that I so oft
Have curled about these fingers, even now
Are foul with blood and dust, like a lamb's
fleece,
Slain in the shambles. — Not a sound I hear.
This silence is more terrible to me
Than any sound, than any cry of pain,
That might escape the lips of one who dies.
Doth his heart fail him? Doth he fall away
In the last hour from God? O Sirion, Sir-
ion,
Art thou afraid? I do not hear thy voice.
Die as thy brothers died. Thou must not
live!

SCENE II. — THE MOTHER; ANTIOCHUS; SIRION.

The Mother. Are they all dead?
Ant. Of all thy Seven Sons
One only lives. Behold them where they lie;
How dost thou like this picture?
The Mother. God in heaven?
Can a man do such deeds, and yet not die
By the recoil of his own wickedness?
Ye murdered, bleeding, mutilated bodies
That were my children once, and still are
mine,
I cannot watch o'er you as Rispah watched
In sackcloth o'er the seven sons of Saul,
Till water drop upon you out of heaven
And wash this blood away! I cannot mourn
As she, the daughter of Aiah, mourned the
dead,
From the beginning of the barley-harvest

Until the autumn rains, and suffered not
The birds of air to rest on them by day,
Nor the wild beasts by night. For ye have
    died
A better death; a death so full of life
That I ought rather to rejoice than mourn. —
Wherefore art thou not dead, O Sirion?
Wherefore art thou the only living thing
Among thy brothers dead? Art thou afraid?
    Ant. O woman, I have spared him for thy
        sake,
For he is fair to look upon and comely;
And I have sworn to him by all the gods
That I would crown his life with joy and
    honor,
Heap treasures on him, luxuries, delights,
Make him my friend and keeper of my se-
    crets,
If he would turn from your Mosaic Law
And be as we are; but he will not listen.
    The Mother. My noble Sirion!
    Ant.   Therefore I beseech thee,
Who art his mother, thou wouldst speak
    with him,

And wouldst persuade him. I am sick of
    blood.
    The Mother. Yea, I will speak with him
        and will persuade him.
O Sirion, my son! have pity on me,
On me that bare thee, and that gave thee
    suck,
And fed and nourished thee, and brought
    thee up
With the dear trouble of a mother's care
Unto this age. Look on the heavens above
    thee,
And on the earth and all that is therein;
Consider that God made them out of things
That were not; and that likewise in this
    manner
Mankind was made. Then fear not this tor-
    mentor;
But, being worthy of thy brethren, take
Thy death as they did, that I may receive
    thee
Again in mercy with them.
    Ant.   I am mocked,
Yea, I am laughed to scorn.

Sirion.   Whom wait ye for?
Never will I obey the King's commandment,
But the commandment of the ancient Law,
That was by Moses given unto our fathers.
And thou, O godless man, that of all others
Art the most wicked, be not lifted up,
Nor puffed up with uncertain hopes, uplift-
        ing
Thy hand against the servants of the Lord,
For thou hast not escaped the righteous
        judgment
Of the Almighty God, who seeth all things!
    Ant. He is no God of mine; I fear Him
        not.
    Sirion. My brothers, who have suffered a
        brief pain,
Are dead; but thou, Antiochus, shalt suffer
The punishment of pride. I offer up
My body and my life, beseeching God
That He would speedily be merciful
Unto our nation, and that thou by plagues
Mysterious and by torments mayest confess
That He alone is God.
    Ant.   Ye both shall perish
By torments worse than any that your God,
Here or hereafter, hath in store for me.
    The Mother. My Sirion, I am proud of
        thee!
    Ant.   Be silent!
Go to thy bed of torture in yon chamber,
Where lie so many sleepers, heartless mother!
Thy footsteps will not wake them, nor thy
        voice,
Nor wilt thou hear, amid thy troubled dreams,
Thy children crying for thee in the night!
    The Mother. O Death, that stretchest thy
        white hands to me,
I fear them not, but press them to my lips,
That are as white as thine; for I am Death,
Nay, am the Mother of Death, seeing these
        sons
All lying lifeless. — Kiss me, Sirion.

ACT III.

The Battle-field of Beth-horon.

SCENE I. — JUDAS MACCABÆUS *in armor before his tent.*

Judas. The trumpets sound; the echoes of
        the mountains
Answer them, as the Sabbath morning breaks

97

Over Beth-horon and its battle-field,
Where the great captain of the hosts of
        God,
A slave brought up in the brick-fields of
        Egypt,
O'ercame the Amorites. There was no day
Like that, before or after it, nor shall be.
The sun stood still; the hammers of the
        hail
Beat on their harness; and the captains set
Their weary feet upon the necks of kings,
As I will upon thine, Antiochus,
Thou man of blood! — Behold the rising
        sun
Strikes on the golden letters of my banner,
Be Elohim Yehovah! Who is like
To thee, O Lord, among the gods? — Alas!
I am not Joshua, I cannot say,
"Sun, stand thou still on Gibeon, and thou
        Moon,
In Ajalon!" Nor am I one who wastes
The fateful time in useless lamentation;
But one who bears his life upon his hand
To lose it or to save it, as may best
Serve the designs of Him who giveth life.

SCENE II. — JUDAS MACCABÆUS; JEWISH FUGI-
        TIVES.

    Judas. Who and what are ye, that with
        furtive steps
Steal in among our tents?
    Fugitives.   O Maccabæus,
Outcasts are we, and fugitives as thou art,
Jews of Jerusalem, that have escaped
From the polluted city, and from death.
    Judas. None can escape from death.
            Say that ye come
To die for Israel, and ye are welcome.
What tidings bring ye?
    Fugitives.   Tidings of despair.
The Temple is laid waste; the precious
        vessels,
Censers of gold, vials and veils and crowns,
And golden ornaments, and hidden treas-
        ures,
Have all been taken from it, and the Gen-
        tiles
With revelling and with riot fill its courts,
And dally with harlots in the holy places.
    Judas. All this I knew before.

Fugitives.   Upon the altar
Are things profane, things by the law forbidden ;
Nor can we keep our Sabbaths or our Feasts,
But on the festivals of Dionysus
Must walk in their processions, bearing ivy
To crown a drunken god.
   Judas.   This too I know.
But tell me of the Jews. How fare the Jews?
   Fugitives.   The coming of this mischief hath been sore
And grievous to the people. All the land
Is full of lamentation and of mourning.
The Princes and the Elders weep and wail ;
The young men and the maidens are made feeble ;
The beauty of the women hath been changed.
   Judas. And are there none to die for Israel?
'Tis not enough to mourn. Breastplate and harness
Are better things than sackcloth. Let the women
Lament for Israel ; the men should die.
   Fugitives. Both men and women die ; old men and young :
Old Eleazer died : and Máhala
With all her Seven Sons.
   Judas.   Antiochus,
At every step thou takest there is left
A bloody footprint in the street, by which
The avenging wrath of God will track thee out !
It is enough. Go to the sutler's tents :
Those of you who are men, put on such armor
As ye may find ; those of you who are women,
Buckle that armor on ; and for a watch-word
Whisper, or cry aloud, " The help of God."

SCENE III. — JUDAS MACCABÆUS ; NICANOR.

Nicanor. Hail, Judas Maccabæus !
   Judas.   Hail !— Who art thou
That comest here in this mysterious guise
Into our camp unheralded ?
   Nic.   A herald
Sent from Nicanor.

   Judas.   Heralds come not thus.
Armed with thy shirt of mail from head to heel,
Thou glidest like a serpent silently
Into my presence. Wherefore dost thou turn
Thy face from me? A herald speaks his errand
With forehead unabashed. Thou art a spy
Sent by Nicanor.
   Nic.   No disguise avails !
Behold my face ; I am Nicanor's self.
   Judas. Thou art indeed Nicanor. I salute thee.
What brings thee hither to this hostile camp
Thus unattended ?
   Nic.   Confidence in thee.
Thou hast the nobler virtues of thy race,
Without the failings that attend those virtues.
Thou canst be strong, and yet not tyrannous,
Canst righteous be and not intolerant.
Let there be peace between us.
   Judas.   What is peace?
Is it to bow in silence to our victors?
Is it to see our cities sacked and pillaged,
Our people slain, or sold as slaves, or fleeing
At night-time by the blaze of burning towns ;
Jerusalem laid waste ; the Holy Temple
Polluted with strange gods? Are these things peace?
   Nic. These are the dire necessities that wait
On war, whose loud and bloody enginery
I seek to stay. Let there be peace between
Antiochus and thee.
   Judas.   Antiochus?
What is Antiochus, that he should prate
Of peace to me, who am a fugitive?
To-day he shall be lifted up ; to-morrow
Shall not be found, because he is returned
Unto his dust ; his thought has come to nothing.
There is no peace between us, nor can be,
Until this banner floats upon the walls
Of our Jerusalem.
   Nic.   Between that city
And thee there lies a waving wall of tents
Held by a host of forty thousand foot,
And horsemen seven thousand. What hast thou
To bring against all these ?

Judas.   The power of God,
Whose breath shall scatter your white tents
    abroad,
As flakes of snow.

    Nic.   Your Mighty One in heaven
Will not do battle on the Seventh Day;
It is his day of rest.

    Judas.   Silence, blasphemer.
Go to thy tents.

    Nic.   Shall it be war or peace?

    Judas. War, war, and only war. Go to
    thy tents
That shall be scattered, as by you were scat-
    tered
The torn and trampled pages of the Law,
Blown through the windy streets.

    Nic.   Farewell, brave foe!

    Judas. Ho, there, my captains! Have safe-
    conduct given
Unto Nicanor's herald through the camp,
And come yourselves to me. — Farewell, Ni-
    canor!

Scene IV. — Judas Maccabæus; Captains and
    Soldiers.

    Judas. The hour is come. Gather the
    host together
For battle. Lo, with trumpets and with
    songs
The army of Nicanor comes against us.
Go forth to meet them, praying in your
    hearts,
And fighting with your hands.

    Captains.   Look forth and see!
The morning sun is shining on their shields
Of gold and brass; the mountains glisten
    with them,
And shine like lamps. And we who are
    so few
And poorly armed, and ready to faint with
    fasting,
How shall we fight against this multi-
    tude?

    Judas. The victory of a battle standeth
    not

In multitudes, but in the strength that
 cometh
From heaven above. The Lord forbid that I
Should do this thing, and flee away from
 them.
Nay, if our hour be come, then let us die;
Let us not stain our honor.

 Captains.   'T is the Sabbath.
Wilt thou fight on the Sabbath, Maccabæus?

 Judas. Ay; when I fight the battles of the
 Lord,
I fight them on his day, as on all others.
Have ye forgotten certain fugitives
That fled once to these hills, and hid them-
 selves
In caves? How their pursuers camped
 against them
Upon the Seventh Day, and challenged
 them?
And how they answered not, nor cast a
 stone,
Nor stopped the places where they lay con-
 cealed,
But meekly perished with their wives and
 children,
Even to the number of a thousand souls?
We who are fighting for our laws and lives
Will not so perish.

 Captains.   Lead us to the battle!

 Judas. And let our watchword be, " The
 Help of God!"
Last night I dreamed a dream; and in my
 vision
Beheld Onias, our High-Priest of old,
Who holding up his hands prayed for the
 Jews.
This done, in the like manner there ap-
 peared
An old man, and exceeding glorious,
With hoary hair, and of a wonderful
And excellent majesty. And Onias said:
" This is a lover of the Jews, who prayeth
Much for the people and the Holy City,—
God's prophet Jeremias." And the prophet
Held forth his right hand and gave unto me
A sword of gold; and giving it he said:
" Take thou this holy sword, a gift from God,
And with it thou shalt wound thine adver-
 saries."

 Captains. The Lord is with us!

 Judas.   Hark! I hear the trumpets
Sound from Beth-horon; from the battle-
 field
Of Joshua, where he smote the Amorites,
Smote the Five Kings of Eglon and of Jar-
 muth,
Of Hebron, Lachish, and Jerusalem,
As we to-day will smite Nicanor's hosts
And leave a memory of great deeds behind
 us.

 Captains and Soldiers. The Help of God!

 Judas.   *Be Elohim Yehovah!*
Lord, thou didst send thine Angel in the
 time
Of Esekias, King of Israel,
And in the armies of Sennacherib
Didst slay a hundred fourscore and five thou-
 sand.
Wherefore, O Lord of heaven, now also send
Before us a good angel for a fear,
And through the might of thy right arm let
 those
Be stricken with terror that have come this
 day
Against thy holy people to blaspheme!

ACT IV.

The Outer Courts of the Temple at Jerusalem.

Scene I. — Judas Maccabæus; Captains;
 Jews.

 Judas. Behold, our enemies are discom-
 fited.
Jerusalem is fallen; and our banners
Float from her battlements, and o'er her
 gates
Nicanor's severed head, a sign of terror,
Blackens in wind and sun.

 Captains.   O Maccabæus,
The citadel of Antiochus, wherein
The Mother with her Seven Sons was mur-
 dered,
Is still defiant.

 Judas. Wait.

 Captains.   Its hateful aspect
Insults us with the bitter memories
Of other days.

 Judas.   Wait; it shall disappear
And vanish as a cloud. First let us cleanse

The Sanctuary. See, it is become
Waste like a wilderness. Its golden gates
Wrenched from their hinges and consumed by
 fire;
Shrubs growing in its courts as in a for-
 est;
Upon its altars hideous and strange idols;
And strewn about its pavement at my feet
Its Sacred Books, half-burned and painted
 o'er
With images of heathen gods.
 Jews.   Woe! woe!
Our beauty and our glory are laid waste!
The Gentiles have profaned our holy places!
  (*Lamentation and alarm of trumpets.*)

 Judas. This sound of trumpets, and this
  lamentation,
The heart-cry of a people toward the heavens
Stir me to wrath and vengeance. Go, my
 captains;
I hold you back no longer. Batter down
The citadel of Antiochus, while here
We sweep away his altars and his gods.

  Scene II. — Judas Maccabæus; Jason;
    Jews.

 Jews. Lurking among the ruins of the Tem-
  ple,
Deep in its inner courts, we found this man,
Clad as High-Priest.
 Judas.   I ask not who thou art,
I know thy face, writ over with deceit
As are these tattered volumes of the Law
With heathen images. A priest of God
Wast thou in other days, but thou art now
A priest of Satan. Traitor, thou art Ja-
 son.
 Jason. I am thy prisoner, Judas Macca-
  bæus,
And it would ill become me to conceal
My name or office.
 Judas.   Over yonder gate
There hangs the head of one who was a
 Greek.
What should prevent me now, thou man of
 sin,
From hanging at its side the head of one
Who born a Jew hath made himself a Greek?
 Jason. Justice prevents thee.
 Judas.   Justice? Thou art stained

With every crime 'gainst which the Deca-
 logue
Thunders with all its thunder.
 Jason.   If not Justice,
Then Mercy, her handmaiden.
 Judas.   When hast thou
At any time, to any man or woman,
Or even to any little child, shown mercy?
 Jason. I have but done what King Antio-
  chus
Commanded me.
 Judas.   True, thou hast been the
  weapon
With which he struck; but hast been such a
 weapon,
So flexible, so fitted to his hand,
It tempted him to strike. So thou hast urged
 him
To double wickedness, thine own and his.
Where is this King? Is he in Antioch
Among his women still, and from his win-
 dows
Throwing down gold by handfuls, for the
 rabble
To scramble for?
 Jason.   Nay, he is gone from there,
Gone with an army into the far East.
 Judas. And wherefore gone?
 Jason.   I know not. For the space
Of forty days almost were horsemen seen
Running in air, in cloth of gold, and armed
With lances, like a band of soldiery;
It was a sign of triumph.
 Judas.   Or of death.
Wherefore art thou not with him?
 Jason.   I was left
For service in the Temple.
 Judas.   To pollute it,
And to corrupt the Jews; for there are men
Whose presence is corruption; to be with
 them
Degrades us and deforms the things we do.
 Jason. I never made a boast, as some men
  do,
Of my superior virtue, nor denied
The weakness of my nature, that hath made
 me
Subservient to the will of other men.
 Judas. Upon this day, the five-and-twen-
  tieth day

Of the month Caslan, was the Temple here
Profaned by strangers, — by Antiochus
And thee, his instrument. Upon this day
Shall it be cleansed. Thou, who didst lend
    thyself
Unto this profanation, canst not be
A witness of these solemn services.
There can be nothing clean where thou art
    present.
The people put to death Callisthenes,
Who burned the Temple gates; and if they
    find thee
Will surely slay thee. I will spare thy life
To punish thee the longer. Thou shalt wan-
    der
Among strange nations. Thou, that hast cast
    out
So many from their native land, shalt per-
    ish
In a strange land. Thou, that hast left so
    many

Unburied, shalt have none to mourn for thee,
Nor any solemn funerals at all,
Nor sepulchre with thy fathers. — Get thee
    hence!
(*Music. Procession of Priests and people, with citherns,
harps, and cymbals.* JUDAS MACCABÆUS *puts himself
at their head, and they go into the inner courts.*)

SCENE III. — JASON, *alone.*

Jason. Through the Gate Beautiful I see
    them come
With branches and green boughs and leaves
    of palm,
And pass into the inner courts. Alas!
I should be with them, should be one of them,
But in an evil hour, an hour of weakness,
That cometh unto all, I fell away
From the old faith, and did not clutch the
    new,
Only an outward semblance of belief;
For the new faith I cannot make mine own,

Not being born to it. It hath no root
Within me. I am neither Jew nor Greek,
But stand between them both, a renegade
To each in turn; having no longer faith
In gods or men. Then what mysterious charm,
What fascination is it chains my feet,
And keeps me gazing like a curious child
Into the holy places, where the priests
Have raised their altar? — Striking stones to-
gether,
They take fire out of them, and light the
lamps
In the great candlestick. They spread the
veils,
And set the loaves of showbread on the table.
The incense burns; the well-remembered odor
Comes wafted unto me, and takes me back
To other days. I see myself among them
As I was then; and the old superstition
Creeps over me again! — A childish fancy! —
And hark! they sing with citherns and with
cymbals,
And all the people fall upon their faces,
Praying and worshipping! — I will away
Into the East, to meet Antiochus
Upon his homeward journey, crowned with
triumph.
Alas! to-day I would give everything
To see a friend's face, or to hear a voice
That had the slightest tone of comfort in it!

ACT V.

The Mountains of Ecbatana.

Scene I. — Antiochus; Philip; Attendants.

Ant. Here let us rest awhile. Where are
we, Philip?
What place is this?
Philip. Ecbatana, my Lord;
And yonder mountain range is the Orontes.
Ant. The Orontes is my river at Anti-
och.
Why did I leave it? Why have I been
tempted
By coverings of gold and shields and breast-
plates
To plunder Elymais, and be driven
From out its gates, as by a fiery blast
Out of a furnace?
Philip. These are fortune's changes.

Ant. What a defeat it was! The Persian
horsemen
Came like a mighty wind, the wind Khamá-
seen,
And melted us away, and scattered us
As if we were dead leaves, or desert sand.
Philip. Be comforted, my Lord; for thou
hast lost
But what thou hadst not.
Ant. I, who made the Jews
Skip like the grasshoppers, am made myself
To skip among these stones.
Philip. Be not discouraged.
Thy realm of Syria remains to thee;
That is not lost nor marred.
Ant. Oh, where are now
The splendors of my court, my baths and
banquets?
Where are my players and my dancing women?
Where are my sweet musicians with their
pipes,
That made me merry in the olden time?
I am a laughing-stock to man and brute.
The very camels, with their ugly faces,
Mock me and laugh at me.
Philip. Alas! my Lord,
It is not so. If thou wouldst sleep awhile,
All would be well.
Ant. Sleep from mine eyes is gone,
And my heart faileth me for very care.
Dost thou remember, Philip, the old fable
Told us when we were boys, in which the bear
Going for honey overturns the hive,
And is stung blind by bees? I am that beast,
Stung by the Persian swarms of Elymais.
Philip. When thou art come again to
Antioch
These thoughts will be as covered and forgot-
ten
As are the tracks of Pharaoh's chariot-wheels
In the Egyptian sands.
Ant. Ah! when I come
Again to Antioch! When will that be?
Alas! alas!

Scene II. — Antiochus; Philip; A Messenger.

Messenger. May the King live forever!
Ant. Who art thou, and whence comest
thou?
Messenger. My Lord,

I am a messenger from Antioch,
Sent here by Lysias.

    Ant.   A strange foreboding
Of something evil overshadows me.
I am no reader of the Jewish Scriptures;
I know not Hebrew; but my High-Priest Jason,
As I remember, told me of a Prophet
Who saw a little cloud rise from the sea
Like a man's hand, and soon the heaven was
    black
With clouds and rain.   Here, Philip, read; I
    cannot;
I see that cloud.   It makes the letters dim
Before mine eyes.

    Philip (reading).   " To King Antiochus,
The God, Epiphanes."

    Ant.   Oh mockery!
Even Lysias laughs at me! — Go on, go on!

    Philip (reading).   " We pray thee hasten
    thy return.   The realm
Is falling from thee.   Since thou hast gone
    from us
The victories of Judas Maccabæus
Form all our annals.   First he overthrew
Thy forces at Beth-horon, and passed on,
And took Jerusalem, the Holy City.
And then Emmaus fell; and then Bethsura;
Ephron and all the towns of Galaad,
And Maccabæus marched to Carnion."

    Ant.   Enough, enough!   Go call my char-
    iot-men;
We will drive forward, forward, without ceasing,
Until we come to Antioch.   My captains,
My Lysias, Gorgias, Seron, and Nicanor,
Are babes in battle, and this dreadful Jew
Will rob me of my kingdom and my crown.
My elephants shall trample him to dust;
I will wipe out his nation, and will make
Jerusalem a common burying-place,
And every home within its walls a tomb!

*(Throws up his hands, and sinks into the arms of at-
tendants, who lay him upon a bank.)*

    Philip.   Antiochus! Antiochus! Alas,
The King is ill!   What is it, O my Lord?

    Ant.   Nothing.   A sudden and sharp spasm
    of pain,
As if the lightning struck me, or the knife
Of an assassin smote me to the heart.
'Tis passed, even as it came.   Let us set forward.

    Philip.   See that the chariots be in read-
    iness;
We will depart forthwith.

    Ant.   A moment more.
I cannot stand.   I am become at once
Weak as an infant.   Ye will have to lead me.
Jove, or Jehovah, or whatever name
Thou wouldst be named, — it is alike to me, —
If I knew how to pray, I would entreat
To live a little longer.

    Philip.   O my Lord,
Thou shalt not die; we will not let thee die!

    Ant.   How canst thou help it, Philip?   Oh
    the pain!
Stab after stab.   Thou hast no shield against
This unseen weapon.   God of Israel,
Since all the other gods abandon me,
Help me.   I will release the Holy City,
Garnish with goodly gifts the Holy Temple.
Thy people, whom I judged to be unworthy
To be so much as buried, shall be equal
Unto the citizens of Antioch.
I will become a Jew, and will declare
Through all the world that is inhabited
The power of God!

    Philip.   He faints.   It is like death.
Bring here the royal litter.   We will bear him
Into the camp, while yet he lives.

    Ant.   O Philip,
Into what tribulation am I come!
Alas!   I now remember all the evil
That I have done the Jews; and for this cause
These troubles are upon me, and behold
I perish through great grief in a strange land.

    Philip.   Antiochus! my King!

    Ant.   Nay, King no longer.
Take thou my royal robes, my signet ring,
My crown and sceptre, and deliver them
Unto my son, Antiochus Eupator;
And unto the good Jews, my citizens,
In all my towns, say that their dying monarch
Wisheth them joy, prosperity, and health.
I who, puffed up with pride and arrogance,
Thought all the kingdoms of the earth mine
    own,
If I would but outstretch my hand and take
    them,
Meet face to face a greater potentate,
King Death — Epiphanes — the Illustrious!
                   [*Dies.*

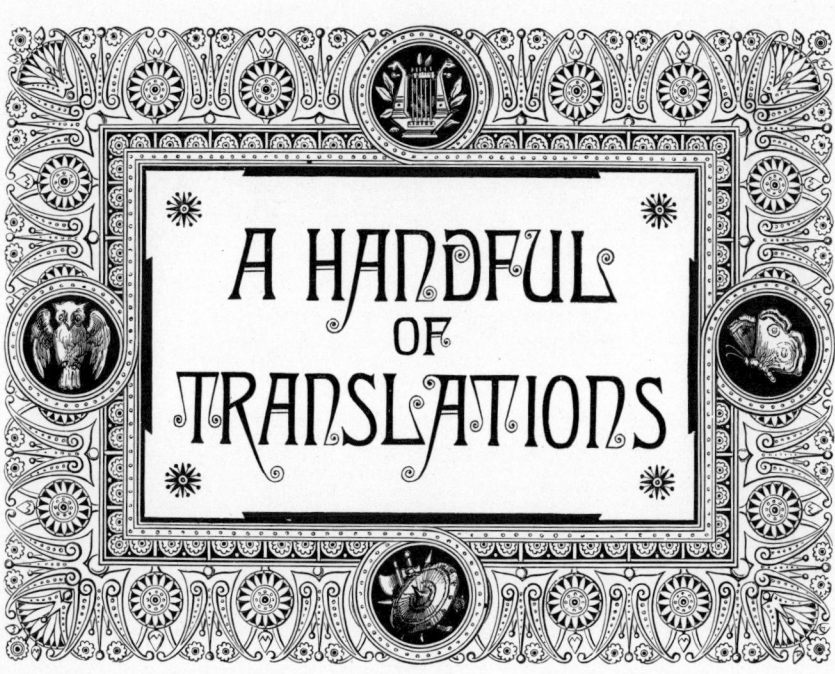

A HANDFUL
OF
TRANSLATIONS

A HANDFUL OF TRANSLATIONS

THE FUGITIVE.

TARTAR SONG, FROM THE PROSE VERSION OF CHODZKO.

I.

"He is gone to the desert land!
  I can see the shining mane
  Of his horse on the distant plain,
  As he rides with his Kossak band!

"Come back, rebellious one!
  Let thy proud heart relent;
  Come back to my tall, white tent,
  Come back, my only son!

"Thy hand in freedom shall
  Cast thy hawks, when morning breaks,
  On the swans of the Seven Lakes,
  On the lakes of Karajal.

"I will give thee leave to stray
  And pasture thy hunting steeds
  In the long grass and the reeds
  Of the meadows of Karaday.

"I will give thee my coat of mail,
  Of softest leather made,
  With choicest steel inlaid;
  Will not all this prevail?"

II.

"This hand no longer shall
  Cast my hawks, when morning breaks,
  On the swans of the Seven Lakes,
  On the lakes of Karajal.

"I will no longer stray
  And pasture my hunting steeds
  In the long grass and the reeds
  Of the meadows of Karaday.

"Though thou give me thy coat of mail,
  Of softest leather made,
  With choicest steel inlaid,
  All this cannot prevail.

"What right hast thou, O Khan,
  To me, who am mine own,
  Who am slave to God alone,
  And not to any man?

"God will appoint the day
  When I again shall be
  By the blue, shallow sea,
  Where the steel-bright sturgeons play.

"God, who doth care for me,
  In the barren wilderness,
  On unknown hills, no less
  Will my companion be.

"When I wander lonely and lost
  In the wind; when I watch at night
  Like a hungry wolf, and am white
  And covered with hoar-frost;

"Yea, wheresoever I be,
  In the yellow desert sands,
  In mountains or unknown lands,
  Allah will care for me!"

III.

Then Sobra, the old, old man, —
  Three hundred and sixty years
  Had he lived in this land of tears,
  Bowed down and said, "O Khan!

"If you bid me, I will speak.
  There's no sap in dry grass,
  No marrow in dry bones! Alas,
  The mind of old men is weak!

"I am old, I am very old:
  I have seen the primeval man,
  I have seen the great Gengis Khan,
  Arrayed in his robes of gold.

"What I say to you is the truth;
  And I say to you, O Khan,
  Pursue not the star-white man,
  Pursue not the beautiful youth.

"Him the Almighty made,
  And brought him forth of the light
  At the verge and end of the night,
  When men on the mountain prayed.

"He was born at the break of day,
  When abroad the angels walk;
  He hath listened to their talk,
  And he knoweth what they say.

"Gifted with Allah's grace,
  Like the moon of Ramazan
  When it shines in the skies, O Khan,
  Is the light of his beautiful face.

"When first on earth he trod,
  The first words that he said
  Were these, as he stood and prayed,
'There is no God but God!'

"And he shall be king of men,
  For Allah hath heard his prayer,
  And the Archangel in the air,
  Gabriel, hath said, Amen!"

THE SIEGE OF KAZAN.

TARTAR SONG, FROM THE PROSE VERSION OF CHODZKO.

BLACK are the moors before Kazan,
  And their stagnant waters smell of blood:
I said in my heart, with horse and man,
  I will swim across this shallow flood.

Under the feet of Argamack,
  Like new moons were the shoes he bare,
Silken trappings hung on his back,
  In a talisman on his neck, a prayer.

My warriors, thought I, are following me;
  But when I looked behind, alas!

Not one of all the band could I see,
  All had sunk in the black morass!

Where are our shallow fords? and where
  The power of Kazan with its fourfold gates?
From the prison windows our maidens fair
  Talk of us still through the iron grates.

We cannot hear them; for horse and man
  Lie buried deep in the dark abyss!
Ah! the black day hath come down on Kazan!
  Ah! was ever a grief like this?

THE BOY AND THE BROOK.

ARMENIAN POPULAR SONG, FROM THE PROSE VERSION OF ALISHAN.

Down from yon distant mountain height
  The brooklet flows through the village
      street;
A boy comes forth to wash his hands,
Washing, yes washing, there he stands,
  In the water cool and sweet.

Brook, from what mountain dost thou come?
  O my brooklet cool and sweet!
I come from yon mountain high and cold,
Where lieth the new snow on the old,
  And melts in the summer heat.

Brook, to what river dost thou go?
  O my brooklet cool and sweet!
I go to the river there below

Where in bunches the violets grow,
  And sun and shadow meet.

Brook, to what garden dost thou go?
  O my brooklet cool and sweet!
I go to the garden in the vale
Where all night long the nightingale
  Her love-song doth repeat.

Brook, to what fountain dost thou go?
  O my brooklet cool and sweet!
I go to the fountain at whose brink
The maid that loves thee comes to drink,
And whenever she looks therein,
I rise to meet her, and kiss her chin,
  And my joy is then complete.

TO THE STORK.

ARMENIAN POPULAR SONG, FROM THE PROSE VERSION OF ALISHAN.

WELCOME, O Stork! that dost wing
  Thy flight from the far-away!
Thou hast brought us the signs of Spring,
  Thou hast made our sad hearts gay.

Descend, O Stork! descend
  Upon our roof to rest;
In our ash-tree, O my friend,
  My darling, make thy nest.

To thee, O Stork, I complain,
  O Stork, to thee I impart
The thousand sorrows, the pain
  And aching of my heart.

When thou away didst go,
  Away from this tree of ours,

The withering winds did blow,
  And dried up all the flowers.

Dark grew the brilliant sky,
  Cloudy and dark and drear;
They were breaking the snow on high,
  And winter was drawing near.

From Varaca's rocky wall,
  From the rock of Varaca unrolled.
The snow came and covered all,
  And the green meadow was cold.

O Stork, our garden with snow
  Was hidden away and lost,
And the rose-trees that in it grow
  Were withered by snow and frost.

CONSOLATION.

TO M. DUPERRIER, GENTLEMAN OF AIX IN PROVENCE, ON THE DEATH OF HIS DAUGHTER.

FROM MALHERBE.

WILL then, Duperrier, thy sorrow be eternal?
  And shall the sad discourse
Whispered within thy heart, by tenderness
    paternal,
  Only augment its force?

Thy daughter's mournful fate, into the tomb
    descending
  By death's frequented ways,
Has it become to thee a labyrinth never ending,
  Where thy lost reason strays?

I know the charms that made her youth a
    benediction:
  Nor should I be content,
As a censorious friend, to solace thine afflic-
    tion
  By her disparagement.

But she was of the world, which fairest
    things exposes
  To fates the most forlorn;
A rose, she too hath lived as long as live the
    roses,
  The space of one brief morn.

   .   .   .   .   .   .

Death has his rigorous laws, unparalleled, un-
    feeling;

All prayers to him are vain;
Cruel, he stops his ears, and, deaf to our ap-
    pealing,
  He leaves us to complain.

The poor man in his hut, with only thatch
    for cover,
  Unto these laws must bend;
The sentinel that guards the barriers of the
    Louvre
  Cannot our kings defend.

To murmur against death, in petulant de-
    fiance,
  Is never for the best;
To will what God doth will, that is the
    only science
  That gives us any rest.

TO CARDINAL RICHELIEU.

FROM MALHERBE.

THOU mighty Prince of Church and State,
Richelieu! until the hour of death,
Whatever road man chooses, Fate
Still holds him subject to her breath.
Spun of all silks, our days and nights
Have sorrows woven with delights;
And of this intermingled shade
Our various destiny appears,
Even as one sees the course of years
Of summers and of winters made.

Sometimes the soft, deceitful hours
Let us enjoy the halcyon wave;
Sometimes impending peril lowers
Beyond the seaman's skill to save.
The Wisdom, infinitely wise,
That gives to human destinies
Their foreordained necessity,
Has made no law more fixed below,
Than the alternate ebb and flow
Of Fortune and Adversity.

THE ANGEL AND THE CHILD.

FROM JEAN REBOUL, THE BAKER OF NISMES.

AN angel with a radiant face,
  Above a cradle bent to look,
Seemed his own image there to trace,
  As in the waters of a brook.

"Dear child! who me resemblest so,"
  It whispered, "come, O come with me!
Happy together let us go,
  The earth unworthy is of thee!

"Here none to perfect bliss attain;
  The soul in pleasure suffering lies;
Joy hath an undertone of pain,
  And even the happiest hours their sighs.

"Fear doth at every portal knock;
  Never a day serene and pure
From the o'ershadowing tempest's shock
  Hath made the morrow's dawn secure.

"What, then, shall sorrows and shall fears
  Come to disturb so pure a brow?
And with the bitterness of tears
  These eyes of azure troubled grow?

"Ah no! into the fields of space,
  Away shalt thou escape with me;
And Providence will grant thee grace
  Of all the days that were to be.

"Let no one in thy dwelling cower,
  In sombre vestments draped and veiled;

But let them welcome thy last hour,
  As thy first moments once they hailed.

"Without a cloud be there each brow;
  There let the grave no shadow cast;
When one is pure as thou art now,
  The fairest day is still the last."

And waving wide his wings of white,
  The angel, at these words, had sped
Towards the eternal realms of light! —
  Poor mother! see, thy son is dead!

TO ITALY.

FROM FILICAJA.

ITALY! Italy! thou who 'rt doomed to wear
  The fatal gift of beauty, and possess
  The dower funest of infinite wretched-
    ness
Written upon thy forehead by despair;

Ah! would that thou wert stronger, or less fair,
  That they might fear thee more, or love thee
    less,
  Who in the splendor of thy loveliness
  Seem wasting, yet to mortal combat dare!

Then from the Alps I should not see descend-
ing
Such torrents of armed men, nor Gallic horde
Drinking the wave of Po, distained with gore,

Nor should I see thee girded with a sword
Not thine, and with the stranger's arm
contending,
Victor or vanquished, slave forevermore.

WANDERER'S NIGHT-SONGS.

FROM GOETHE.

I.

THOU that from the heavens art,
Every pain and sorrow stillest,
And the doubly wretched heart
Doubly with refreshment fillest,
I am weary with contending!
Why this rapture and unrest?
Peace descending
Come, ah, come into my breast!

II.

O'er all the hill-tops
Is quiet now,
In all the tree-tops
Hearest thou
Hardly a breath;
The birds are asleep in the trees:
Wait; soon like these
Thou too shalt rest.

REMORSE.

FROM AUGUST VON PLATEN.

How I started up in the night, in the night,
Drawn on without rest or reprieval!
The streets, with their watchmen, were lost to
my sight,
As I wandered so light
In the night, in the night,
Through the gate with the arch mediæval.

The mill-brook rushed from the rocky height,
I leaned o'er the bridge in my yearning;
Deep under me watched I the waves in their
flight,
As they glided so light
In the night, in the night,
Yet backward not one was returning.

O'erhead were revolving, so countless and
bright,
The stars in melodious existence;
And with them the moon, more serenely be-
dight; —
They sparkled so light
In the night, in the night,
Through the magical, measureless distance.

And upward I gazed in the night, in the night,
And again on the waves in their fleeting;
Ah woe! thou hast wasted thy days in delight,
Now silence thou light,
In the night, in the night,
The remorse in thy heart that is beating.

SANTA TERESA'S BOOK-MARK.

FROM THE SPANISH OF SANTA TERESA.

LET nothing disturb thee,
Nothing affright thee;
All things are passing;

God never changeth;
Patient endurance
Attaineth to all things;

Who God possesseth
In nothing is wanting;
Alone God sufficeth.

ARTIST: MARY HALLOCK FOOTE.

THALIA.

The Masque of Pandora.

THE MASQVE OF PANDORA

I.

THE WORKSHOP OF HEPHÆSTUS.

HEPHÆSTUS, *standing before the statue of* PANDORA.

NOT fashioned out of gold, like Hera's throne,
Nor forged of iron like the thunderbolts
Of Zeus omnipotent, or other works
Wrought by my hands at Lemnos or Olym-
     pus,
But moulded in soft clay, that unresisting
Yields itself to the touch, this lovely form

Before me stands, perfect in every part.
Not Aphrodite's self appeared more fair,
When first upwafted by caressing winds
She came to high Olympus, and the gods
Paid homage to her beauty. Thus her hair
Was cinctured; thus her floating drapery
Was like a cloud about her, and her face
Was radiant with the sunshine and the sea.

THE VOICE OF ZEUS.

Is thy work done, Hephæstus?

HEPHÆSTUS.

It is finished!

THE VOICE.

Not finished till I breathe the breath of life
Into her nostrils, and she moves and speaks.

HEPHÆSTUS.

Will she become immortal like ourselves?

THE VOICE.

The form that thou hast fashioned out of
    clay
Is of the earth and mortal; but the spirit,
The life, the exhalation of my breath,
Is of diviner essence and immortal.
The gods shall shower on her their benefac-
    tions,
She shall possess all gifts: the gift of song,
The gift of eloquence, the gift of beauty,
The fascination and the nameless charm
That shall lead all men captive.

HEPHÆSTUS.

Wherefore? wherefore?
A wind shakes the house.

I hear the rushing of a mighty wind
Through all the halls and chambers of my
    house!
Her parted lips inhale it, and her bosom
Heaves with the inspiration. As a reed
Beside a river in the rippling current
Bends to and fro, she bows or lifts her head.
She gazes round about as if amazed;
She is alive; she breathes, but yet she speaks
    not!

PANDORA *descends from the pedestal.*

CHORUS OF THE GRACES.

AGLAIA.

In the workshop of Hephæstus
    What is this I see?
Have the Gods to four increased us
    Who were only three?
Beautiful in form and feature,
    Lovely as the day,
Can there be so fair a creature
    Formed of common clay?

THALIA.

O sweet, pale face! O lovely eyes of azure,
    Clear as the waters of a brook that run
    Limpid and laughing in the summer sun!
O golden hair, that like a miser's treasure
In its abundance overflows the measure!
    O graceful form, that cloudlike floatest on
    With the soft, undulating gait of one
Who moveth as if motion were a pleasure!
By what name shall I call thee? Nymph or
    Muse,
    Callirrhoë or Urania? Some sweet name
    Whose every syllable is a caress
Would best befit thee; but I cannot choose,
    Nor do I care to choose; for still the same,
    Nameless or named, will be thy loveliness.

EUPHROSYNE.

Dowered with all celestial gifts,
    Skilled in every art
That ennobles and uplifts
    And delights the heart,
Fair on earth shall be thy fame
    As thy face is fair,
And Pandora be the name
    Thou henceforth shalt bear.

II.

OLYMPUS.

HERMES, *putting on his sandals.*

MUCH must he toil who serves the Immortal
    Gods,
And I, who am their herald, most of all.
No rest have I, nor respite. I no sooner
Unclasp the winged sandals from my feet,

Than I again must clasp them, and depart
Upon some foolish errand. But to-day
The errand is not foolish. Never yet
With greater joy did I obey the summons
That sends me earthward. I will fly so
    swiftly

That my caduceus in the whistling air
Shall make a sound like the Pandæan pipes,
Cheating the shepherds; for to-day I go,
Commissioned by high-thundering Zeus, to
    lead
A maiden to Prometheus, in his tower,
And by my cunning arguments persuade him
To marry her. What mischief lies concealed
In this design I know not; but I know

Who thinks of marrying hath already taken
One step upon the road to penitence.
Such embassies delight me. Forth I launch
On the sustaining air, nor fear to fall
Like Icarus, nor swerve aside like him
Who drove amiss Hyperion's fiery steeds.
I sink, I fly! The yielding element
Folds itself round about me like an arm,
And holds me as a mother holds her child.

III.

TOWER OF PROMETHEUS ON MOUNT CAUCASUS.

PROMETHEUS.

I HEAR the trumpet of Alectryon
Proclaim the dawn. The stars begin to fade,
And all the heavens are full of prophecies
And evil auguries. Blood-red last night
I saw great Kronos rise; the crescent moon
Sank through the mist, as if it were the scythe
His parricidal hand had flung far down
The western steeps. O ye Immortal Gods,
What evil are ye plotting and contriving?

HERMES *and* PANDORA *at the threshold.*

PANDORA.

I cannot cross the threshold. An unseen
And icy hand repels me. These blank walls
Oppress me with their weight!

PROMETHEUS.

           Powerful ye are,
But not omnipotent. Ye cannot fight

Against Necessity. The Fates control you,
As they do us, and so far we are equals!

PANDORA.

Motionless, passionless, companionless,
He sits there muttering in his beard. His
　　　voice
Is like a river flowing underground!

HERMES.

Prometheus, hail!

PROMETHEUS.

　　　　　Who calls me?

HERMES.

　　　　　　　　　　It is I.
Dost thou not know me?

PROMETHEUS.

　　　　　　　　By thy winged cap
And winged heels I know thee. Thou art
　　　Hermes,
Captain of thieves! Hast thou again been
　　　stealing
The heifers of Admetus in the sweet
Meadows of asphodel? or Hera's girdle?
Or the earth-shaking trident of Poseidon?

HERMES.

And thou, Prometheus; say, hast thou again
Been stealing fire from Helios' chariot-wheels
To light thy furnaces?

PROMETHEUS.

　　　　　Why comest thou hither
So early in the dawn?

HERMES.

　　　　　The Immortal Gods
Know naught of late or early. Zeus himself
The omnipotent hath sent me.

PROMETHEUS.

　　　　　For what purpose?

HERMES.

To bring this maiden to thee.

PROMETHEUS.

　　　　　　　　I mistrust

The Gods and all their gifts. If they have
　　　sent her
It is for no good purpose.

HERMES.

　　　　　　　What disaster
Could she bring on thy house, who is a
　　　woman?

PROMETHEUS.

The Gods are not my friends, nor am I theirs.
Whatever comes from them, though in a shape
As beautiful as this, is evil only.
Who art thou?

PANDORA.

　　　　　One who, though to thee unknown,
Yet knoweth thee.

PROMETHEUS.

　　How shouldst thou know me, woman?

PANDORA.

Who knoweth not Prometheus the humane?

PROMETHEUS.

Prometheus the unfortunate; to whom
Both Gods and men have shown themselves
　　　ungrateful.
When every spark was quenched on every
　　　hearth
Throughout the earth, I brought to man the
　　　fire
And all its ministrations. My reward
Hath been the rock and vulture.

HERMES.

　　　　　　　　But the Gods
At last relent and pardon.

PROMETHEUS.

　　　　　　　　They relent not;
They pardon not; they are implacable,
Revengeful, unforgiving!

HERMES.

　　　　　　　As a pledge
Of reconciliation they have sent to thee
This divine being, to be thy companion,
And bring into thy melancholy house
The sunshine and the fragrance of her youth.

PROMETHEUS.

I need them not. I have within myself
All that my heart desires; the ideal beauty
Which the creative faculty of mind
Fashions and follows in a thousand shapes
More lovely than the real. My own thoughts
Are my companions; my designs and labors
And aspirations are my only friends.

HERMES.

Decide not rashly. The decision made
Can never be recalled. The Gods implore not,
Plead not, solicit not; they only offer
Choice and occasion, which once being passed
Return no more. Dost thou accept the gift?
100

PROMETHEUS.

No gift of theirs, in whatsoever shape
It comes to me, with whatsoever charm
To fascinate my sense, will I receive.
Leave me.

PANDORA.

Let us go hence. I will not stay.

HERMES.

We leave thee to thy vacant dreams, and
     all
The silence and the solitude of thought,
The endless bitterness of unbelief,
The loneliness of existence without love.

CHORUS OF THE FATES.

CLOTHO.

How the Titan, the defiant,
The self-centred, self-reliant,
Wrapped in visions and illusions,
Robs himself of life's best gifts!
Till by all the storm-winds shaken,
By the blast of fate o'ertaken,
Hopeless, helpless, and forsaken,
In the mists of his confusions
To the reefs of doom he drifts!

LACHESIS.

Sorely tried and sorely tempted,
From no agonies exempted.
In the penance of his trial,
And the discipline of pain;

Often by illusions cheated,
Often baffled and defeated
In the tasks to be completed,
He, by toil and self-denial,
To the highest shall attain.

ATROPOS.

Tempt no more the noble schemer;
Bear unto some idle dreamer
This new toy and fascination,
This new dalliance and delight!
To the garden where reposes
Epimetheus crowned with roses,
To the door that never closes
Upon pleasure and temptation,
Bring this vision of the night!

IV.

THE AIR.

HERMES, *returning to Olympus.*

As lonely as the tower that he inhabits,
As firm and cold as are the crags about him
Prometheus stands. The thunderbolts of Zeus
Alone can move him; but the tender heart
Of Epimetheus, burning at white heat,
Hammers and flames like all his brother's
        forges!
Now as an arrow from Hyperion's bow,
My errand done, I fly, I float, I soar

Into the air, returning to Olympus.
O joy of motion! O delight to cleave
The infinite realms of space, the liquid ether,
Through the warm sunshine and the cooling
        cloud,
Myself as light as sunbeam or as cloud!
With one touch of my swift and winged feet,
I spurn the solid earth, and leave it rocking
As rocks the bough from which a bird takes
        wing.

V.

THE HOUSE OF EPIMETHEUS.

EPIMETHEUS.

BEAUTIFUL apparition! go not hence!
Surely thou art a Goddess, for thy voice
Is a celestial melody, and thy form
Self-poised as if it floated on the air!

PANDORA.

No Goddess am I, nor of heavenly birth,
But a mere woman fashioned out of clay
And mortal as the rest.

EPIMETHEUS.

                Thy face is fair;
There is a wonder in thine azure eyes
That fascinates me. Thy whole presence
        seems
A soft desire, a breathing thought of love.
Say, would thy star like Merope's grow
        dim
If thou shouldst wed beneath thee?

PANDORA.

                    Ask me not;
I cannot answer thee. I only know
The Gods have sent me hither.

EPIMETHEUS.

                    I believe,
And thus believing am most fortunate.
It was not Hermes led thee here, but Eros,
And swifter than his arrows were thine eyes
In wounding me. There was no moment's
        space
Between my seeing thee and loving thee.
Oh, what a telltale face thou hast! Again
I see the wonder in thy tender eyes.

PANDORA.

They do but answer to the love in thine,
Yet secretly I wonder thou shouldst love me.
Thou knowest me not.

EPIMETHEUS.

                    Perhaps I know thee better
Than had I known thee longer. Yet it seems
That I have always known thee, and but
        now
Have found thee. Ah, I have been waiting
        long.

PANDORA.

How beautiful is this house! The atmosphere
Breathes rest and comfort, and the many
        chambers
Seem full of welcomes.

EPIMETHEUS.

                    They not only seem,
But truly are. This dwelling and its master
Belong to thee.

PANDORA.

                    Here let me stay forever!
There is a spell upon me.

EPIMETHEUS.

                    Thou thyself
Art the enchantress, and I feel thy power
Envelop me, and wrap my soul and sense
In an Elysian dream.

PANDORA.

                    Oh, let me stay.
How beautiful are all things round about
        me,
Multiplied by the mirrors on the walls!
What treasures hast thou here! Yon oaken
        chest,
Carven with figures and embossed with gold,
Is wonderful to look upon! What choice
And precious things dost thou keep hidden
        in it?

EPIMETHEUS.

I know not. 'T is a mystery.

PANDORA.

                    Hast thou never
Lifted the lid?

EPIMETHEUS.

                    The oracle forbids.
Safely concealed there from all mortal eyes
Forever sleeps the secret of the Gods.
Seek not to know what they have hidden
        from thee,
Till they themselves reveal it.

PANDORA.

                    As thou wilt.

EPIMETHEUS.

Let us go forth from this mysterious place.
The garden walks are pleasant at this hour;
The nightingales among the sheltering boughs
Of populous and many-nested trees
Shall teach me how to woo thee, and shall
        tell me
By what resistless charms or incantations
They won their mates.

PANDORA.

        Thou dost not need a teacher.
            They go out.

CHORUS OF THE EUMENIDES.

What the Immortals
Confide to thy keeping,
Tell unto no man;
Waking or sleeping,

Closed be thy portals
To friend as to foeman.

Silence conceals it;
The word that is spoken
Betrays and reveals it;
By breath or by token
The charm may be broken.

With shafts of their splendors
The Gods unforgiving
Pursue the offenders,
The dead and the living!
Fortune forsakes them,
Nor earth shall abide them,

Nor Tartarus hide them;
Swift wrath overtakes them.

With useless endeavor,
Forever, forever,
Is Sisyphus rolling
His stone up the mountain!
Immersed in the fountain,
Tantalus tastes not
The water that wastes not!
Through ages increasing
The pangs that afflict him,
With motion unceasing
The wheel of Ixion
Shall torture its victim!

VI.

IN THE GARDEN.

EPIMETHEUS.

YON snow-white cloud that sails sublime in
ether
Is but the sovereign Zeus, who like a swan
Flies to fair-ankled Leda!

PANDORA.

Or perchance
Ixion's cloud, the shadowy shape of Hera,
That bore the Centaurs.

EPIMETHEUS.

The divine and human.

CHORUS OF BIRDS.

Gently swaying to and fro,
Rocked by all the winds that blow,
Bright with sunshine from above
Dark with shadow from below,
Beak to beak and breast to breast
In the cradle of their nest,
Lie the fledglings of our love.

ECHO.

Love! love!

EPIMETHEUS.

Hark! listen! Hear how sweetly overhead

The feathered flute-players pipe their songs
of love,
And Echo answers, love and only love.

CHORUS OF BIRDS.

Every flutter of the wing,
Every note of song we sing,
Every murmur, every tone,
Is of love and love alone.

ECHO.

Love alone!

EPIMETHEUS.

Who would not love, if loving she might be
Changed like Callisto to a star in heaven?

PANDORA.

Ah, who would love, if loving she might
be
Like Semele consumed and burnt to ashes?

EPIMETHEUS.

Whence knowest thou these stories?

PANDORA.

Hermes taught me;
He told me all the history of the Gods.

CHORUS OF REEDS.

Evermore a sound shall be
In the reeds of Arcady,
Evermore a low lament
Of unrest and discontent,
As the story is retold
Of the nymph so coy and cold,
Who with frightened feet outran
The pursuing steps of Pan.

EPIMETHEUS.

The pipe of Pan out of these reeds is made,
And when he plays upon it to the shep-
   herds
They pity him, so mournful is the sound.
Be thou not coy and cold as Syrinx was.

PANDORA.

Nor thou as Pan be rude and mannerless.

PROMETHEUS, *without.*

Ho! Epimetheus!

EPIMETHEUS.

      'T is my brother's voice;
A sound unwelcome and inopportune
As was the braying of Silenus' ass,
Once heard in Cybele's garden.

PANDORA.

                Let me go.
I would not be found here. I would not see
   him.

She escapes among the trees.

CHORUS OF DRYADES.

Haste and hide thee,

Ere too late,
In these thickets intricate;
Lest Prometheus
See and chide thee,
Lest some hurt
Or harm betide thee,
Haste and hide thee!

PROMETHEUS, *entering.*

Who was it fled from here?   I saw a shape
Flitting among the trees.

EPIMETHEUS.

It was Pandora.

PROMETHEUS.

O Epimetheus!   Is it then in vain
That I have warned thee?   Let me now im-
plore.
Thou harborest in thy house a dangerous guest.

EPIMETHEUS.

Whom the Gods love they honor with such
guests.

PROMETHEUS.

Whom the Gods would destroy they first make
mad.

EPIMETHEUS.

Shall I refuse the gifts they send to me?

PROMETHEUS.

Reject all gifts that come from higher powers.

EPIMETHEUS.

Such gifts as this are not to be rejected.

PROMETHEUS.

Make not thyself the slave of any woman.

EPIMETHEUS.

Make not thyself the judge of any man.

PROMETHEUS.

I judge thee not; for thou art more than
man;
Thou art descended from Titanic race,
And hast a Titan's strength, and faculties

That make thee godlike; and thou sittest
here
Like Heracles spinning Omphale's flax,
And beaten with her sandals.

EPIMETHEUS.

O my brother!
Thou drivest me to madness with thy taunts.

PROMETHEUS.

And me thou drivest to madness with thy
follies.
Come with me to my tower on Caucasus:
See there my forges in the roaring caverns,
Beneficent to man, and taste the joy
That springs from labor.   Read with me the
stars,
And learn the virtues that lie hidden in plants,
And all things that are useful.

EPIMETHEUS.

O my brother
I am not as thou art.   Thou dost inherit
Our father's strength, and I our mother's
weakness:
The softness of the Oceanides,
The yielding nature that cannot resist.

PROMETHEUS.

Because thou wilt not.

EPIMETHEUS.

Nay; because I cannot.

PROMETHEUS.

Assert thyself; rise up to thy full height;
Shake from thy soul these dreams effeminate
These passions born of indolence and ease.
Resolve, and thou art free.   But breathe the
air
Of mountains, and their unapproachable sum-
mits
Will lift thee to the level of themselves.

EPIMETHEUS.

The roar of forests and of waterfalls,
The rushing of a mighty wind, with loud
And undistinguishable voices calling,
Are in my ear!

PROMETHEUS.

Oh, listen and obey.

EPIMETHEUS.

Thou leadest me as a child. I follow thee.

They go out.

CHORUS OF OREADES.

Centuries old are the mountains;
Their foreheads wrinkled and rifted
Helios crowns by day,
Pallid Selene by night;
From their bosoms uptossed
The snows are driven and drifted,
Like Tithonus' beard
Streaming dishevelled and white.

Thunder and tempest of wind
Their trumpets blow in the vastness;
Phantoms of mist and rain,
Cloud and the shadow of cloud,
Pass and repass by the gates

Of their inaccessible fastness;
Ever unmoved they stand,
Solemn, eternal, and proud.

VOICES OF THE WATERS.

Flooded by rain and snow
In their inexhaustible sources,
Swollen by affluent streams
Hurrying onward and hurled
Headlong over the crags,
The impetuous water-courses
Rush and roar and plunge
Down to the nethermost world.

Say, have the solid rocks
Into streams of silver been melted,
Flowing over the plains,
Spreading to lakes in the fields?
Or have the mountains, the giants,
The ice-helmed, the forest-belted,
Scattered their arms abroad;
Flung in the meadows their shields?

VOICES OF THE WINDS.

High on their turreted cliffs
That bolts of thunder have shattered,
Storm-winds muster and blow
Trumpets of terrible breath;
Then from the gateways rush,
And before them routed and scattered
Sullen the cloud-rack flies,
Pale with the pallor of death.

Onward the hurricane rides,
And flee for shelter the shepherds;
White are the frightened leaves,
Harvests with terror are white;
Panic seizes the herds,
And even the lions and leopards,
Prowling no longer for prey,
Crouch in their caverns with fright.

VOICES OF THE FORESTS.

Guarding the mountains around
Majestic the forests are standing,
Bright are their crested helms,
Dark is their armor of leaves;
Filled with the breath of freedom
Each bosom subsiding, expanding,
Now like the ocean sinks,
Now like the ocean upheaves.

Planted firm on the rock,
With foreheads stern and defiant,
Loud they shout to the winds,
Loud to the tempest they call;
Naught but Olympian thunders,
That blasted Titan and Giant,
Them can uproot and o'erthrow,
Shaking the earth with their fall.

CHORUS OF OREADES.

These are the Voices Three
Of winds and forests and fountains,
Voices of earth and of air,
Murmur and rushing of streams,
Making together one sound,
The mysterious voice of the mountains,
Waking the sluggard that sleeps,
Waking the dreamer of dreams.

These are the Voices Three,
That speak of endless endeavor,
Speak of endurance and strength,
Triumph and fulness of fame,
Sounding about the world,
An inspiration forever,
Stirring the hearts of men,
Shaping their end and their aim.

VII.

THE HOUSE OF EPIMETHEUS.

PANDORA.

Left to myself I wander as I will,
And as my fancy leads me, through this house,
Nor could I ask a dwelling more complete
Were I indeed the Goddess that he deems me.
No mansion of Olympus, framed to be
The habitation of the Immortal Gods,
Can be more beautiful. And this is mine,
And more than this, the love wherewith he
 crowns me.
As if impelled by powers invisible
And irresistible, my steps return
Unto this spacious hall. All corridors
And passages lead hither, and all doors
But open into it. Yon mysterious chest
Attracts and fascinates me. Would I knew

What there lies hidden! But the oracle
Forbids. Ah me! The secret then is safe.
So would it be if it were in my keeping.
A crowd of shadowy faces from the mirrors
That line these walls are watching me. I
 dare not
Lift up the lid. A hundred times the act
Would be repeated, and the secret seen
By twice a hundred incorporeal eyes.
 She walks to the other side of the hall.
My feet are weary, wandering to and fro,
My eyes with seeing and my heart with
 waiting.
I will lie here and rest till he returns,
Who is my dawn, my day, my Helios.
 Throws herself upon a couch, and falls asleep.

ZEPHYRUS.

Come from thy caverns dark and
    deep,
O son of Erebus and Night;
All sense of hearing and of sight
Enfold in the serene delight
And quietude of sleep!

Set all thy silent sentinels
To bar and guard the Ivory Gate,
And keep the evil dreams of fate
And falsehood and infernal hate
Imprisoned in their cells.

But open wide the Gate of Horn,
Whence, beautiful as planets, rise
The dreams of truth, with starry eyes,
And all the wondrous prophecies
And visions of the morn.

CHORUS OF DREAMS FROM THE IVORY GATE.

Ye sentinels of sleep,
It is in vain ye keep
Your drowsy watch before the Ivory Gate;
Though closed the portal seems,
The airy feet of dreams
Ye cannot thus in walls incarcerate.

We phantoms are and dreams
Born by Tartarean streams,
As ministers of the infernal powers;
O son of Erebus
And Night, behold! we thus
Elude your watchful warders on the towers!
101

From gloomy Tartarus
The Fates have summoned us
To whisper in her ear, who lies asleep,
A tale to fan the fire
Of her insane desire
To know a secret that the Gods would keep.

This passion, in their ire,
The Gods themselves inspire,
To vex mankind with evils manifold,
So that disease and pain
O'er the whole earth may reign,
And nevermore return the Age of Gold.

PANDORA, *waking.*

A voice said in my sleep: "Do not de-
lay:
Do not delay; the golden moments fly!
The oracle hath forbidden; yet not thee
Doth it forbid, but Epimetheus only!"
I am alone. These faces in the mirrors
Are but the shadows and phantoms of myself;
They cannot help nor hinder. No one sees
me,
Save the all-seeing Gods, who, knowing good
And knowing evil, have created me
Such as I am, and filled me with desire
Of knowing good and evil like themselves.

She approaches the chest.

I hesitate no longer. Weal or woe,
Or life or death, the moment shall decide.

*She lifts the lid. A dense mist rises from the chest, and fills
the room.* PANDORA *falls senseless on the floor. Storm
without.*

CHORUS OF DREAMS FROM THE GATE OF HORN.

Yes, the moment shall decide!
It already hath decided;
And the secret once confided
To the keeping of the Titan
Now is flying far and wide,
Whispered, told on every side,
To disquiet and to frighten.

Fever of the heart and brain,
Sorrow, pestilence, and pain,
Moans of anguish, maniac laughter,
All the evils that hereafter
Shall afflict and vex mankind,
All into the air have risen
From the chambers of their prison;
Only Hope remains behind.

VIII.

IN THE GARDEN.

EPIMETHEUS.

THE storm is past, but it hath left behind it
Ruin and desolation. All the walks
Are strewn with shattered boughs; the birds
    are silent;
The flowers, downtrodden by the wind, lie
    dead;
The swollen rivulet sobs with secret pain;
The melancholy reeds whisper together
As if some dreadful deed had been committed
They dare not name, and all the air is heavy
With an unspoken sorrow! Premonitions,
Foreshadowings of some terrible disaster
Oppress my heart. Ye Gods, avert the omen!

PANDORA, *coming from the house.*

O Epimetheus, I no longer dare
To lift mine eyes to thine, nor hear thy voice,
Being no longer worthy of thy love.

EPIMETHEUS.

What hast thou done?

PANDORA.

      Forgive me not, but kill me.

EPIMETHEUS.

What hast thou done?

PANDORA.

      I pray for death, not pardon.

EPIMETHEUS.

What hast thou done?

PANDORA.

      I dare not speak of it.

EPIMETHEUS.

Thy pallor and thy silence terrify me!

PANDORA.

I have brought wrath and ruin on thy house!

My heart hath braved the oracle that guarded
The fatal secret from us, and my hand
Lifted the lid of the mysterious chest!

EPIMETHEUS.

Then all is lost! I am indeed undone.

PANDORA.

I pray for punishment, and not for pardon.

EPIMETHEUS.

Mine is the fault, not thine. On me shall fall
The vengeance of the Gods, for I betrayed
Their secret when, in evil hour, I said
It was a secret; when, in evil hour,
I left thee here alone to this temptation.
Why did I leave thee?

PANDORA.

      Why didst thou return?
Eternal absence would have been to me
The greatest punishment. To be left alone
And face to face with my own crime, had
    been
Just retribution. Upon me, ye Gods,
Let all your vengeance fall!

EPIMETHEUS.

      On thee and me.
I do not love thee less for what is done,
And cannot be undone. Thy very weakness
Hath brought thee nearer to me, and hence-
    forth
My love will have a sense of pity in it,
Making it less a worship than before.

PANDORA.

Pity me not; pity is degradation.
Love me and kill me.

EPIMETHEUS.

      Beautiful Pandora!
Thou art a Goddess still!

PANDORA.

    I am a woman;
And the insurgent demon in my nature,
That made me brave the oracle, revolts
At pity and compassion. Let me die;
What else remains for me?

EPIMETHEUS.

    Youth, hope, and love:
To build a new life on a ruined life,
To make the future fairer than the past,
And make the past appear a troubled dream.
Even now in passing through the garden
  walks
Upon the ground I saw a fallen nest
Ruined and full of rain; and over me
Beheld the uncomplaining birds already
Busy in building a new habitation.

PANDORA.

Auspicious omen!

EPIMETHEUS.

    May the Eumenides
Put out their torches and behold us not,
And fling away their whips of scorpions
And touch us not.

PANDORA.

    Me let them punish.
Only through punishment of our evil deeds,
Only through suffering, are we reconciled
To the immortal Gods and to ourselves.

CHORUS OF THE EUMENIDES.

Never shall souls like these.
 Escape the Eumenides,
The daughters dark of Acheron and Night!
  Unquenched our torches glare,
  Our scourges in the air
Send forth prophetic sounds before they smite.

  Never by lapse of time
  The soul defaced by crime
Into its former self returns again;
  For every guilty deed
  Holds in itself the seed
Of retribution and undying pain.

  Never shall be the loss
  Restored, till Helios
Hath purified them with his heavenly fires;
  Then what was lost is won,
  And the new life begun,
Kindled with nobler passions and desires.

THE HANGING OF THE CRANE

I.

THE lights are out, and gone are all the guests
That thronging came with merriment and jests
To celebrate the Hanging of the Crane
In the new house, — into the night are gone;
But still the fire upon the hearth burns on,
And I alone remain.

O fortunate, O happy day,
When a new household finds its place
Among the myriad homes of earth,
Like a new star just sprung to birth,
And rolled on its harmonious way
Into the boundless realms of space!

So said the guests in speech and song,
As in the chimney, burning bright,
We hung the iron crane to-night,
And merry was the feast and long.

II.

AND now I sit and muse on what may be,
And in my vision see, or seem to see,
  Through floating vapors interfused with
        light,
Shapes indeterminate, that gleam and fade,
As shadows passing into deeper shade
  Sink and elude the sight.

For two alone, there in the hall,
Is spread the table round and small;
Upon the polished silver shine
The evening lamps, but, more divine,
The light of love shines over all;
Of love, that says not mine and thine,
But ours, for ours is thine and mine.

They want no guests, to come between
Their tender glances like a screen,
And tell them tales of land and sea,
And whatsoever may betide
The great, forgotten world outside;
They want no guests; they needs must be
Each other's own best company.

III.

THE picture fades; as at a village fair
A showman's views, dissolving into air,
  Again appear transfigured on the screen,
So in my fancy this; and now once more,
In part transfigured, through the open door
  Appears the selfsame scene.

Seated, I see the two again,
But not alone; they entertain
A little angel unaware,
With face as round as is the moon,
A royal guest with flaxen hair,

Who, throned upon his lofty chair,
Drums on the table with his spoon,
Then drops it careless on the floor,
To grasp at things unseen before.

Are these celestial manners? these
The ways that win, the arts that please?
Ah yes; consider well the guest,
And whatsoe'er he does seems best;
He ruleth by the right divine
Of helplessness, so lately born
In purple chambers of the morn,
As sovereign over thee and thine.
He speaketh not; and yet there lies
A conversation in his eyes;
The golden silence of the Greek,
The gravest wisdom of the wise,
Not spoken in language, but in looks
More legible than printed books,
As if he could but would not speak.
And now, O monarch absolute,
Thy power is put to proof; for, lo!
Resistless, fathomless, and slow,
The nurse comes rustling like the sea,
And pushes back thy chair and thee,
And so good night to King Canute.

IV.

As one who walking in a forest sees
A lovely landscape through the parted trees,
  Then sees it not, for boughs that intervene;
Or as we see the moon sometimes revealed
Through drifting clouds, and then again con-
        cealed,
  So I behold the scene.

There are two guests at table now;
The king, deposed and older grown,
No longer occupies the throne, —
The crown is on his sister's brow;
A Princess from the Fairy Isles,
The very pattern girl of girls,
All covered and embowered in curls,
Rose-tinted from the Isle of Flowers,
And sailing with soft, silken sails
From far-off Dreamland into ours.
Above their bowls with rims of blue
Four azure eyes of deeper hue
Are looking, dreamy with delight;
Limpid as planets that emerge

Above the ocean's rounded verge,
Soft-shining through the summer night.
Steadfast they gaze, yet nothing see
Beyond the horizon of their bowls;
Nor care they for the world that rolls
With all its freight of troubled souls
Into the days that are to be.

v.

AGAIN the tossing boughs shut out the scene,
Again the drifting vapors intervene,
  And the moon's pallid disk is hidden quite;
And now I see the table wider grown,
As round a pebble into water thrown
    Dilates a ring of light.

I see the table wider grown,
I see it garlanded with guests,
As if fair Ariadne's Crown
Out of the sky had fallen down;

Maidens within whose tender breasts
A thousand restless hopes and fears,
Forth reaching to the coming years,
Flutter awhile, then quiet lie,
Like timid birds that fain would fly,
But do not dare to leave their nests; —
And youths, who in their strength elate
Challenge the van and front of fate,
Eager as champions to be
In the divine knight-errantry
Of youth, that travels sea and land
Seeking adventures, or pursues,
Through cities, and through solitudes
Frequented by the lyric Muse,
The phantom with the beckoning hand,
That stills allures and still eludes.
O sweet illusions of the brain!
O sudden thrills of fire and frost!
The world is bright while ye remain,
And dark and dead when ye are lost!

VI.

The meadow-brook, that seemeth to stand still,
Quickens its current as it nears the mill;
  And so the stream of Time that lingereth
In level places, and so dull appears,
Runs with a swifter current as it nears
    The gloomy mills of Death.

And now, like the magician's scroll,
That in the owner's keeping shrinks
With every wish he speaks or thinks,
Till the last wish consumes the whole,
The table dwindles, and again
I see the two alone remain.
The crown of stars is broken in parts;
Its jewels, brighter than the day,
Have one by one been stolen away
To shine in other homes and hearts.
One is a wanderer now afar
In Ceylon or in Zanzibar,
Or sunny regions of Cathay;
And one is in the boisterous camp
Mid clink of arms and horses' tramp,
And battle's terrible array.
I see the patient mother read,
With aching heart, of wrecks that float
Disabled on those seas remote,
Or of some great heroic deed
On battle-fields, where thousands bleed
To lift one hero into fame.
Anxious she bends her graceful head
Above these chronicles of pain,
And trembles with a secret dread
Lest there among the drowned or slain
She find the one beloved name.

VII.

AFTER a day of cloud and wind and rain
Sometimes the setting sun breaks out again,

And, touching all the darksome woods with
    light,
Smiles on the fields, until they laugh and
    sing,
Then like a ruby from the horizon's ring
    Drops down into the night.

What see I now? The night is fair,
The storm of grief, the clouds of care,
The wind, the rain, have passed away;
The lamps are lit, the fires burn bright,
The house is full of life and light;
It is the Golden Wedding day.
The guests come thronging in once
    more,
Quick footsteps sound along the floor,
The trooping children crowd the stair,
And in and out and everywhere
Flashes along the corridor
The sunshine of their golden hair.
On the round table in the hall
Another Ariadne's Crown
Out of the sky hath fallen down;
More than one Monarch of the Moon
Is drumming with his silver spoon;
The light of love shines over all.

O fortunate, O happy day!
The people sing, the people say.
The ancient bridegroom and the bride,
Smiling contented and serene
Upon the blithe, bewildering scene,
Behold, well pleased, on every side
Their forms and features multiplied,
As the reflection of a light
Between two burnished mirrors gleams,
Or lamps upon a bridge at night
Stretch on and on before the sight,
Till the long vista endless seems.

POEM FOR THE FIFTIETH ANNIVERSARY OF THE CLASS OF 1825 IN
BOWDOIN COLLEGE.

Tempora labuntur, tacitisque senescimus annis,
Et fugiunt freno non remorante dies.

OVID, *Fastorum*, Lib. vi.

"O CÆSAR, we who are about to die
Salute you!" was the gladiators' cry
In the arena, standing face to face
With death and with the Roman popu-
lace.

O ye familiar scenes, — ye groves of pine,
That once were mine and are no longer
mine, —
Thou river, widening through the meadows
green

To the vast sea, so near and yet unseen, —
Ye halls, in whose seclusion and repose
Phantoms of fame, like exhalations, rose
And vanished, — we who are about to die,
Salute you; earth and air and sea and sky,
And the Imperial Sun that scatters down
His sovereign splendors upon grove and
    town.

Ye do not answer us! ye do not hear!
We are forgotten; and in your austere
And calm indifference, ye little care
Whether we come or go, or whence or
    where.
What passing generations fill these halls,
What passing voices echo from these walls,
Ye heed not; we are only as the blast,
A moment heard, and then forever past.

Not so the teachers who in earlier days
Led our bewildered feet through learning's
    maze;
They answer us —alas! what have I said?
What greetings come there from the voice-
    less dead?
What salutation, welcome, or reply?
What pressure from the hands that lifeless
    lie?
They are no longer here; they all are gone
Into the land of shadows, — all save one.
Honor and reverence, and the good repute
That follows faithful service as its fruit,
Be unto him, whom living we salute.

The great Italian poet, when he made
His dreadful journey to the realms of shade,
Met there the old instructor of his youth,
And cried in tones of pity and of ruth:
" Oh, never from the memory of my heart
Your dear, paternal image shall depart,
Who while on earth, ere yet by death sur-
    prised,
Taught me how mortals are immortalized;
How grateful am I for that patient care
All my life long my language shall de-
    clare."

To-day we make the poet's words our own,
And utter them in plaintive undertone;
Nor to the living only be they said,

But to the other living called the dead,
Whose dear, paternal images appear
Not wrapped in gloom, but robed in sun-
    shine here;
Whose simple lives, complete and without
    flaw,
Were part and parcel of great Nature's law;
Who said not to their Lord, as if afraid,
" Here is thy talent in a napkin laid,"
But labored in their sphere, as men who live
In the delight that work alone can give.
Peace be to them; eternal peace and rest,
And the fulfilment of the great behest:
" Ye have been faithful over a few things,
Over ten cities shall ye reign as kings."

And ye who fill the places we once filled,
And follow in the furrows that we tilled,
Young men, whose generous hearts are beat-
    ing high,
We who are old, and are about to die,
Salute you; hail you; take your hands in ours,
And crown you with our welcome as with
    flowers!

How beautiful is youth! how bright it
    gleams
With its illusions, aspirations, dreams!
Book of Beginnings, Story without End,
Each maid a heroine, and each man a
    friend!
Aladdin's Lamp, and Fortunatus' Purse,
That holds the treasures of the universe!
All possibilities are in its hands,
No danger daunts it, and no foe with-
    stands;
In its sublime audacity of faith,
" Be thou removed!" it to the mountain
    saith,
And with ambitious feet, secure and proud,
Ascends the ladder leaning on the cloud!

As ancient Priam at the Scæan gate
Sat on the walls of Troy in regal state
With the old men, too old and weak to fight,
Chirping like grasshoppers in their delight
To see the embattled hosts, with spear and
    shield,
Of Trojans and Achaians in the field;
So from the snowy summits of our years

We see you in the plain, as each appears,
And question of you; asking, "Who is he
That towers above the others? Which may
    be
Atreides, Menelaus, Odysseus,
Ajax the great, or bold Idomeneus?"

Let him not boast who puts his armor on
As he who puts it off, the battle done.
Study yourselves; and most of all note well
Wherein kind Nature meant you to excel.
Not every blossom ripens into fruit;
Minerva, the inventress of the flute,
Flung it aside, when she her face surveyed
Distorted in a fountain as she played;
The unlucky Marsyas found it, and his fate
Was one to make the bravest hesitate.

Write on your doors the saying wise and old,
"Be bold! be bold!" and everywhere —
    "Be bold;

Be not too bold!" Yet better the excess
Than the defect; better the more than less;
Better like Hector in the field to die,
Than like a perfumed Paris turn and fly.

And now, my classmates; ye remaining few
That number not the half of those we
    knew,
Ye, against whose familiar names not yet
The fatal asterisk of death is set,
Ye I salute! The horologe of Time
Strikes the half-century with a solemn
    chime,
And summons us together once again,
The joy of meeting not unmixed with pain.

Where are the others? Voices from the
    deep
Caverns of darkness answer me: "They
    sleep!"
I name no names; instinctively I feel

Each at some well-remembered grave will
    kneel,
And from the inscription wipe the weeds
    and moss,
For every heart best knoweth its own loss.
I see their scattered gravestones gleaming
    white
Through the pale dusk of the impending
    night;
O'er all alike the impartial sunset throws
Its golden lilies mingled with the rose;
We give to each a tender thought, and
    pass
Out of the graveyards with their tangled
    grass,
Unto these scenes frequented by our feet
When we were young, and life was fresh
    and sweet.

What shall I say to you? What can I
    say
Better than silence is? When I survey
This throng of faces turned to meet my
    own,
Friendly and fair, and yet to me unknown,
Transformed the very landscape seems to be;
It is the same, yet not the same to me.
So many memories crowd upon my brain,
So many ghosts are in the wooded plain,
I fain would steal away, with noiseless
    tread,
As from a house where some one lieth
    dead.
I cannot go; — I pause; — I hesitate;
My feet reluctant linger at the gate;
As one who struggles in a troubled dream
To speak and cannot, to myself I seem.

Vanish the dream! Vanish the idle fears!
Vanish the rolling mists of fifty years!
Whatever time or space may intervene,
I will not be a stranger in this scene.
Here every doubt, all indecision, ends;
Hail, my companions, comrades, classmates,
    friends!

Ah me! the fifty years since last we met
Seem to me fifty folios bound and set
By Time, the great transcriber, on his
    shelves,

Wherein are written the histories of our-
    selves.
What tragedies, what comedies, are there;
What joy and grief, what rapture and de-
    spair!
What chronicles of triumph and defeat,
Of struggle, and temptation, and retreat!
What records of regrets, and doubts, and
    fears!
What pages blotted, blistered by our tears!
What lovely landscapes on the margin shine,
What sweet, angelic faces, what divine
And holy images of love and trust,
Undimmed by age, unsoiled by damp or
    dust!

Whose hand shall dare to open and explore
These volumes, closed and clasped forever-
    more?
Not mine. With reverential feet I pass;
I hear a voice that cries, " Alas! alas!
Whatever hath been written shall remain,
Nor be erased nor written o'er again;
The unwritten only still belongs to thee:
Take heed, and ponder well what that
    shall be."

As children frightened by a thundercloud
Are reassured if some one reads aloud
A tale of wonder, with enchantment fraught,
Or wild adventure, that diverts their thought,
Let me endeavor with a tale to chase
The gathering shadows of the time and
    place,
And banish what we all too deeply feel
Wholly to say, or wholly to conceal.

In mediæval Rome, I know not where,
There stood an image with its arm in air,
And on its lifted finger, shining clear,
A golden ring with the device, " Strike
    here!"
Greatly the people wondered, though none
    guessed
The meaning that these words but half ex-
    pressed,
Until a learned clerk, who at noonday
With downcast eyes was passing on his way,
Paused, and observed the spot, and marked
    it well,

Whereon the shadow of the finger fell;
And, coming back at midnight, delved, and
  found
A secret stairway leading under ground.
Down this he passed into a spacious hall,
Lit by a flaming jewel on the wall;
And opposite, in threatening attitude,
With bow and shaft a brazen statue stood.
Upon its forehead, like a coronet,
Were these mysterious words of menace set:
"That which I am, I am; my fatal aim
None can escape, not even yon luminous
  flame!"

Midway the hall was a fair table placed,
With cloth of gold, and golden cups en-
  chased
With rubies, and the plates and knives
  were gold,
And gold the bread and viands manifold.
Around it, silent, motionless, and sad,
Were seated gallant knights in armor clad,
And ladies beautiful with plume and zone,
But they were stone, their hearts within
  were stone;
And the vast hall was filled in every part
With silent crowds, stony in face and heart.

Long at the scene, bewildered and amazed
The trembling clerk in speechless wonder
  gazed;
Then from the table, by his greed made
  bold,
He seized a goblet and a knife of gold,
And suddenly from their seats the guests
  upsprang,
The vaulted ceiling with loud clamors rang,
The archer sped his arrow, at their call,
Shattering the lambent jewel on the wall,
And all was dark around and overhead; —
Stark on the floor the luckless clerk lay
  dead!

The writer of this legend then records
Its ghostly application in these words:
The image is the Adversary old,
Whose beckoning finger points to realms of
  gold;
Our lusts and passions are the downward
  stair

That leads the soul from a diviner air;
The archer, Death; the flaming jewel, Life;
Terrestrial goods, the goblet and the knife;
The knights and ladies, all whose flesh and
  bone
By avarice have been hardened into stone;
The clerk, the scholar whom the love of
  pelf
Tempts from his books and from his nobler
  self.

The scholar and the world! The endless
  strife,
The discord in the harmonies of life!
The love of learning, the sequestered nooks,
And all the sweet serenity of books;
The market-place, the eager love of gain,
Whose aim is vanity, and whose end is
  pain!

But why, you ask me, should this tale be
  told
To men grown old, or who are growing
  old?
It is too late! Ah, nothing is too late
Till the tired heart shall cease to palpitate.
Cato learned Greek at eighty; Sophocles
Wrote his grand Œdipus, and Simonides
Bore off the prize of verse from his com-
  peers,
When each had numbered more than four-
  score years,
And Theophrastus, at fourscore and ten,
Had but begun his "Characters of Men."
Chaucer, at Woodstock with the night-
  ingales,
At sixty wrote the Canterbury Tales;
Goethe at Weimar, toiling to the last,
Completed Faust when eighty years were
  past.
These are indeed exceptions; but they
  show
How far the gulf-stream of our youth may
  flow
Into the arctic regions of our lives,
Where little else than life itself survives.

As the barometer foretells the storm
While still the skies are clear, the weather
  warm,

So something in us, as old age draws near,
Betrays the pressure of the atmosphere.
The nimble mercury, ere we are aware,
Descends the elastic ladder of the air;
The telltale blood in artery and vein
Sinks from its higher levels in the brain;
Whatever poet, orator, or sage
May say of it, old age is still old age.
It is the waning, not the crescent moon;
The dusk of evening, not the blaze of noon;
It is not strength, but weakness; not desire,
But its surcease; not the fierce heat of fire,
The burning and consuming element,
But that of ashes and of embers spent,
In which some living sparks we still dis-
      cern,
Enough to warm, but not enough to burn.

What then? Shall we sit idly down and
      say
The night hath come; it is no longer day?
The night hath not yet come; we are not
      quite
Cut off from labor by the failing light;
Something remains for us to do or dare;
Even the oldest tree some fruit may bear;
Not Œdipus Coloneus, or Greek Ode,
Or tales of pilgrims that one morning rode
Out of the gateway of the Tabard Inn,
But other something, would we but begin;
For age is opportunity no less
Than youth itself, though in another dress,
And as the evening twilight fades away
The sky is filled with stars, invisible by
      day.

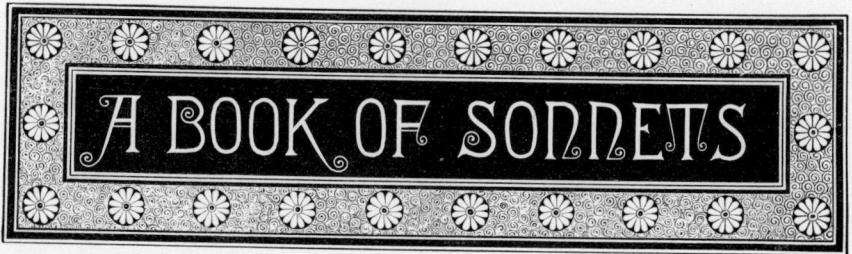

A BOOK OF SONNETS

THREE FRIENDS OF MINE.

I.

When I remember them, those friends of
  mine,
  Who are no longer here, the noble three,
  Who half my life were more than friends
    to me,
  And whose discourse was like a generous
    wine,
I most of all remember the divine
  Something, that shone in them, and made
    us see

The archetypal man, and what might be
The amplitude of Nature's first design.
In vain I stretch my hands to clasp their
  hands;
  I cannot find them. Nothing now is left
  But a majestic memory. They meanwhile
Wander together in Elysian lands,
  Perchance remembering me, who am bereft
  Of their dear presence, and, remembering,
    smile.

II.

In Attica thy birthplace should have been,
  Or the Ionian Isles, or where the seas
  Encircle in their arms the Cyclades,
  So wholly Greek wast thou in thy serene
And childlike joy of life, O Philhellene!
  Around thee would have swarmed the Attic
    bees;
  Homer had been thy friend, or Socrates,

And Plato welcomed thee to his demesne.
For thee old legends breathed historic breath;
  Thou sawest Poseidon in the purple sea,
  And in the sunset Jason's fleece of gold!
Oh, what hadst thou to do with cruel Death,
  Who wast so full of life, or Death with thee,
  That thou shouldst die before thou hadst
    grown old!

III.

I stand again on the familiar shore,
  And hear the waves of the distracted sea
  Piteously calling and lamenting thee,
  And waiting restless at thy cottage door.
The rocks, the sea-weed on the ocean floor,
  The willows in the meadow, and the free
  Wild winds of the Atlantic welcome me;
  Then why shouldst thou be dead, and come
    no more?

Ah, why shouldst thou be dead, when com-
  mon men
  Are busy with their trivial affairs,
  Having and holding? Why, when thou
    hadst read
Nature's mysterious manuscript, and then
  Wast ready to reveal the truth it bears,
  Why art thou silent? Why shouldst thou
    be dead?

IV.

River, that stealest with such silent pace
  Around the City of the Dead, where lies

A friend who bore thy name, and whom
  these eyes

Shall see no more in his accustomed place,
Linger and fold him in thy soft embrace
   And say good night, for now the western
     skies
   Are red with sunset, and gray mists arise
   Like damps that gather on a dead man's face.

Good night! good night! as we so oft have said
   Beneath this roof at midnight, in the days
   That are no more, and shall no more return.
Thou hast but taken thy lamp and gone to bed;
   I stay a little longer, as one stays
   To cover up the embers that still burn.

V.

THE doors are all wide open; at the gate
   The blossomed lilacs counterfeit a blaze,
   And seem to warm the air; a dreamy haze
   Hangs o'er the Brighton meadows like a
     fate,
And on their margin, with sea-tides elate,
   The flooded Charles, as in the happier days,
   Writes the last letter of his name, and stays
   His restless steps, as if compelled to wait.

I also wait; but they will come no more,
   Those friends of mine, whose presence sat-
     isfied
   The thirst and hunger of my heart. Ah
     me!
They have forgotten the pathway to my door!
   Something is gone from nature since they
     died,
   And summer is not summer, nor can be.

CHAUCER.

An old man in a lodge within a park :
  The chamber walls depicted all around
  With portraitures of huntsman, hawk, and
    hound,
  And the hurt deer. He listeneth to the
    lark,
Whose song comes with the sunshine through
  the dark
  Of painted glass in leaden lattice bound ;
  He listeneth and he laugheth at the
    sound,
  Then writeth in a book like any clerk.
He is the poet of the dawn, who wrote
  The Canterbury Tales, and his old age
  Made beautiful with song ; and as I
    read
I hear the crowing cock, I hear the
  note
  Of lark and linnet, and from every
    page
  Rise odors of ploughed field or flowery
    mead.

SHAKESPEARE.

A vision as of crowded city streets,
  With human life in endless overflow ;
  Thunder of thoroughfares ; trumpets that
    blow
  To battle ; clamor, in obscure retreats,
Of sailors landed from their anchored fleets ;
  Tolling of bells in turrets, and below
  Voices of children, and bright flowers that
    throw
  O'er garden-walls their intermingled sweets !
This vision comes to me when I unfold
  The volume of the Poet paramount,
  Whom all the Muses loved, not one
    alone ; —
Into his hands they put the lyre of gold,
  And, crowned with sacred laurel at their
    fount,
  Placed him as Musagetes on their throne.

MILTON.

I PACE the sounding sea-beach and behold
  How the voluminous billows roll and run,
  Upheaving and subsiding, while the sun
  Shines through their sheeted emerald far
    unrolled,
And the ninth wave, slow gathering fold by
    fold
  All its loose-flowing garments into one,
  Plunges upon the shore, and floods the
    dun
  Pale reach of sands, and changes them to
    gold.
So in majestic cadênce rise and fall
  The mighty undulations of thy song,
  O sightless bard, England's Mæonides!
And ever and anon, high over all
  Uplifted, a ninth wave superb and strong,
  Floods all the soul with its melodious
    seas.

KEATS.

THE young Endymion sleeps Endymion's
    sleep;
  The shepherd-boy whose tale was left half
    told!
  The solemn grove uplifts its shield of gold
  To the red rising moon, and loud and
    deep
The nightingale is singing from the steep;
  It is midsummer, but the air is cold;
  Can it be death? Alas, beside the fold
  A shepherd's pipe lies shattered near his
    sheep.
Lo! in the moonlight gleams a marble white,
  On which I read: "Here lieth one whose
    name
  Was writ in water." And was this the
    meed
Of his sweet singing? Rather let me write:
  "The smoking flax before it burst to flame
  Was quenched by death, and broken the
    bruised reed."

THE GALAXY.

Torrent of light and river of the air,
  Along whose bed the glimmering stars are
     seen
  Like gold and silver sands in some ravine
  Where mountain streams have left their
     channels bare !
The Spaniard sees in thee the pathway, where
  His patron saint descended in the sheen
  Of his celestial armor, on serene
  And quiet nights, when all the heavens
     were fair.

Not this I see, nor yet the ancient fable
  Of Phaeton's wild course, that scorched the
     skies
  Where'er the hoofs of his hot coursers
     trod ;
But the white drift of worlds o'er chasms of
     sable,
  The star-dust, that is whirled aloft and
     flies
  From the invisible chariot-wheels of God.

THE SOUND OF THE SEA.

The sea awoke at midnight from its sleep,
  And round the pebbly beaches far and
     wide
  I heard the first wave of the rising tide
  Rush onward with uninterrupted sweep ;
A voice out of the silence of the deep,
  A sound mysteriously multiplied
  As of a cataract from the mountain's side,

Or roar of winds upon a wooded steep.
So comes to us at times, from the unknown
  And inaccessible solitudes of being,
  The rushing of the sea-tides of the soul ;
And inspirations, that we deem our own,
  Are some divine foreshadowing and fore-
     seeing
Of things beyond our reason or control.

A SUMMER DAY BY THE SEA.

THE sun is set ; and in his latest beams
 Yon little cloud of ashen gray and gold,
 Slowly upon the amber air unrolled,
 The falling mantle of the Prophet seems.
From the dim headlands many a light-house
   gleams,
 The street-lamps of the ocean ; and behold,
 O'erhead the banners of the night unfold ;

The day hath passed into the land of
   dreams.
O summer day beside the joyous sea !
 O summer day so wonderful and white,
 So full of gladness and so full of pain ?
Forever and forever shalt thou be
 To some the gravestone of a dead delight,
 To some the landmark of a new domain.

THE TIDES.

I SAW the long line of the vacant shore,
 The sea-weed and the shells upon the sand,
 And the brown rocks left bare on every hand,
 As if the ebbing tide would flow no more.
Then heard I, more distinctly than before,
 The ocean breathe and its great breast ex-
   pand,
 And hurrying came on the defenceless land

The insurgent waters with tumultuous roar,
All thought and feeling and desire, I said,
 Love, laughter, and the exultant joy of song
 Have ebbed from me forever ! Suddenly
   o'er me
They swept again from their deep ocean bed,
 And in a tumult of delight, and strong
 As youth, and beautiful as youth, upbore me.

A SHADOW.

I said unto myself, if I were dead,
  What would befall these children? What
    would be
  Their fate, who now are looking up to me
  For help and furtherance? Their lives, I
    said,
Would be a volume wherein I have read
  But the first chapters, and no longer see
  To read the rest of their dear history,

So full of beauty and so full of dread.
Be comforted; the world is very old,
  And generations pass, as they have passed,
  A troop of shadows moving with the sun;
Thousands of times has the old tale been told;
  The world belongs to those who come the
    last,
  They will find hope and strength as we
    have done.

A NAMELESS GRAVE.

"A soldier of the Union mustered out,"
  Is the inscription on an unknown grave
  At Newport News, beside the salt-sea
    wave,
  Nameless and dateless; sentinel or scout
Shot down in skirmish, or disastrous rout
  Of battle, when the loud artillery drave
  Its iron wedges through the ranks of brave

And doomed battalions, storming the re-
    doubt.
Thou unknown hero sleeping by the sea
  In thy forgotten grave! with secret shame
  I feel my pulses beat, my forehead burn,
When I remember thou hast given for me
  All that thou hadst, thy life, thy very name,
  And I can give thee nothing in return.

SLEEP.

Lull me to sleep, ye winds, whose fitful sound
    Seems from some faint Æolian harpstring
        caught;
    Seal up the hundred wakeful eyes of thought
    As Hermes with his lyre in sleep profound
The hundred wakeful eyes of Argus bound;
    For I am weary, and am overwrought
    With too much toil, with too much care
        distraught,

And with the iron crown of anguish crowned.
Lay thy soft hand upon my brow and
        cheek,
    O peaceful Sleep! until from pain released
    I breathe again uninterrupted breath!
Ah, with what subtile meaning did the
        Greek
    Call thee the lesser mystery at the feast
    Whereof the greater mystery is death!

THE OLD BRIDGE AT FLORENCE.

Taddeo Gaddi built me. I am old,
    Five centuries old. I plant my foot of
        stone
    Upon the Arno, as St. Michael's own
    Was planted on the dragon. Fold by fold
Beneath me as it struggles, I behold
    Its glistening scales. Twice hath it over-
        thrown

My kindred and companions. Me alone
    It moveth not, but is by me controlled.
I can remember when the Medici
    Were driven from Florence; longer still ago
    The final wars of Ghibelline and Guelf.
Florence adorns me with her jewelry;
    And when I think that Michael Angelo
    Hath leaned on me, I glory in myself.

IL PONTE VECCHIO DI FIRENZE.

Gaddi mi fece; il Ponte Vecchio sono;
    Cinquecent' anni già sull' Arno pianto
    Il piede, come il suo Michele Santo
    Piantò sul draco. Mentre ch' io ragiono
Lo vedo torcere con flebil suono
    Le rilucenti scaglie. Ha questi affranto
    Due volte i miei maggior. Me solo intanto

Neppure muove, ed io non l' abbandono.
Io mi rammento quando fur cacciati
    I Medici; pur quando Ghibellino
    E Guelfo fecer pace mi rammento.
Fiorenza i suoi giojelli m' ha prestati;
    E quando penso ch' Agnolo il divino
    Su me posava, insuperbir mi sento.

NATURE.

As a fond mother, when the day is o'er,
  Leads by the hand her little child to bed,
  Half willing, half reluctant to be led,
  And leave his broken playthings on the floor,
Still gazing at them through the open door,
  Nor wholly reassured and comforted
  By promises of others in their stead,
  Which, though more splendid, may not
    please him more ;

So Nature deals with us, and takes away
  Our playthings one by one, and by the
    hand
  Leads us to rest so gently, that we go
Scarce knowing if we wish to go or stay,
  Being too full of sleep to understand
  How far the unknown transcends the what
    we know.

IN THE CHURCHYARD AT TARRYTOWN.

HERE lies the gentle humorist, who died
  In the bright Indian Summer of his fame !
  A simple stone, with but a date and name,
  Marks his secluded resting-place beside
The river that he loved and glorified.
  Here in the autumn of his days he came,
  But the dry leaves of life were all aflame
  With tints that brightened and were mul-
    tiplied.

How sweet a life was his ; how sweet a
    death !
  Living, to wing with mirth the weary hours,
  Or with romantic tales the heart to cheer ;
Dying, to leave a memory like the breath
  Of summers full of sunshine and of show-
    ers,
  A grief and gladness in the atmosphere.

ELIOT'S OAK.

THOU ancient oak! whose myriad leaves are
    loud
  With sounds of unintelligible speech,
  Sounds as of surges on a shingly beach,
  Or multitudinous murmurs of a crowd;
With some mysterious gift of tongues en-
    dowed,
  Thou speakest a different dialect to each;

To me a language that no man can teach,
  Of a lost race, long vanished like a cloud.
For underneath thy shade, in days remote,
  Seated like Abraham at eventide
  Beneath the oaks of Mamre, the unknown
Apostle of the Indians, Eliot, wrote
  His Bible in a language that hath died
  And is forgotten, save by thee alone.

THE DESCENT OF THE MUSES.

NINE sisters, beautiful in form and face,
  Came from their convent on the shining
    heights
  Of Pierus, the mountain of delights,
  To dwell among the people at its base.
Then seemed the world to change. All time
    and space,
  Splendor of cloudless days and starry nights,
  And men and manners, and all sounds and
    sights,

Had a new meaning, a diviner grace.
Proud were these sisters, but were not too
    proud
  To teach in schools of little country towns
  Science and song, and all the arts that please;
So that while housewives span, and farmers
    ploughed,
  Their comely daughters, clad in homespun
    gowns,
  Learned the sweet songs of the Pierides.

VENICE.

WHITE swan of cities, slumbering in thy nest
  So wonderfully built among the reeds
  Of the lagoon, that fences thee and feeds,
  As sayeth thy old historian and thy guest!
White water-lily, cradled and caressed
  By ocean streams, and from the silt and
    weeds
  Lifting thy golden filaments and seeds,

Thy sun-illumined spires, thy crown and
    crest!
White phantom city, whose untrodden streets
  Are rivers, and whose pavements are the
    shifting
  Shadows of palaces and strips of sky;
I wait to see thee vanish like the fleets
  Seen in mirage, or towers of cloud uplifting
  In air their unsubstantial masonry.

ARTIST: SANFORD R. GIFFORD.

VENICE.

THE POETS.

O YE dead Poets, who are living still
  Immortal in your verse, though life be fled,
  And ye, O living Poets, who are dead
  Though ye are living, if neglect can kill,
Tell me if in the darkest hours of ill,
  With drops of anguish falling fast and red
  From the sharp crown of thorns upon your
    head,

Ye were not glad your errand to fulfil?
Yes; for the gift and ministry of Song
  Have something in them so divinely sweet,
  It can assuage the bitterness of wrong;
Not in the clamor of the crowded street,
  Not in the shouts and plaudits of the throng,
  But in ourselves, are triumph and defeat.

PARKER CLEAVELAND.

WRITTEN ON REVISITING BRUNSWICK IN THE SUMMER OF 1875.

AMONG the many lives that I have known.
  None I remember more serene and sweet,
  More rounded in itself and more complete,
  Than his, who lies beneath this funeral
    stone.
These pines, that murmur in low monotone,
  These walks frequented by scholastic feet,
  Were all his world; but in this calm re-
    treat

For him the Teacher's chair became a throne.
With fond affection memory loves to dwell
  On the old days, when his example made
  A pastime of the toil of tongue and pen;
And now, amid the groves he loved so well
  That naught could lure him from their
    grateful shade,
  He sleeps, but wakes elsewhere, for God
    hath said, Amen!

THE HARVEST MOON.

IT is the Harvest Moon! On gilded vanes
  And roofs of villages, on woodland crests
  And their aerial neighborhoods of nests
  Deserted, on the curtained window-panes
Of rooms where children sleep, on country lanes
  And harvest-fields, its mystic splendor rests!
  Gone are the birds that were our summer
    guests;

With the last sheaves return the laboring
    wains!
All things are symbols: the external shows
  Of Nature have their image in the mind,
  As flowers and fruits and falling of the leaves;
The song-birds leave us at the summer's close,
  Only the empty nests are left behind,
  And pipings of the quail among the sheaves.

TO THE RIVER RHONE.

THOU Royal River, born of sun and shower
  In chambers purple with the Alpine glow,
  Wrapped in the spotless ermine of the snow
  And rocked by tempests! — at the appointed
    hour
Forth, like a steel-clad horseman from a tower,
  With clang and clink of harness dost thou
    go

To meet thy vassal torrents, that below
  Rush to receive thee and obey thy power.
And now thou movest in triumphal march,
  A king among the rivers! On thy way
  A hundred towns await and welcome thee;
Bridges uplift for thee the stately arch,
  Vineyards encircle thee with garlands gay,
  And fleets attend thy progress to the sea!

THE THREE SILENCES OF MOLINOS.

TO JOHN GREENLEAF WHITTIER.

THREE Silences there are : the first of speech,
　The second of desire, the third of thought ;
　This is the lore a Spanish monk, distraught
With dreams and visions, was the first to
　　teach.
These Silences, commingling each with each,
　Made up the perfect Silence that he sought
　And prayed for, and wherein at times he
　　caught
Mysterious sounds from realms beyond our
　　reach.
O thou, whose daily life anticipates
　The life to come, and in whose thought
　　and word
　The spiritual world preponderates,
Hermit of Amesbury ! thou too hast heard
　Voices and melodies from beyond the gates,
　And speakest only when thy soul is stirred !

THE TWO RIVERS.

I.

SLOWLY the hour-hand of the clock moves
　　round ;
　So slowly that no human eye hath power
　To see it move ! Slowly in shine or shower
　The painted ship above it, homeward bound,
Sails, but seems motionless, as if aground ;
　Yet both arrive at last ; and in his tower
　The slumberous watchman wakes and strikes
　　the hour,
A mellow, measured, melancholy sound.
Midnight ! the outpost of advancing day !
　The frontier town and citadel of night !
　The watershed of Time, from which the
　　streams
Of Yesterday and To-morrow take their way,
　One to the land of promise and of light,
　One to the land of darkness and of dreams !

II.

O River of Yesterday, with current swift
　Through chasms descending, and soon lost
　　to sight,
　I do not care to follow in their flight
　The faded leaves, that on thy bosom drift !
O River of To-morrow, I uplift
　Mine eyes, and thee I follow, as the night
Wanes into morning, and the dawning light
Broadens, and all the shadows fade and
　　shift !
I follow, follow, where thy waters run
　Through unfrequented, unfamiliar fields,
　Fragrant with flowers and musical with song ;
Still follow, follow ; sure to meet the sun,
　And confident, that what the future yields
　Will be the right, unless myself be wrong.

III.

Yet not in vain, O River of Yesterday,
　Through chasms of darkness to the deep
　　descending,
　I heard thee sobbing in the rain, and
　　blending
Thy voice with other voices far away.
I called to thee, and yet thou wouldst not stay,
　But turbulent, and with thyself contending,
　And torrent-like thy force on pebbles spend-
　　ing,

Thou wouldst not listen to a poet's lay.
Thoughts, like a loud and sudden rush of
    wings,
  Regrets and recollections of things past,
  With hints and prophecies of things to be,

And inspirations, which, could they be things,
  And stay with us, and we could hold them
    fast,
  Were our good angels, — these I owe to
    thee.

IV.

And thou, O River of To-morrow, flowing
  Between thy narrow adamantine walls,
    But beautiful, and white with waterfalls,
    And wreaths of mist, like hands the path-
      way showing;
I hear the trumpets of the morning blowing,
  I hear thy mighty voice, that calls and
    calls,
    And see, as Ossian saw in Morven's halls,
    Mysterious phantoms, coming, beckoning,
      going!
It is the mystery of the unknown
  That fascinates us; we are children still,
    Wayward and wistful; with one hand we
      cling
To the familiar things we call our own,
  And with the other, resolute of will,
  Grope in the dark for what the day will
    bring.

105

BOSTON.

ST. BOTOLPH'S TOWN! Hither across the
    plains
  And fens of Lincolnshire, in garb austere,
  There came a Saxon monk, and founded
    here
A Priory, pillaged by marauding Danes,
So that thereof no vestige now remains;
  Only a name, that, spoken loud and clear,
  And echoed in another hemisphere,

Survives the sculptured walls and painted
    panes.
St. Botolph's Town! Far over leagues of land
  And leagues of sea looks forth its noble
    tower,
  And far around the chiming bells are heard;
So may that sacred name forever stand
  A landmark, and a symbol of the power,
  That lies concentred in a single word.

ST. JOHN'S, CAMBRIDGE.

I STAND beneath the tree, whose branches
    shade
  Thy western window, Chapel of St. John!
  And hear its leaves repeat their benison
  On him, whose hand thy stones memorial
    laid;
Then I remember one of whom was said
  In the world's darkest hour, "Behold thy
    son!"
  And see him living still, and wandering on

And waiting for the advent long delayed.
Not only tongues of the apostles teach
  Lessons of love and light, but these ex-
    panding
  And sheltering boughs with all their leaves
    implore,
And say in language clear as human speech,
  "The peace of God, that passeth under-
    standing,
  Be and abide with you forevermore!"

MOODS.

OH that a Song would sing itself to me
  Out of the heart of Nature, or the heart
  Of man, the child of Nature, not of Art,
  Fresh as the morning, salt as the salt sea,
With just enough of bitterness to be
  A medicine to this sluggish mood, and
    start
  The life-blood in my veins, and so impart
  Healing and help in this dull lethargy!

Alas! not always doth the breath of song
  Breathe on us. It is like the wind that
    bloweth
  At its own will, not ours, nor tarrieth long;
We hear the sound thereof, but no man
    knoweth
  From whence it comes, so sudden and swift
    and strong,
  Nor whither in its wayward course it goeth.

WOODSTOCK PARK.

HERE in a little rustic hermitage
  Alfred the Saxon King, Alfred the Great,
  Postponed the cares of king-craft to trans-
    late
  The Consolations of the Roman sage.
Here Geoffrey Chaucer, in his ripe old age
  Wrote the unrivalled Tales, which soon or
    late
  The venturous hand that strives to imitate

  Vanquished must fall on the unfinished page.
Two kings were they, who ruled by right
    divine,
  And both supreme; one in the realm of
    Truth,
  One in the realm of Fiction and of Song.
What prince hereditary of their line,
  Uprising in the strength and flush of youth,
  Their glory shall inherit and prolong?

THE FOUR PRINCESSES AT WILNA.

A PHOTOGRAPH.

SWEET faces, that from pictured casements lean
  As from a castle window, looking down
  On some gay pageant passing through a town,
  Yourselves the fairest figures in the scene;
With what a gentle grace, with what serene
  Unconsciousness ye wear the triple crown
  Of youth and beauty and the fair renown
  Of a great name, that ne'er hath tarnished
    been !

From your soft eyes, so innocent and sweet,
  Four spirits, sweet and innocent as they,
  Gaze on the world below, the sky above;
Hark ! there is some one singing in the street;
  " Faith, Hope, and Love ! these three," he
    seems to say;
" These three; and greatest of the three is
  Love."

HOLIDAYS.

THE holiest of all holidays are those
  Kept by ourselves in silence and apart;
  The secret anniversaries of the heart,
  When the full river of feeling overflows; —
The happy days unclouded to their close;
  The sudden joys that out of darkness start
  As flames from ashes; swift desires that
    dart

Like swallows singing down each wind that
    blows!
White as the gleam of a receding sail,
  White as a cloud that floats and fades in air,
  White as the whitest lily on a stream,
These tender memories are; — a fairy tale
  Of some enchanted land we know not where,
  But lovely as a landscape in a dream.

WAPENTAKE.

TO ALFRED TENNYSON.

POET ! I come to touch thy lance with mine;
  Not as a knight, who on the listed field
  Of tourney touched his adversary's shield
  In token of defiance, but in sign
Of homage to the mastery, which is thine,
  In English song; nor will I keep con-
    cealed,
  And voiceless as a rivulet frost-congealed,

My admiration for thy verse divine.
Not of the howling dervishes of song,
  Who craze the brain with their delirious
    dance,
  Art thou, O sweet historian of the heart !
Therefore to thee the laurel-leaves belong,
  To thee our love and our allegiance,
  For thy allegiance to the poet's art.

THE BROKEN OAR.

ONCE upon Iceland's solitary strand
  A poet wandered with his book and pen,
  Seeking some final word, some sweet Amen,
  Wherewith to close the volume in his hand.
The billows rolled and plunged upon the sand,
  The circling sea-gulls swept beyond his ken,
  And from the parting cloud-rack now and then

Flashed the red sunset over sea and land.
Then by the billows at his feet was tossed
  A broken oar; and carved thereon he read;
  " Oft was I weary, when I toiled at thee";
And like a man, who findeth what was lost,
  He wrote the words, then lifted up his head,
  And flung his useless pen into the sea.

ARTIST: A. FREDERICKS.

THE POTTER AT HIS WHEEL.

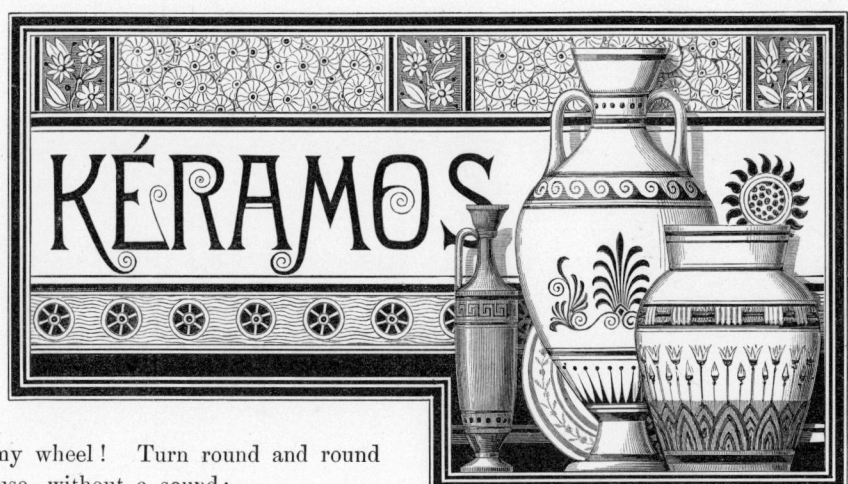

KÉRAMOS

TURN, turn, my wheel! Turn round and round
Without a pause, without a sound:
   So spins the flying world away!
This clay, well mixed with marl and sand,
Follows the motion of my hand;
For some must follow, and some command,
   Though all are made of clay!

Thus sang the Potter at his task
Beneath the blossoming hawthorn-tree,
While o'er his features, like a mask,
The quilted sunshine and leaf-shade
Moved, as the boughs above him swayed,
And clothed him, till he seemed to be
A figure woven in tapestry,
So sumptuously was he arrayed
In that magnificent attire
Of sable tissue flaked with fire.
Like a magician he appeared,
A conjurer without book or beard;
And while he plied his magic art —
For it was magical to me —
I stood in silence and apart,
And wondered more and more to see
That shapeless, lifeless mass of clay
Rise up to meet the master's hand,
And now contract and now expand,
And even his slightest touch obey;
While ever in a thoughtful mood
He sang his ditty, and at times
Whistled a tune between the rhymes,
As a melodious interlude.

Turn, turn, my wheel! All things must change
To something new, to something strange;
   Nothing that is can pause or stay;

The moon will wax, the moon will wane,
The mist and cloud will turn to rain,
The rain to mist and cloud again,
   To-morrow be to-day.

Thus still the Potter sang, and still,
By some unconscious act of will,
The melody and even the words
Were intermingled with my thought,
As bits of colored thread are caught
And woven into nests of birds.
And thus to regions far remote,
Beyond the ocean's vast expanse,
This wizard in the motley coat
Transported me on wings of song,
And by the northern shores of France
Bore me with restless speed along.

What land is this that seems to be
A mingling of the land and sea?
This land of sluices, dikes, and dunes?
This water-net, that tessellates
The landscape? this unending maze
Of gardens, through whose latticed gates
The imprisoned pinks and tulips gaze;
Where in long summer afternoons
The sunshine, softened by the haze,
Comes streaming down as through a screen;
Where over fields and pastures green
The painted ships float high in air,
And over all and everywhere
The sails of windmills sink and soar
Like wings of sea-gulls on the shore?

What land is this ? Yon pretty town
Is Delft, with all its wares displayed ;
The pride, the market-place, the crown
And centre of the Potter's trade.
See ! every house and room is bright
With glimmers of reflected light
From plates that on the dresser shine ;
Flagons to foam with Flemish beer,
Or sparkle with the Rhenish wine,
And pilgrim flasks with fleurs-de-lis,
And ships upon a rolling sea,
And tankards pewter topped, and
    queer
With comic mask and musketeer !
Each hospitable chimney smiles

A welcome from its painted tiles ;
The parlor walls, the chamber floors,
The stairways and the corridors,
The borders of the garden walks,
Are beautiful with fadeless flowers,
That never droop in winds or showers,
And never wither on their stalks.

Turn, turn, my wheel ! All life is brief ;
What now is bud will soon be leaf,
    What now is leaf will soon decay ;
The wind blows east, the wind blows west ;
The blue eggs in the robin's nest
Will soon have wings and beak and breast,
    And flutter and fly away.

Now southward through the air I glide,
The song my only pursuivant,
And see across the landscape wide
The blue Charente, upon whose tide
The belfries and the spires of Saintes
Ripple and rock from side to side,
As, when an earthquake rends its
    walls,
A crumbling city reels and falls.

Who is it in the suburbs here,
This Potter, working with such cheer,
In this mean house, this mean attire,
His manly features bronzed with fire,
Whose figulines and rustic wares

Scarce find him bread from day to day?
This madman, as the people say,
Who breaks his tables and his chairs
To feed his furnace fires, nor cares
Who goes unfed if they are fed,
Nor who may live if they are dead?
This alchemist with hollow cheeks
And sunken, searching eyes, who seeks,
By mingled earths and ores combined
With potency of fire, to find
Some new enamel, hard and bright,
His dream, his passion, his delight?

O Palissy! within thy breast
Burned the hot fever of unrest;

Thine was the prophet's vision, thine
The exultation, the divine
Insanity of noble minds,
That never falters nor abates,
But labors and endures and waits,
Till all that it foresees it finds,
Or what it cannot find creates!

106

Turn, turn, my wheel! This earthern jar
A touch can make, a touch can mar;
    And shall it to the Potter say,
What makest thou? Thou hast no hand?
As men who think to understand
A world by their Creator planned,
    Who wiser is than they.

Still guided by the dreamy song,
As in a trance I float along
Above the Pyrenean chain,
Above the fields and farms of Spain,
Above the bright Majorcan isle,
That lends its softened name to art, —
A spot, a dot upon the chart,
Whose little towns, red-roofed with tile,
Are ruby-lustred with the light
Of blazing furnaces by night,
And crowned by day with wreaths of smoke.
Then eastward, wafted in my flight
On my enchanter's magic cloak,
I sail across the Tyrrhene Sea
Into the land of Italy,
And o'er the windy Apennines,
Mantled and musical with pines.

The palaces, the princely halls,
The doors of houses and the walls
Of churches and of belfry towers,
Cloister and castle, street and mart,
Are garlanded and gay with flowers
That blossom in the fields of art.
Here Gubbio's workshops gleam and glow
With brilliant, iridescent dyes,
The dazzling whiteness of the snow,
The cobalt blue of summer skies ;
And vase and scutcheon, cup and plate,
In perfect finish emulate
Faenza, Florence, Pesaro.

Forth from Urbino's gate there came
A youth with the angelic name
Of Raphael, in form and face
Himself angelic, and divine
In arts of color and design.
From him Francesco Xanto caught
Something of his transcendent grace,
And into fictile fabrics wrought
Suggestions of the master's thought.
Nor less Maestro Giorgio shines
With madre-perl and golden lines

Mingle in one harmonious whole!
With large blue eyes and steadfast gaze,
Her yellow hair in net and braid,
Necklace and ear-rings all ablaze
With golden lustre o'er the glaze,
A woman's portrait; on the scroll,
Cana, the Beautiful! A name
Forgotten save for such brief fame
As this memorial can bestow, —
A gift some lover long ago
Gave with his heart to this fair dame.

A nobler title to renown
Is thine, O pleasant Tuscan town,
Seated beside the Arno's stream;
For Luca della Robbia there
Created forms so wondrous fair,
They made thy sovereignty supreme.
These choristers with lips of stone,
Whose music is not heard, but seen,
Still chant, as from their organ-screen,
Their Maker's praise; nor these alone,
But the more fragile forms of clay,
Hardly less beautiful than they,
These saints and angels that adorn
The walls of hospitals, and tell
The story of good deeds so well
That poverty seems less forlorn,
And life more like a holiday.

Of arabesques, and interweaves
His birds and fruits and flowers and leaves
About some landscape, shaded brown,
With olive tints on rock and town.

Behold this cup within whose bowl,
Upon a ground of deepest blue
With yellow-lustred stars o'erlaid,
Colors of every tint and hue

Here in this old neglected church,
That long eludes the traveller's search,
Lies the dead bishop on his tomb;
Earth upon earth he slumbering lies,
Life-like and death-like in the gloom;
Garlands of fruit and flowers in
        bloom
And foliage deck his resting-place;
A shadow in the sightless eyes,
A pallor on the patient face,
Made perfect by the furnace heat;
All earthly passions and desires
Burnt out by purgatorial fires;
Seeming to say, " Our years are fleet,
And to the weary death is sweet."

But the most wonderful of all
The ornaments on tomb or wall
That grace the fair Ausonian shores
Are those the faithful earth restores,
Near some Apulian town concealed,
In vineyard or in harvest field, —
Vases and urns and bas-reliefs,
Memorials of forgotten griefs,

Or records of heroic deeds
Of demigods and mighty chiefs :
Figures that almost move and speak,
And, buried amid mould and weeds,
Still in their attitudes attest
The presence of the graceful Greek, —
Achilles in his armor dressed,
Alcides with the Cretan bull,
And Aphrodite with her boy,
Or lovely Helena of Troy,
Still living and still beautiful.

Turn, turn, my wheel ! 'T is nature's plan
The child should grow into the man,
    The man grow wrinkled, old, and gray;
In youth the heart exults and sings,
The pulses leap, the feet have wings;
In age the cricket chirps, and brings
    The harvest-home of day.

And now the winds that southward blow,
And cool the hot Sicilian isle,
Bear me away. I see below
The long line of the Libyan Nile,

Flooding and feeding the parched lands
With annual ebb and overflow,
A fallen palm whose branches lie
Beneath the Abyssinian sky,
Whose roots are in Egyptian sands.
On either bank huge water-wheels,
Belted with jars and dripping weeds,
Send forth their melancholy moans,
As if, in their gray mantles hid,
Dead anchorites of the Thebaid
Knelt on the shore and told their beads,
Beating their breasts with loud ap-
        peals
And penitential tears and groans.

This city, walled and thickly set
With glittering mosque and minaret,
Is Cairo, in whose gay bazaars
The dreaming traveller first inhales
The perfume of Arabian gales,
And sees the fabulous earthen jars,
Huge as were those wherein the maid
Morgiana found the Forty Thieves
Concealed in midnight ambuscade;
And seeing, more than half believes
The fascinating tales that run

Through all the Thousand Nights and One,
Told by the fair Scheherezade.

More strange and wonderful than these
Are the Egyptian deities,
Ammon, and Emeth, and the grand
Osiris, holding in his hand
The lotus; Isis, crowned and veiled;
The sacred Ibis, and the Sphinx;
Bracelets with blue enamelled links;
The Scarabee in emerald mailed,
Or spreading wide his funeral wings;
Lamps that perchance their night-watch kept
O'er Cleopatra while she slept, —
All plundered from the tombs of kings.

Turn, turn, my wheel! The human race,
Of every tongue, of every place,
    Caucasian, Coptic, or Malay,
All that inhabit this great earth,
Whatever be their rank or worth,
Are kindred and allied by birth,
    And made of the same clay.

O'er desert sands, o'er gulf and bay,
O'er Ganges and o'er Himalay,

Bird-like I fly, and flying sing,
To flowery kingdoms of Cathay,
And bird-like poise on balanced wing
Above the town of King-te-tching,
A burning town, or seeming so, —
Three thousand furnaces that glow
Incessantly, and fill the air
With smoke uprising, gyre on gyre,
And painted by the lurid glare,
Of jets and flashes of red fire.

As leaves that in the autumn fall,
Spotted and veined with various hues,
Are swept along the avenues,
And lie in heaps by hedge and wall,
So from this grove of chimneys whirled
To all the markets of the world,
These porcelain leaves are wafted on,
Light yellow leaves with spots and stains
Of violet and of crimson dye,
Or tender azure of a sky
Just washed by gentle April rains,
And beautiful with celadon.

Nor less the coarser household wares,
The willow pattern, that we knew
In childhood, with its bridge of blue
Leading to unknown thoroughfares;
The solitary man who stares
At the white river flowing through
Its arches, the fantastic trees
And wild perspective of the view;
And intermingled among these
The tiles that in our nurseries
Filled us with wonder and delight,
Or haunted us in dreams at night.

And yonder by Nankin, behold!
The Tower of Porcelain, strange and
          old,
Uplifting to the astonished skies
Its ninefold painted balconies,
With balustrades of twining leaves,
And roofs of tile, beneath whose eaves
Hang porcelain bells that all the time
Ring with a soft, melodious chime;
While the whole fabric is ablaze
With varied tints, all fused in one
Great mass of color, like a maze
Of flowers illumined by the sun.

Turn, turn, my, wheel! What is begun
At daybreak must at dark be done,
    To-morrow will be another day;
To-morrow the hot furnace flame
Will search the heart and try the frame,
And stamp with honor or with shame
    These vessels made of clay.

Cradled and rocked in Eastern seas,
The islands of the Japanese
Beneath me lie; o'er lake and plain
The stork, the heron, and the crane
Through the clear realms of azure drift,
And on the hillside I can see
The villages of Imari,
Whose thronged and flaming workshops lift
Their twisted columns of smoke on high,
Cloud cloisters that in ruins lie,

With sunshine streaming through each rift,
And broken arches of blue sky.

All the bright flowers that fill the land,
Ripple of waves on rock or sand,
The snow on Fusiyama's cone,
The midnight heaven so thickly sown
With constellations of bright stars,
The leaves that rustle, the reeds that
    make
A whisper by each stream and lake,
The saffron dawn, the sunset red,
Are painted on these lovely jars;
Again the skylark sings, again
The stork, the heron, and the crane
Float through the azure overhead,
The counterfeit and counterpart
Of Nature reproduced in Art.

Art is the child of Nature; yes,
Her darling child, in whom we trace
The features of the mother's face,
Her aspect and her attitude;
All her majestic loveliness
Chastened and softened and subdued
Into a more attractive grace,
And with a human sense imbued.
He is the greatest artist, then,
Whether of pencil or of pen,
Who follows Nature. Never man,
As artist or as artisan,
Pursuing his own fantasies,
Can touch the human heart, or please,
Or satisfy our nobler needs,
As he who sets his willing feet
In Nature's footprints, light and fleet,
And follows fearless where she leads.

Thus mused I on that morn in May,
Wrapped in my visions like the Seer,

Whose eyes behold not what is near,
But only what is far away,
When, suddenly sounding peal on peal,
The church-bell from the neighboring town
Proclaimed the welcome hour of noon.
The Potter heard, and stopped his wheel,
His apron on the grass threw down,
Whistled his quiet little tune,
Not overloud nor overlong,
And ended thus his simple song:

Stop, stop, my wheel! Too soon, too soon
The noon will be the afternoon,
    Too soon to-day be yesterday;
Behind us in our path we cast
The broken potsherds of the past,
And all are ground to dust at last,
    And trodden into clay!

BIRDS OF PASSAGE

THE HERONS OF ELMWOOD.

WARM and still is the summer night,
  As here by the river's brink I wander;
White overhead are the stars, and white
  The glimmering lamps on the hillside yonder.

Silent are all the sounds of day;
  Nothing I hear but the chirp of crickets,
And the cry of the herons winging their way
  O'er the poet's house in the Elmwood thickets.

Call to him, herons, as slowly you pass
　　To your roosts in the haunts of the exiled
　　　　thrushes,
Sing him the song of the green morass,
　　And the tides that water the reeds and rushes.

Sing him the mystical Song of the Hern,
　　And the secret that baffles our utmost seek-
　　　　ing ;
For only a sound of lament we discern,
　　And cannot interpret the words you are
　　　　speaking.

Sing of the air, and the wild delight
　　Of wings that uplift and winds that up-
　　　　hold you,
The joy of freedom, the rapture of flight
　　Through the drift of the floating mists that
　　　　infold you ;

Of the landscape lying so far below,
　　With its towns and rivers and desert places ;

And the splendor of light above, and the
　　　　glow
　　Of the limitless, blue, ethereal spaces.

Ask him if songs of the Troubadours,
　　Or of Minnesingers in old black-letter,
Sound in his ears more sweet than yours,
　　And if yours are not sweeter and wilder
　　　　and better.

Sing to him, say to him, here at his gate,
　　Where the boughs of the stately elms are
　　　　meeting,
Some one hath lingered to meditate,
　　And send him unseen this friendly greet-
　　　　ing;

That many another hath done the same,
　　Though not by a sound was the silence
　　　　broken ;
The surest pledge of a deathless name
　　Is the silent homage of thoughts unspoken.

A DUTCH PICTURE.

Simon Danz has come home again,
　　From cruising about with his buccaneers ;
He has singed the beard of the King of Spain,
And carried away the Dean of Jaen
　　And sold him in Algiers.

In his house by the Maese, with its roof of
　　　　tiles,
　　And weathercocks flying aloft in air,
There are silver tankards of antique styles,
Plunder of convent and castle, and piles
　　Of carpets rich and rare.

In his tulip-garden there by the town,
　　Overlooking the sluggish stream,
With his Moorish cap and dressing-gown,
The old sea-captain, hale and brown,
　　Walks in a waking dream.

A smile in his gray mustachio lurks
　　Whenever he thinks of the King of Spain,
And the listed tulips look like Turks,
And the silent gardener as he works
　　Is changed to the Dean of Jaen.

The windmills on the outermost
　　Verge of the landscape in the haze,
To him are towers on the Spanish coast,
With whiskered sentinels at their post,
　　Though this is the river Maese.

But when the winter rains begin,
　　He sits and smokes by the blazing brands,
And old seafaring men come in,
Goat-bearded, gray, and with double chin,
　　And rings upon their hands.

They sit there in the shadow and shine
　　Of the flickering fire of the winter night ;
Figures in color and design
Like those by Rembrandt of the Rhine,
　　Half darkness and half light.

And they talk of ventures lost or won,
　　And their talk is ever and ever the same,
While they drink the red wine of Tarra-
　　　　gon,
From the cellars of some Spanish Don,
　　Or convent set on flame.

Restless at times with heavy strides
  He paces his parlor to and fro;
He is like a ship that at anchor rides,
And swings with the rising and falling tides,
  And tugs at her anchor-tow.

Voices mysterious far and near,
  Sound of the wind and sound of the sea,
Are calling and whispering in his ear.

"Simon Danz! Why stayest thou here?
  Come forth and follow me!"

So he thinks he shall take to the sea again
  For one more cruise with his bucca-
      neers,
To singe the beard of the King of Spain,
And capture another Dean of Jaen
  And sell him in Algiers.

CASTLES IN SPAIN.

How much of my young heart, O Spain,
  Went out to thee in days of yore!
What dreams romantic filled my brain,
And summoned back to life again
The Paladins of Charlemagne
  The Cid Campeador!

And shapes more shadowy than these,
  In the dim twilight half revealed;
Phœnician galleys on the seas,

The Roman camps like hives of bees,
The Goth uplifting from his knees
  Pelayo on his shield.

It was these memories perchance,
  From annals of remotest eld,
That lent the colors of romance
To every trivial circumstance,
And changed the form and countenance
  Of all that I beheld.

Old towns, whose history lies hid
　　In monkish chronicle or rhyme, —
Burgos, the birthplace of the Cid,
Zamora and Valladolid,
Toledo, built and walled amid
　　The wars of Wamba's time;

The long, straight line of the highway,
　　The distant town that seems so near,
The peasants in the fields, that stay
Their toil to cross themselves and pray,
When from the belfry at midday
　　The Angelus they hear;

White crosses in the mountain pass,
　　Mules gay with tassels, the loud din
Of muleteers, the tethered ass
That crops the dusty wayside grass,
And cavaliers with spurs of brass
　　Alighting at the inn;

White hamlets hidden in fields of wheat,
　　White cities slumbering by the sea,
White sunshine flooding square and street,
Dark mountain ranges, at whose feet
The river beds are dry with heat, —
　　All was a dream to me.

Yet something sombre and severe
　　O'er the enchanted landscape reigned;
A terror in the atmosphere
As if King Philip listened near,
Or Torquemada, the austere,
　　His ghostly sway maintained.

The softer Andalusian skies
　　Dispelled the sadness and the gloom;
There Cadiz by the seaside lies,
And Seville's orange-orchards rise,
Making the land a paradise
　　Of beauty and of bloom.

There Cordova is hidden among
　　The palm, the olive, and the vine;
Gem of the South, by poets sung,
And in whose Mosque Almanzor hung
As lamps the bells that once had rung
　　At Compostella's shrine.

But over all the rest supreme,
　　The star of stars, the cynosure,
The artist's and the poet's theme,
The young man's vision, the old man's dream, —
Granada by its winding stream,
　　The city of the Moor!

And there the Alhambra still recalls
　　Aladdin's palace of delight:
Allah il Allah! through its halls
Whispers the fountain as it falls,
The Darro darts beneath its walls,
　　The hills with snow are white.

Ah yes, the hills are white with snow,
　　And cold with blasts that bite and freeze;
But in the happy vale below
The orange and pomegranate grow,
And wafts of air toss to and fro
　　The blossoming almond trees.

The Vega cleft by the Xenil,
　　The fascination and allure
Of the sweet landscape chains the will;
The traveller lingers on the hill,
His parted lips are breathing still
　　The last sigh of the Moor.

How like a ruin overgrown
　　With flowers that hide the rents of time,
Stands now the Past that I have known;
Castles in Spain, not built of stone
But of white summer clouds, and blown
　　Into this little mist of rhyme!

VITTORIA COLONNA.

VITTORIA COLONNA, on the death of her husband, the Marchese di Pescara, retired to her castle at Ischia (Inarimé), and there wrote the Ode upon his death, which gained her the title of Divine.

ONCE more, once more, Inarimé
  I see thy purple hills ! — once more
I hear the billows of the bay
  Wash the white pebbles on thy shore.

High o'er the sea-surge and the sands,
  Like a great galleon wrecked and cast
Ashore by storms, thy castle stands,
  A mouldering landmark of the Past.

Upon its terrace-walk I see
  A phantom gliding to and fro;
It is Colonna, — it is she
  Who lived and loved so long ago.

Pescara's beautiful young wife,
  The type of perfect womanhood,
Whose life was love, the life of life,
  That time and change and death withstood.

For death, that breaks the marriage band
  In others, only closer pressed
The wedding-ring upon her hand
  And closer locked and barred her breast.

She knew the life-long martyrdom,
  The weariness, the endless pain
Of waiting for some one to come
  Who nevermore would come again.

The shadows of the chestnut trees,
  The odor of the orange blooms,
The song of birds, and, more than these,
  The silence of deserted rooms;

The respiration of the sea,
  The soft caresses of the air,
All things in nature seemed to be
  But ministers of her despair;

Till the o'erburdened heart, so long
  Imprisoned in itself, found vent
And voice in one impassioned song
  Of inconsolable lament.

Then as the sun, though hidden from sight,
  Transmutes to gold the leaden mist,

Her life was interfused with light,
  From realms that, though unseen, exist.

Inarimé! Inarimé!
  Thy castle on the crags above
In dust shall crumble and decay,
  But not the memory of her love.

THE REVENGE OF RAIN-IN-THE-FACE.

In that desolate land and lone,
Where the Big Horn and Yellowstone
  Roar down their mountain path,
By their fires the Sioux Chiefs
Muttered their woes and griefs
  And the menace of their wrath.

" Revenge! " cried Rain-in-the-Face,
" Revenge upon all the race
  Of the White Chief with yellow hair! "
And the mountains dark and high
From their crags reëchoed the cry
  Of his anger and despair.

In the meadow, spreading wide
By woodland and riverside
  The Indian village stood;
All was silent as a dream,
Save the rushing of the stream
  And the blue-jay in the wood.

In his war paint and his beads,
Like a bison among the reeds,
  In ambush the Sitting Bull
Lay with three thousand braves
Crouched in the clefts and caves,
  Savage, unmerciful!

Into the fatal snare
The White Chief with yellow hair
  And his three hundred men
Dashed headlong, sword in hand;
But of that gallant band
  Not one returned again.

The sudden darkness of death
Overwhelmed them like the breath
  And smoke of a furnace fire:
By the river's bank, and between
The rocks of the ravine,
  They lay in their bloody attire.

But the foemen fled in the night,
And Rain-in-the-Face, in his flight,
  Uplifted high in air
As a ghastly trophy, bore
The brave heart, that beat no more,
  Of the White Chief with yellow hair.

Whose was the right and the wrong?
Sing it, O funeral song,
  With a voice that is full of tears,
And say that our broken faith
Wrought all this ruin and scathe,
  In the Year of a Hundred Years.

TO THE RIVER YVETTE.

O LOVELY river of Yvette!
  O darling river! like a bride,
Some dimpled, bashful, fair Lisette,
  Thou goest to wed the Orge's tide.

Maincourt, and lordly Dampierre,
  See and salute thee on thy way,
And, with a blessing and a prayer,
  Ring the sweet bells of St. Forget.

The valley of Chevreuse in vain
  Would hold thee in its fond embrace;

Thou glidest from its arms again
  And hurriest on with swifter pace.

Thou wilt not stay; with restless feet
  Pursuing still thine onward flight,
Thou goest as one in haste to meet
  Her sole desire, her heart's delight.

O lovely river of Yvette!
  O darling stream! on balanced wings
The wood-birds sang the chansonnette
  That here a wandering poet sings.

THE EMPEROR'S GLOVE.

"COMBIEN faudrait-il de peaux d'Espagne pour faire un gant de cette grandeur?" A play upon the words *gant*, a glove, and *Gand*, the French for Ghent.

ON St. Bavon's tower, commanding
  Half of Flanders, his domain,
Charles the Emperor once was standing,
While beneath him on the landing
  Stood Duke Alva and his train.

Like a print in books of fables,
  Or a model made for show,
With its pointed roofs and gables,
Dormer windows, scrolls and labels,
  Lay the city far below.

Through its squares and streets and al-
    leys
  Poured the populace of Ghent;
As a routed army rallies,
Or as rivers run through valleys,
  Hurrying to their homes they went.

"Nest of Lutheran misbelievers!"
  Cried Duke Alva as be gazed;

"Haunt of traitors and deceivers,
Stronghold of insurgent weavers,
  Let it to the ground be razed!"

On the Emperor's cap the feather
  Nods, as laughing he replies:
"How many skins of Spanish leather,
Think you, would, if stitched together
  Make a glove of such a size?"

A BALLAD OF THE FRENCH FLEET.

OCTOBER, 1746.

MR. THOMAS PRINCE *loquitur.*

A FLEET with flags arrayed
  Sailed from the port of Brest,
And the Admiral's ship displayed
  The signal: "Steer southwest."
For this Admiral D'Anville
  Had sworn by cross and crown
To ravage with fire and steel
  Our helpless Boston Town.

There were rumors in the street,
  In the houses there was fear
Of the coming of the fleet,
  And the danger hovering near.
And while from mouth to mouth
  Spread the tidings of dismay,
I stood in the Old South,
  Saying humbly: "Let us pray!

"O Lord! we would not advise;
  But if in thy Providence
A tempest should arise
  To drive the French Fleet hence,
And scatter it far and wide,
  Or sink it in the sea,
We should be satisfied,
  And thine the glory be."

This was the prayer I made,
  For my soul was all on flame,
And even as I prayed
  The answering tempest came;
It came with a mighty power,
  Shaking the windows and walls,
And tolling the bell in the tower,
  As it tolls at funerals.

The lightning suddenly
  Unsheathed its flaming sword,
And I cried: "Stand still, and see
  The salvation of the Lord!"

The heavens were black with cloud,
  The sea was white with hail,
And ever more fierce and loud
  Blew the October gale.

The fleet it overtook,
  And the broad sails in the van
Like the tents of Cushan shook,
  Or the curtains of Midian.
Down on the reeling decks
  Crashed the o'erwhelming seas;
Ah, never were there wrecks
  So pitiful as these!

Like a potter's vessel broke
  The great ships of the line;
They were carried away as a smoke,
  Or sank like lead in the brine.
O Lord! before thy path
  They vanished and ceased to be,
When thou didst walk in wrath
  With thine horses through the sea!

THE LEAP OF ROUSHAN BEG.

Mounted on Kyrat strong and fleet,
His chestnut steed with four white feet,
  Roushan Beg, called Kurroglou,
Son of the road and bandit chief,
Seeking refuge and relief,
  Up the mountain pathway flew.

Such was Kyrat's wondrous speed,
Never yet could any steed
  Reach the dust-cloud in his course.
More than maiden, more than wife,
More than gold and next to life
  Roushan the Robber loved his horse.

In the land that lies beyond
Erzeroum and Trebizond,
  Garden-girt his fortress stood;
Plundered khan, or caravan
Journeying north from Koordistan,
  Gave him wealth and wine and food.

Seven hundred and fourscore
Men at arms his livery wore,
  Did his bidding night and day;

Now, through regions all unknown,
He was wandering, lost, alone,
  Seeking without guide his way.

Suddenly the pathway ends,
Sheer the precipice descends,
  Loud the torrent roars unseen;
Thirty feet from side to side
Yawns the chasm; on air must ride
  He who crosses this ravine.

Following close in his pursuit,
At the precipice's foot
  Reyhan the Arab of Orfah
Halted with his hundred men,
Shouting upward from the glen,
  "La Illáh illa Alláh!"

Gently Roushan Beg caressed
Kyrat's forehead, neck, and breast;
  Kissed him upon both his eyes,
Sang to him in his wild way,
As upon the topmost spray
  Sings a bird before it flies.

" O my Kyrat, O my steed,
Round and slender as a reed,
　Carry me this peril through !
Satin housings shall be thine,
Shoes of gold, O Kyrat mine,
　O thou soul of Kurroglou !

"Soft thy skin as silken skein,
Soft as woman's hair thy mane,
　Tender are thine eyes and true ;
All thy hoofs like ivory shine,
Polished bright ; O life of mine,
　Leap, and rescue Kurroglou !"

Kyrat, then, the strong and fleet,
Drew together his four white feet,
　Paused a moment on the verge,
Measured with his eye the space,
And into the air's embrace
　Leaped as leaps the ocean surge.

As the ocean surge o'er sand
Bears a swimmer safe to land,
　Kyrat safe his rider bore ;

Rattling down the deep abyss
Fragments of the precipice
　Rolled like pebbles on a shore.

Roushan's tasselled cap of red
Trembled not upon his head,
　Careless sat he and upright ;
Neither hand nor bridle shook,
Nor his head he turned to look,
　As he galloped out of sight.

Flash of harness in the air,
Seen a moment like the glare
　Of a sword drawn from its sheath ;
Thus the phantom horseman passed,
And the shadow that he cast
　Leaped the cataract underneath.

Reyhan the Arab held his breath
While this vision of life and death
　Passed above him. " Allahu !"
Cried he. " In all Koordistan
Lives there not so brave a man
　As this Robber Kurroglou !"

HAROUN AL RASCHID.

ONE day, Haroun Al Raschid read
A book wherein the poet said : —

" Where are the kings, and where the rest
Of those who once the world possessed ?

" They 're gone with all their pomp and show,
They 're gone the way that thou shalt go.

" O thou who choosest for thy share
The world, and what the world calls fair,

" Take all that it can give or lend,
But know that death is at the end ! "

Haroun Al Raschid bowed his head :
Tears fell upon the page he read.

KING TRISANKU.

VISWAMITRA the Magician,
    By his spells and incantations,
Up to Indra's realms elysian
    Raised Trisanku, king of nations.

Indra and the gods offended
    Hurled him downward, and descending

In the air he hung suspended,
    With these equal powers contending.

Thus by aspirations lifted,
    By misgivings downward driven,
Human hearts are tossed and drifted
    Midway between earth and heaven.

A WRAITH IN THE MIST.

" SIR, I should build me a fortification, if I came to live here." — BOSWELL's *Johnson.*

ON the green little isle of Inchkenneth,
    Who is it that walks by the shore,
So gay with his Highland blue bonnet,
    So brave with his targe and claymore ?

His form is the form of a giant,
    But his face wears an aspect of pain ;

Can this be the Laird of Inchkenneth ?
    Can this be Sir Allan McLean ?

Ah no ! It is only the Rambler,
    The Idler, who lives in Bolt Court,
And who says, were he Laird of Inchkenneth,
    He would wall himself round with a fort.

THE THREE KINGS.

THREE Kings came riding from far away,
    Melchior and Gaspar and Baltasar ;
Three Wise Men out of the East were they,
And they travelled by night and they slept
        by day,
    For their guide was a beautiful, wonderful
        star.

The star was so beautiful, large, and clear,
    That all the other stars of the sky
Became a white mist in the atmosphere,

And by this they knew that the coming was
        near
    Of the Prince foretold in the prophecy.

Three caskets they bore on their saddle-
        bows,
    Three caskets of gold with golden keys ;
Their robes were of crimson silk with rows
Of bells and pomegranates and furbelows,
    Their turbans like blossoming almond-
        trees.

And so the Three Kings rode into the West,
   Through the dusk of night, over hill and
      dell,
And sometimes they nodded with beard on
      breast,
And sometimes talked, as they paused to rest,
   With the people they met at some wayside
      well.

"Of the child that is born," said Baltasar,
   "Good people, I pray you, tell us the
      news;
For we in the East have seen his star,
And have ridden fast, and have ridden
      far,
   To find and worship the King of the
      Jews."

And the people answered, "You ask in
   vain;
   We know of no king but Herod the
      Great!"
They thought the Wise Men were men in-
      sane,
As they spurred their horses across the plain,
   Like riders in haste, and who cannot wait.

And when they came to Jerusalem,
   Herod the Great, who had heard this
      thing,
Sent for the Wise Men and questioned them;
And said, "Go down unto Bethlehem,
   And bring me tidings of this new king."

So they rode away; and the star stood still,
   The only one in the gray of morn;
Yes, it stopped, — it stood still of its own
      free will,
Right over Bethlehem on the hill,
   The city of David where Christ was born.

And the Three Kings rode through the gate
   and the guard,
   Through the silent street, till their horses
      turned
And neighed as they entered the great inn-yard;
But the windows were closed, and the doors
      were barred,
   And only a light in the stable burned.

And cradled there in the scented hay,
  In the air made sweet by the breath of kine,
The little child in the manger lay,
The child, that would be king one day
  Of a kingdom not human but divine.

His mother Mary of Nazareth
  Sat watching beside his place of rest,
Watching the even flow of his breath,
For the joy of life and the terror of death
  Were mingled together in her breast.

They laid their offerings at his feet:
  The gold was their tribute to a King,
The frankincense, with its odor sweet,

Was for the Priest, the Paraclete,
  The myrrh for the body's burying.

And the mother wondered and bowed her
    head,
  And sat as still as a statue of stone;
Her heart was troubled yet comforted,
Remembering what the Angel had said
  Of an endless reign and of David's throne.

Then the Kings rode out of the city gate,
  With a clatter of hoofs in proud array;
But they went not back to Herod the Great,
For they knew his malice and feared his hate,
  And returned to their homes by another way.

SONG.

STAY, stay at home, my heart, and rest;
Home-keeping hearts are happiest,
For those that wander they know not where
Are full of trouble and full of care;
  To stay at home is best.

Weary and homesick and distressed,
They wander east, they wander west,
And are baffled and beaten and blown about
By the winds of the wilderness of doubt;
  To stay at home is best.

Then stay at home, my heart, and rest;
The bird is safest in its nest;
O'er all that flutter their wings and fly
A hawk is hovering in the sky;
  To stay at home is best.

THE WHITE CZAR.

THE White Czar is Peter the Great. Batyushka, *Father dear,* and Gosudar, *Sovereign,* are titles the Russian people are fond of giving to the Czar in their popular songs.

DOST thou see on the rampart's height
That wreath of mist, in the light
Of the midnight moon? Oh, hist!
It is not a wreath of mist;
It is the Czar, the White Czar,
  Batyushka! Gosudar!

He has heard, among the dead,
The artillery roll o'erhead;
The drums and the tramp of feet
Of his soldiery in the street;
He is awake! the White Czar,
  Batyushka! Gosudar!

He has heard in the grave the cries
Of his people: " Awake ! arise ! "
He has rent the gold brocade
Whereof his shroud was made ;
He is risen ! the White Czar,
    Batyushka ! Gosudar !

From the Volga and the Don
He has led his armies on,
Over river and morass,
Over desert and mountain pass ;
The Czar, the Orthodox Czar,
    Batyushka ! Gosudar !

He looks from the mountain-chain
Toward the seas, that cleave in twain
The continents ; his hand
Points southward o'er the land
Of Roumili ! O Czar,
    Batyushka ! Gosudar !

And the words break from his lips :
" I am the builder of ships,
And my ships shall sail these seas
To the Pillars of Hercules !
I say it ; the White Czar,
    Batyushka ! Gosudar !

" The Bosphorus shall be free ;
It shall make room for me ;
And the gates of its water-streets
Be unbarred before my fleets.
I say it ; the White Czar,
    Batyushka ! Gosudar !

" And the Christian shall no more
Be crushed, as heretofore,
Beneath thine iron rule,
O sultan of Istamboul !
I swear it ! I the Czar,
    Batyushka ! Gosudar ! "

DELIA.

SWEET as the tender fragrance that survives,
When martyred flowers breathe out their little
    lives,
Sweet as a song that once consoled our pain,
But never will be sung to us again,
Is thy remembrance. Now the hour of rest
Hath come to thee. Sleep, darling ; it is best.

Fortunate old man ! Here among familiar rivers,
And these sacred founts, shalt thou take the shadowy coolness.

Virgil's First Eclogue.

MELIBŒUS.

TITYRUS, thou in the shade of a spreading beech tree reclining,
Meditatest, with slender pipe, the Muse of the woodlands.
We our country's bounds and pleasant pastures relinquish,
We our country fly; thou, Tityrus, stretched in the shadow,
Teachest the woods to resound with the name of the fair Amaryllis.

TITYRUS.

O Melibœus, a god for us this leisure created,
For he will be unto me a god forever; his altar
Oftentimes shall imbue a tender lamb from our sheepfolds.
He, my heifers to wander at large, and myself, as thou seest,
On my rustic reed to play what I will, hath permitted.

MELIBŒUS.

Truly I envy not, I marvel rather; on all sides
In all the fields is such trouble. Behold, my goats I am driving,
Heartsick, further away; this one scarce, Tityrus, lead I;
For having here yeaned twins just now among the dense hazels,
Hope of the flock, ah me! on the naked flint she hath left them.
Often this evil to me, if my mind had not been insensate,
Oak trees stricken by heaven predicted, as now I remember;
Often the sinister crow from the hollow ilex predicted.
Nevertheless, who this god may be, O Tityrus, tell me.

TITYRUS.

O Melibœus, the city that they call Rome, I imagined,
Foolish I! to be like this of ours, where often we shepherds
Wonted are to drive down of our ewes the delicate offspring.
Thus whelps like unto dogs had I known, and kids to their mothers,
Thus to compare great things with small had I been accustomed.
But this among other cities its head as far hath exalted
As the cypresses do among the lissome viburnums.

MELIBŒUS.

And what so great occasion of seeing Rome hath possessed thee?

TITYRUS.

Liberty, which, though late, looked upon me in my inertness,
After the time when my beard fell whiter from me in shaving, —
Yet she looked upon me, and came to me after a long while,

Since Amaryllis possesses and Galatea hath left me.
For I will even confess that while Galatea possessed me
Neither care of my flock nor hope of liberty was there.
Though from my wattled folds there went forth many a victim,
And the unctuous cheese was pressed for the city ungrateful,
Never did my right hand return home heavy with money.

MELIBŒUS.

I have wondered why sad thou invokedst the gods, Amaryllis,
And for whom thou didst suffer the apples to hang on the branches!
Tityrus hence was absent! Thee, Tityrus, even the pine trees,
Thee, the very fountains, the very copses were calling.

TITYRUS.

What could I do? No power had I to escape from my bondage,
Nor had I power elsewhere to recognize gods so propitious.
Here I beheld that youth, to whom each year, Melibœus,
During twice six days ascends the smoke of our altars.
Here first gave he response to me soliciting favor:
"Feed as before your heifers, ye boys, and yoke up your bullocks."

MELIBŒUS.

Fortunate old man! So then thy fields will be left thee,
And large enough for thee, though naked stone and the marish
All thy pasture-lands with the dreggy rush may encompass.
No unaccustomed food thy gravid ewes shall endanger,
Nor of the neighboring flock the dire contagion infect them.
Fortunate old man! Here among familiar rivers,
And these sacred founts, shalt thou take the shadowy coolness.
On this side, a hedge along the neighboring cross-road,
Where Hyblæan bees ever feed on the flower of the willow,
Often with gentle susurrus to fall asleep shall persuade thee.
Yonder, beneath the high rock, the pruner shall sing to the breezes,
Nor meanwhile shall thy heart's delight, the hoarse wood-pigeons,
Nor the turtle-dove cease to mourn from aerial elm trees.

TITYRUS.

Therefore the agile stags shall sooner feed in the ether,
And the billows leave the fishes bare on the sea-shore,
Sooner, the border-lands of both overpassed, shall the exiled
Parthian drink of the Saone, or the German drink of the Tigris,
Than the face of him shall glide away from my bosom!

MELIBŒUS.

But we hence shall go, a part to the thirsty Africs,
Part to Scythia come, and the rapid Cretan Oaxes,
And to the Britons from all the universe utterly sundered.
Ah, shall I ever, a long time hence, the bounds of my country
And the roof of my lowly cottage covered with greensward
Seeing, with wonder behold, — my kingdoms, a handful of wheat-ears!
Shall an impious soldier possess these lands newly cultured,
And these fields of corn a barbarian? Lo, whither discord
Us wretched people hath brought! for whom our fields we have planted!
Graft, Melibœus, thy pear trees, now, put in order thy vineyards.
Go, my goats, go hence, my flocks so happy aforetime.
Never again henceforth outstretched in my verdurous cavern
Shall I behold you afar from the bushy precipice hanging.
Songs no more shall I sing; not with me, ye goats, as your shepherd,
Shall ye browse on the bitter willow or blooming laburnum.

TITYRUS.

Nevertheless, this night together with me canst thou rest thee
Here on the verdant leaves; for us there are mellowing apples,
Chestnuts soft to the touch, and clouted cream in abundance;
And the high roofs now of the villages smoke in the distance,
And from the lofty mountains are falling larger the shadows.

AT TOMIS, IN BESSARABIA, NEAR THE MOUTHS OF THE DANUBE.

Tristia, Book III., Elegy X.

Should any one there in Rome remember Ovid the exile,
  And, without me, my name still in the city survive;

Tell him that under stars which never set in the ocean
  I am existing still, here in a barbarous land.

Fierce Sarmatians encompass me round, and the Bessi and Getæ;
  Names how unworthy to be sung by a genius like mine!

Yet when the air is warm, intervening Ister defends us:
  He, as he flows, repels inroads of war with his waves.

But when the dismal winter reveals its hideous aspect,
  When all the earth becomes white with a marble-like frost;

And when Boreas is loosed, and the snow hurled under Arcturus,
  Then these nations, in sooth, shudder and shiver with cold.

Deep lies the snow, and neither the sun nor the rain can dissolve it;
  Boreas hardens it still, makes it forever remain.

Hence, ere the first has melted away, another succeeds it,
  And two years it is wont, in many places, to lie.

And so great is the power of the North-wind awakened, it levels
  Lofty towers with the ground, roofs uplifted bears off.

Wrapped in skins, and with trousers sewed, they contend with the weather,
  And their faces alone of the whole body are seen.

Often their tresses, when shaken, with pendent icicles tinkle,
  And their whitened beards shine with the gathering frost.

Wines consolidate stand, preserving the form of the vessels;
   No more draughts of wine, — pieces presented they drink.

Why should I tell you how all the rivers are frozen and solid,
   And from out of the lake frangible water is dug?

Ister, — no narrower stream than the river that bears the papyrus, —
   Which through its many mouths mingles its waves with the deep;

Ister, with hardening winds, congeals its cerulean waters,
   Under a roof of ice winding its way to the sea.

There where ships have sailed, men go on foot; and the billows,
   Solid made by the frost, hoof-beats of horses indent.

Over unwonted bridges, with water gliding beneath them,
   The Sarmatian steers drag their barbarian carts.

Scarcely shall I be believed; yet when naught is gained by a falsehood,
   Absolute credence then should to a witness be given.

I have beheld the vast Black Sea of ice all compacted,
  And a slippery crust pressing its motionless tides.

'T is not enough to have seen, I have trodden this indurate ocean ;
  Dry shod passed my foot over its uppermost wave.

If thou hadst had of old such a sea as this is, Leander !
  Then thy death had not been charged as a crime to the Strait.

Nor can the curvéd dolphins uplift themselves from the water ;
  All their struggles to rise merciless winter prevents ;

And though Boreas sound with roar of wings in commotion,
  In the blockaded gulf never a wave will there be ;

And the ships will stand hemmed in by the frost, as in marble,
  Nor will the oar have power through the stiff waters to cleave.

Fast-bound in the ice have I seen the fishes adhering,
  Yet notwithstanding this some of them still were alive.

Hence, if the savage strength of omnipotent Boreas freezes
  Whether the salt-sea wave, whether the refluent stream, —

Straightway, — the Ister made level by arid blasts of the North-wind, —
  Comes the barbaric foe borne on his swiftfooted steed ;

Foe, that powerful made by his steed and his far-flying arrows,
  All the neighboring land void of inhabitants makes.

Some take flight, and none being left to defend their possessions,
  Unprotected, their goods pillage and plunder become ;

Cattle and creaking carts, the little wealth of the country,
  And what riches beside indigent peasants possess.

Some as captives are driven along, their hands bound behind them,
  Looking backward in vain toward their Lares and lands.

Others, transfixed with barbéd arrows, in agony perish,
  For the swift arrow-heads all have in poison been dipped.

What they cannot carry or lead away they demolish,
  And the hostile flames burn up the innocent cots.

Even when there is peace, the fear of war is impending ;
  None, with the ploughshare pressed, furrows the soil any more.

Either this region sees, or fears a foe that it sees not,
  And the sluggish land slumbers in utter neglect.
  110

No sweet grape lies hidden here in the shade of its vine-leaves,
　　No fermenting must fills and o'erflows the deep vats.

Apples the region denies; nor would Acontius have found here
　　Aught upon which to write words for his mistress to read.

Naked and barren plains without leaves or trees we behold here, —
　　Places, alas! unto which no happy man would repair.

Since then this mighty orb lies open so wide upon all sides,
　　Has this region been found only my prison to be?

TRISTIA, Book III., Elegy XII.

Now the zephyrs diminish the cold, and the year being ended,
　　Winter Mæotian seems longer than ever before;

And the Ram that bore unsafely the burden of Helle,
　　Now makes the hours of the day equal with those of the night.

Now the boys and the laughing girls the violet gather,
　　Which the fields bring forth, nobody sowing the seed.

Now the meadows are blooming with flowers of various colors,
   And with untaught throats carol the garrulous birds.

Now the swallow, to shun the crime of her merciless mother,
   Under the rafters builds cradles and dear little homes;

And the blade that lay hid, covered up in the furrows of Ceres,
   Now from the tepid ground raises its delicate head.

Where there is ever a vine, the bud shoots forth from the tendrils,
   But from the Getic shore distant afar is the vine!

Where there is ever a tree, on the tree the branches are swelling,
   But from the Getic land distant afar is the tree!

Now it is holiday there in Rome, and to games in due order
   Give place the windy wars of the vociferous bar.

Now they are riding the horses; with light arms now they are playing,
   Now with the ball, and now round rolls the swift-flying hoop:

Now, when the young athlete with flowing oil is anointed,
   He in the Virgin's Fount bathes, overwearied, his limbs.

Thrives the stage; and applause, with voices at variance, thunders,
   And the Theatres three for the three Forums resound.

Four times happy is he, and times without number is happy,
   Who the city of Rome, uninterdicted, enjoys.

But all I see is the snow in the vernal sunshine dissolving,
  And the waters no more delved from the indurate lake.

Nor is the sea now frozen, nor as before o'er the Ister
  Comes the Sarmatian boor driving his stridulous cart.

Hitherward, nevertheless, some keels already are steering,
  And on this Pontic shore alien vessels will be.

Eagerly shall I run to the sailor, and, having saluted,
  Who he may be, I shall ask; wherefore and whence he hath come.

Strange indeed will it be, if he come not from regions adjacent,
  And incautious unless ploughing the neighboring sea.

Rarely a mariner over the deep from Italy passes,
  Rarely he comes to these shores, wholly of harbors devoid.

Whether he knoweth Greek, or whether in Latin he speaketh,
  Surely on this account he the more welcome will be.

Also perchance from the mouth of the Strait and the waters Propontic,
  Unto the steady South-wind, some one is spreading his sails.

Whosoever he is, the news he can faithfully tell me,
  Which may become a part and an approach to the truth.

He, I pray, may be able to tell me the triumphs of Cæsar,
  Which he has heard of, and vows paid to the Latian Jove;

And that thy sorrowful head, Germania, thou, the rebellious,
  Under the feet, at last, of the Great Captain hast laid.

Whoso shall tell me these things, that not to have seen will afflict me,
  Forthwith unto my house welcomed as guest shall he be.

Woe is me! Is the house of Ovid in Scythian lands now?
  And doth punishment now give me its place for a home?

Grant, ye gods, that Cæsar make this not my house and my homestead,
  But decree it to be only the inn of my pain.

ON THE TERRACE OF THE AIGALADES.

FROM THE FRENCH OF MÉRY.

FROM this high portal, where upsprings
The rose to touch our hands in play,
We at a glance behold three things, —
The Sea, the Town, and the Highway.

And the Sea says: My shipwrecks fear;
I drown my best friends in the deep;
And those who braved my tempests, here
Among my sea-weeds lie asleep!

The Town says: I am filled and fraught
With tumult and with smoke and care;
My days with toil are overwrought,
And in my nights I gasp for air.

The Highway says: My wheel-tracks guide
To the pale climates of the North;

Where my last milestone stands, abide
The people to their death gone forth.

Here, in the shade, this life of ours,
Full of delicious air, glides by
Amid a multitude of flowers
As countless as the stars on high;

These red-tiled roofs, this fruitful soil,
Bathed with an azure all divine,
Where springs the tree that gives us oil,
The grape that giveth us the wine;

Beneath these mountains stripped of trees,
Whose tops with flowers are covered o'er,
Where springtime of the Hesperides
Begins, but endeth nevermore;

Under these leafy vaults and walls,
That unto gentle sleep persuade;
This rainbow of the waterfalls,
Of mingled mist and sunshine made;

Upon these shores, where all invites,
We live our languid life apart;

This air is that of life's delights,
The festival of sense and heart;

This limpid space of time prolong,
Forget to-morrow in to-day,
And leave unto the passing throng
The Sea, the Town, and the Highway.

TO MY BROOKLET.

FROM THE FRENCH OF DUCIS.

Thou brooklet, all unknown to song,
  Hid in the covert of the wood!
Ah, yes, like thee I fear the throng,
  Like thee I love the solitude.

O brooklet, let my sorrows past
  Lie all forgotten in their graves,
Till in my thoughts remain at last
  Only thy peace, thy flowers, thy waves.

The lily by thy margin waits; —
  The nightingale, the marguerite;

In shadow here he meditates
  His nest, his love, his music sweet.

Near thee the self-collected soul
  Knows naught of error or of crime;
Thy waters, murmuring as they roll,
  Transform his musings into rhyme.

Ah, when, on bright autumnal eves,
  Pursuing still thy course, shall I
List the soft shudder of the leaves,
  And hear the lapwing's plaintive cry?

BARRÉGES.

FROM THE FRENCH OF LEFRANC DE POMPIGNAN.

I LEAVE you, ye cold mountain chains,
  Dwelling of warriors stark and frore!
  You, may these eyes behold no more,
Save on the horizon of our plains.

Vanish, ye frightful, gloomy views!
  Ye rocks that mount up to the clouds!
  Of skies, enwrapped in misty shrouds,
Impracticable avenues!

Ye torrents, that with might and main
  Break pathways through the rocky walls,
  With your terrific waterfalls
Fatigue no more my weary brain!

Arise, ye landscapes full of charms,
  Arise, ye pictures of delight!

Ye brooks, that water in your flight
The flowers and harvests of our farms!

You I perceive, ye meadows green,
  Where the Garonne the lowland fills,
  Not far from that long chain of hills,
With intermingled vales between.

Yon wreath of smoke, that mounts so high,
  Methinks from my own hearth must come;
  With speed, to that beloved home,
Fly, ye too lazy coursers, fly!

And bear me thither, where the soul
  In quiet may itself possess,
  Where all things soothe the mind's distress,
Where all things teach me and console.

FORSAKEN.

FROM THE GERMAN.

SOMETHING the heart must have to cherish,
  Must love and joy and sorrow learn,
Something with passion clasp, or perish,
  And in itself to ashes burn.

So to this child my heart is clinging,
  And its frank eyes, with look intense,
Me from a world of sin are bringing
  Back to a world of innocence.

Disdain must thou endure forever;
  Strong may thy heart in danger be !
Thou shalt not fail ! but ah, be never
  False as thy father was to me.

Never will I forsake thee, faithless,
  And thou thy mother ne'er forsake,
Until her lips are white and breathless,
  Until in death her eyes shall break.

ALLAH.

FROM THE GERMAN OF MAHLMANN.

ALLAH gives light in darkness,
  Allah gives rest in pain,
Cheeks that are white with weeping
  Allah paints red again.

The flowers and the blossoms wither,
  Years vanish with flying feet;

But my heart will live on forever,
  That here in sadness beat.

Gladly to Allah's dwelling
  Yonder would I take flight;
There will the darkness vanish,
  There will my eyes have sight.

SEVEN SONNETS AND A CANZONE

[The following translations are from the poems of Michael Angelo as revised by his nephew Michael Angelo the Younger, and were made before the publication of the original text by Guasti.]

SEVEN SONNETS AND A CANZONE

I.

THE ARTIST.

NOTHING the greatest artist can conceive
  That every marble block doth not confine
  Within itself; and only its design
  The hand that follows intellect can achieve.
The ill I flee, the good that I believe,
  In thee, fair lady, lofty and divine,
  Thus hidden lie; and so that death be mine
  Art, of desired success, doth me bereave.
Love is not guilty, then, nor thy fair face,
  Nor fortune, cruelty, nor great disdain,
  Of my disgrace, nor chance nor destiny,
If in thy heart both death and love find place
  At the same time, and if my humble brain,
  Burning, can nothing draw but death from thee.

II.

FIRE.

NOT without fire can any workman mould
  The iron to his preconceived design,
  Nor can the artist without fire refine
  And purify from all its dross the gold;
Nor can revive the phœnix, we are told,
  Except by fire. Hence if such death be mine
  I hope to rise again with the divine,
  Whom death augments, and time cannot
        make old.
O sweet, sweet death! O fortunate fire that burns
  Within me still to renovate my days,
  Though I am almost numbered with the dead!
If by its nature unto heaven returns
  This element, me, kindled in its blaze,
  Will it bear upward when my life is fled.

III.

YOUTH AND AGE.

OH give me back the days when loose and free
    To my blind passion were the curb and
        rein,
    Oh give me back the angelic face again,
    With which all virtue buried seems to be!
Oh give my panting footsteps back to me,
    That are in age so slow and fraught with
        pain,
    And fire and moisture in the heart and brain,
    If thou wouldst have me burn and weep for
        thee!
If it be true thou livest alone, Amor,
    On the sweet-bitter tears of human hearts,
    In an old man thou canst not wake desire;
Souls that have almost reached the other
        shore
    Of a diviner love should feel the darts,
    And be as tinder to a holier fire.

IV.

OLD AGE.

THE course of my long life hath reached at
        last
    In fragile bark o'er a tempestuous sea,
    The common harbor, where must rendered
        be
Account of all the actions of the past.
The impassioned phantasy, that, vague and
        vast,
    Made art an idol and a king to me,
    Was an illusion, and but vanity
    Were the desires that lured me and har-
        assed.
The dreams of love, that were so sweet of
        yore,
    What are they now, when two deaths may
        be mine, —
    One sure, and one forecasting its alarms?
Painting and sculpture satisfy no more
    The soul now turning to the Love Divine,
    That oped, to embrace us, on the cross its
        arms.

V.

TO VITTORIA COLONNA.

LADY, how can it chance — yet this we see
    In long experience — that will longer last
    A living image carved from quarries vast
    Than its own maker, who dies presently?
Cause yieldeth to effect if this so be,
    And even Nature is by Art surpassed;
    This know I, who to Art have given the
        past,
    But see that Time is breaking faith with
        me.
Perhaps on both of us long life can I
    Either in color or in stone bestow,
    By now portraying each in look and mien;
So that a thousand years after we die,
    How fair thou wast, and I how full of
        woe,
    And wherefore I so loved thee, may be
        seen.

VI.

TO VITTORIA COLONNA.

WHEN the prime mover of my many sighs
    Heaven took through death from out her
        earthly place,
    Nature, that never made so fair a face,
    Remained ashamed, and tears were in all
        eyes.
O fate, unheeding my impassioned cries!
    O hopes fallacious! O thou spirit of grace,
    Where art thou now? Earth holds in its
        embrace
    Thy lovely limbs, thy holy thoughts the
        skies.
Vainly did cruel death attempt to stay
    The rumor of thy virtuous renown,
    That Lethe's waters could not wash away!
A thousand leaves, since he hath stricken thee
        down,
    Speak of thee, nor to thee could Heaven
        convey,
    Except through death, a refuge and a
        crown.

VII.

DANTE.

WHAT should be said of him cannot be said;
　By too great splendor is his name attended;
　To blame is easier those who him offended,
　Than reach the faintest glory round him
　　shed.
This man descended to the doomed and dead
　For our instruction; then to God ascended;
　Heaven opened wide to him its portals
　　splendid,
　Who from his country's, closed against him,
　　fled.
Ungrateful land! To its own prejudice
　Nurse of his fortunes; and this showeth
　　well,
　That the most perfect most of grief shall
　　see.
Among a thousand proofs let one suffice,
　That as his exile hath no parallel,
　Ne'er walked the earth a greater man, than
　　he.

VIII.

CANZONE.

AH me! ah me! when thinking of the years,
　The vanished years, alas, I do not find
　Among them all one day that was my own!
Fallacious hopes, desires of the unknown,
　Lamenting, loving, burning, and in tears,
　(For human passions all have stirred my
　　mind),

Have held me, now I feel and know, con-
　fined
Both from the true and good still far away.
I perish day by day;
The sunshine fails, the shadows grow more
　dreary,
And I am near to fall, infirm and weary.

DEDICATION

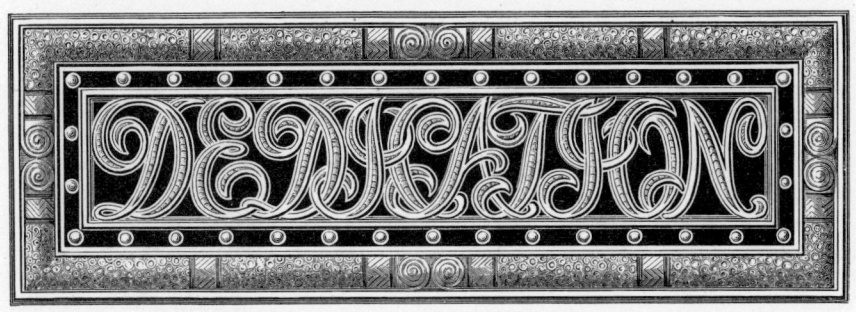

TO G. W. G.

WITH favoring winds, o'er sunlit seas,
We sailed for the Hesperides,
The land where golden apples grow;
But that, ah! that was long ago.

How far, since then, the ocean streams
Have swept us from that land of dreams,
That land of fiction and of truth,
The lost Atlantis of our youth!

Whither, ah, whither? Are not these
The tempest-haunted Orcades,
Where sea-gulls scream, and breakers roar,
And wreck and sea-weed line the shore?

Ultima Thule! Utmost Isle!
Here in thy harbors for a while
We lower our sails; a while we rest,
From the unending, endless quest.

BAYARD TAYLOR.

DEAD he lay among his books!
The peace of God was in his looks.

As the statues in the gloom
Watch o'er Maximilian's tomb,[1]

So those volumes from their shelves
Watched him, silent as themselves.

Ah! his hand will nevermore
Turn their storied pages o'er;

Nevermore his lips repeat
Songs of theirs, however sweet.

Let the lifeless body rest!
He is gone, who was its guest;

Gone, as travellers haste to leave
An inn, nor tarry until eve.

Traveller! in what realms afar,
In what planet, in what star,

In what vast, aerial space,
Shines the light upon thy face?

In what gardens of delight
Rest thy weary feet to-night?

Poet! thou, whose latest verse
Was a garland on thy hearse;

Thou hast sung, with organ tone,
In Deukalion's life, thine own;

On the ruins of the Past
Blooms the perfect flower at last.

Friend! but yesterday the bells
Rang for thee their loud farewells;

And to-day they toll for thee,
Lying dead beyond the sea;

Lying dead among thy books,
The peace of God in all thy looks!

THE CHAMBER OVER THE GATE.

Is it so far from thee
Thou canst no longer see,
In the Chamber over the Gate,
That old man desolate,
Weeping and wailing sore
For his son, who is no more?
    O Absalom, my son!

Is it so long ago
That cry of human woe
From the walled city came,
Calling on his dear name,
That it has died away
In the distance of to-day?
    O Absalom, my son!

[1] In the Hofkirche at Innsbruck.

There is no far or near,
There is neither there nor here,
There is neither soon nor late,
In that Chamber over the Gate,
Nor any long ago
To that cry of human woe,
   O Absalom, my son!

From the ages that are past
The voice sounds like a blast,
Over seas that wreck and drown,
Over tumult of traffic and town;
And from ages yet to be
Come the echoes back to me,
   O Absalom, my son!

Somewhere at every hour
The watchman on the tower
Looks forth, and sees the fleet
Approach of the hurrying feet

Of messengers, that bear
The tidings of despair.
   O Absalom, my son!

He goes forth from the door,
Who shall return no more.
With him our joy departs;
The light goes out in our hearts;
In the Chamber over the Gate
We sit disconsolate.
   O Absalom, my son!

That 't is a common grief
Bringeth but slight relief;
Ours is the bitterest loss,
Ours is the heaviest cross;
And forever the cry will be
"Would God I had died for thee,
   O Absalom, my son!"

FROM MY ARM–CHAIR.

TO THE CHILDREN OF CAMBRIDGE,

Who presented to me, on my Seventy-second Birthday, February 27, 1879, this Chair made from the Wood of the Village Blacksmith's Chestnut Tree.

Am I a king, that I should call my own
   This splendid ebon throne?
Or by what reason, or what right divine,
   Can I proclaim it mine?

Only, perhaps, by right divine of song
   It may to me belong;
Only because the spreading chestnut tree
   Of old was sung by me.

Well I remember it in all its prime,
   When in the summer-time
The affluent foliage of its branches made
   A cavern of cool shade.

There, by the blacksmith's forge, beside
   the street,
   Its blossoms white and sweet
Enticed the bees, until it seemed alive,
   And murmured like a hive.

And when the winds of autumn, with a
       shout,
    Tossed its great arms about,
The shining chestnuts, bursting from the
       sheath,
    Dropped to the ground beneath.

And now some fragments of its branches bare,
    Shaped as a stately chair,
Have by my hearthstone found a home at
       last,
    And whisper of the past.

The Danish king could not in all his pride
    Repel the ocean tide,
But seated in this chair, I can in rhyme
    Roll back the tide of Time.

I see again, as one in vision sees,
    The blossoms and the bees,
And hear the children's voices shout and call,
    And the brown chestnuts fall.

I see the smithy with its fires aglow,
    I hear the bellows blow,
And the shrill hammers on the anvil beat
    The iron white with heat!

And thus, dear children, have ye made for me
    This day a jubilee,
And to my more than three-score years and
       ten
    Brought back my youth again.

The heart hath its own memory, like the
       mind,
    And in it are enshrined
The precious keepsakes, into which is wrought
    The giver's loving thought.

Only your love and your remembrance could
    Give life to this dead wood,
And make these branches, leafless now so
       long,
    Blossom again in song.

JUGURTHA.

How cold are thy baths, Apollo!
    Cried the African monarch, the splendid,
As down to his death in the hollow
    Dark dungeons of Rome he descended,
    Uncrowned, unthroned, unattended;
How cold are thy baths, Apollo!

How cold are thy baths, Apollo!
    Cried the Poet, unknown, unbefriended,
As the vision, that lured him to follow,
    With the mist and the darkness blended,
    And the dream of his life was ended;
How cold are thy baths, Apollo!

THE IRON PEN.

Made from a fetter of Bonnivard, the Prisoner of Chillon; the handle of wood from the Frigate Constitution, and bound with a circlet of gold, inset with three precious stones from Siberia, Ceylon, and Maine.

I THOUGHT this Pen would arise
From the casket where it lies —
    Of itself would arise and write
My thanks and my surprise.

When you gave it me under the pines,
I dreamed these gems from the mines
    Of Siberia, Ceylon, and Maine
Would glimmer as thoughts in the lines;

That this iron link from the chain
Of Bonnivard might retain
    Some verse of the Poet who sang
Of the prisoner and his pain;

That this wood from the frigate's mast
Might write me a rhyme at last,
    As it used to write on the sky
The song of the sea and the blast.

But motionless as I wait,
Like a Bishop lying in state
   Lies the Pen, with its mitre of gold,
And its jewels inviolate.

Then must I speak, and say
That the light of that summer day
   In the garden under the pines
Shall not fade and pass away.

I shall see you standing there,
Caressed by the fragrant air,
   With the shadow on your face,
And the sunshine on your hair.

And in words not idle and vain
I shall answer and thank you again
   For the gift, and the grace of the gift,
O beautiful Helen of Maine!

I shall hear the sweet low tone
Of a voice before unknown,
   Saying, " This is from me to you —
From me, and to you alone."

And forever this gift will be
As a blessing from you to me,
   As a drop of the dew of your youth
On the leaves of an aged tree.

ROBERT BURNS.

I SEE amid the fields of Ayr
A ploughman, who, in foul and fair,
    Sings at his task
So clear, we know not if it is
The laverock's song we hear, or his,
    Nor care to ask.

Is clothed with beauty; gorse and grass
And heather, where his footsteps pass,
    The brighter seem.

For him the ploughing of those fields
A more ethereal harvest yields
    Than sheaves of grain;
Songs flush with purple bloom the rye,
The plover's call, the curlew's cry,
    Sing in his brain.

He sings of love, whose flame illumes
The darkness of lone cottage rooms;
    He feels the force,
The treacherous undertow and stress
Of wayward passions, and no less
    The keen remorse.

Touched by his hand, the wayside weed
Becomes a flower; the lowliest reed
    Beside the stream

At moments, wrestling with his fate,
His voice is harsh, but not with hate;
    The brush-wood, hung
Above the tavern door, lets fall
Its bitter leaf, its drop of gall
    Upon his tongue.

But still the music of his song
Rises o'er all, elate and strong;
    Its master-chords
Are Manhood, Freedom, Brotherhood,
Its discords but an interlude
    Between the words.

And then to die so young and leave
Unfinished what he might achieve!
    Yet better sure
Is this, than wandering up and down
An old man in a country town,
    Infirm and poor.

For now he haunts his native land
As an immortal youth; his hand
    Guides every plough;
He sits beside each ingle-nook,
His voice is in each rushing brook
    Each rustling bough.

His presence haunts this room to-night,
A form of mingled mist and light
    From that far coast.
Welcome beneath this roof of mine!
Welcome! this vacant chair is thine,
    Dear guest and ghost!

HELEN OF TYRE.

WHAT phantom is this that appears
Through the purple mists of the years,
    Itself but a mist like these?
A woman of cloud and of fire;
It is she; it is Helen of Tyre,
    The town in the midst of the seas.

O Tyre! in thy crowded streets
The phantom appears and retreats,
    And the Israelites that sell
Thy lilies and lions of brass,
Look up as they see her pass,
    And murmur "Jezebel!"

Then another phantom is seen
At her side, in a gray gabardine,
    With beard that floats to his waist;
It is Simon Magus, the Seer;
He speaks, and she pauses to hear
    The words he utters in haste.

He says: " From this evil fame,
From this life of sorrow and shame,
    I will lift thee and make thee mine;
Thou hast been Queen Candace,
And Helen of Troy, and shalt be
    The Intelligence Divine ! "

Oh, sweet as the breath of morn,
To the fallen and forlorn
    Are whispered words of praise;

For the famished heart believes
The falsehood that tempts and deceives,
    And the promise that betrays.

So she follows from land to land
The wizard's beckoning hand,
    As a leaf is blown by the gust,
Till she vanishes into night.
O reader, stoop down and write
    With thy finger in the dust.

O town in the midst of the seas,
With thy rafts of cedar trees,
    Thy merchandise and thy ships,
Thou, too, art become as naught,
A phantom, a shadow, a thought,
    A name upon men's lips.

ELEGIAC.

DARK is the morning with mist; in the nar-
    row mouth of the harbor
    Motionless lies the sea, under its curtain of
        cloud;
Dreamily glimmer the sails of ships on the
    distant horizon,
    Like to the towers of a town, built on the
        verge of the sea.

Slowly and stately and still, they sail forth
    into the ocean;
    With them sail my thoughts over the lim-
        itless deep,
Farther and farther away, borne on by un-
    satisfied longings,
    Unto Hesperian isles, unto Ausonian shores.

Now they have vanished away, have disap-
    peared in the ocean;
    Sunk are the towers of the town into the
        depths of the sea!
All have vanished but those that, moored in
    the neighboring roadstead,
    Sailless at anchor ride, looming so large in
        the mist.

Vanished, too, are the thoughts, the dim, un-
    satisfied longings;
    Sunk are the turrets of cloud into the
        ocean of dreams;
While in a haven of rest my heart is riding
    at anchor,
    Held by the chains of love, held by the
        anchors of trust!

OLD ST. DAVID'S AT RADNOR.

WHAT an image of peace and rest
  Is this little church among its graves!
All is so quiet; the troubled breast,
The wounded spirit, the heart oppressed,
  Here may find the repose it craves.

See, how the ivy climbs and expands
  Over this humble hermitage,
And seems to caress with its little hands
The rough, gray stones, as a child that stands
  Caressing the wrinkled cheeks of age!

You cross the threshold; and dim and small
  Is the space that serves for the Shepherd's
    Fold;
The narrow aisle, the bare, white wall,
The pews, and the pulpit quaint and tall,
  Whisper and say: "Alas! we are old."

Herbert's chapel at Bemerton
  Hardly more spacious is than this;

But poet and pastor, blent in one,
Clothed with a splendor, as of the sun,
  That lowly and holy edifice.

It is not the wall of stone without
  That makes the building small or great,
But the soul's light shining round about,
And the faith that overcometh doubt,
  And the love that stronger is than hate.

Were I a pilgrim in search of peace,
  Were I a pastor of Holy Church,
More than a Bishop's diocese
Should I prize this place of rest and release
  From further longing and further search.

Here would I stay, and let the world
  With its distant thunder roar and roll;
Storms do not rend the sail that is furled;
Nor like a dead leaf, tossed and whirled
  In an eddy of wind, is the anchored soul.

THE SIFTING OF PETER.

In St. Luke's Gospel we are told
How Peter in the days of old
    Was sifted;
And now, though ages intervene,
Sin is the same, while time and scene
    Are shifted.

Satan desires us, great and small,
As wheat to sift us, and we all
    Are tempted;
Not one, however rich or great,
Is by his station or estate
    Exempted.

No house so safely guarded is
But he, by some device of his,
    Can enter;
No heart hath armor so complete
But he can pierce with arrows fleet
    Its centre.

For all at last the cock will crow,
Who hear the warning voice, but go
    Unheeding,

Till thrice and more they have denied
The Man of Sorrows, crucified
    And bleeding.

One look of that pale suffering face
Will make us feel the deep disgrace
    Of weakness;
We shall be sifted till the strength
Of self-conceit be changed at length
    To meekness.

Wounds of the soul, though healed, will ache;
The reddening scars remain, and make
    Confession;
Lost innocence returns no more;
We are not what we were before
    Transgression.

But noble souls, through dust and heat,
Rise from disaster and defeat
    The stronger;
And conscious still of the divine
Within them, lie on earth supine
    No longer.

MAIDEN AND WEATHERCOCK.

MAIDEN.

O Weathercock on the village spire,
With your golden feathers all on fire,
Tell me, what can you see from your perch
Above there over the tower of the church?

WEATHERCOCK.

I can see the roofs and the streets below,
And the people moving to and fro,
And beyond, without either roof or street,
The great salt sea, and the fishermen's fleet.

113

I can see a ship come sailing in
Beyond the headlands and harbor of Lynn,
And a young man standing on the deck,
With a silken kerchief round his neck.

Now he is pressing it to his lips,
And now he is kissing his finger-tips,
And now he is lifting and waving his hand,
And blowing the kisses toward the land.

MAIDEN.

Ah, that is the ship from over the sea,
That is bringing my lover back to me,
Bringing my lover so fond and true,
Who does not change with the wind like
        you.

WEATHERCOCK.

If I change with all the winds that blow,
It is only because they made me so,
And people would think it wondrous strange,
If I, a Weathercock, should not change.

O pretty Maiden, so fine and fair,
With your dreamy eyes and your golden hair,
When you and your lover meet to-day
You will thank me for looking some other way.

ARTIST: ERNEST W. LONGFELLOW.

THE WINDMILL.

THE WINDMILL.

BEHOLD! a giant am I!
  Aloft here in my tower,
  With my granite jaws I devour
The maize, and the wheat, and the rye,
  And grind them into flour.

I look down over the farms;
  In the fields of grain I see
  The harvest that is to be,
And I fling to the air my arms,
  For I know it is all for me.

I hear the sound of flails
  Far off, from the threshing-floors
  In barns, with their open doors,
And the wind, the wind in my sails,
  Louder and louder roars.

I stand here in my place,
  With my foot on the rock below,
  And whichever way it may blow
I meet it face to face,
  As a brave man meets his foe.

And while we wrestle and strive
  My master, the miller, stands
  And feeds me with his hands;
For he knows who makes him thrive,
  Who makes him lord of lands.

On Sundays I take my rest;
  Church-going bells begin
  Their low, melodious din;
I cross my arms on my breast,
  And all is peace within.

THE TIDE RISES, THE TIDE FALLS.

THE tide rises, the tide falls,
The twilight darkens, the curlew calls;
Along the sea-sands damp and brown
The traveller hastens toward the town,
  And the tide rises, the tide falls.

Darkness settles on roofs and walls,
But the sea, the sea in the darkness calls;
The little waves, with their soft, white hands,

Efface the footprints in the sands,
  And the tide rises, the tide falls.

The morning breaks; the steeds in their
      stalls
Stamp and neigh, as the hostler calls;
The day returns, but nevermore
Returns the traveller to the shore,
  And the tide rises, the tide falls.

SONNETS

MY CATHEDRAL.

LIKE two cathedral towers these stately pines
   Uplift their fretted summits tipped with
      cones ;
   The arch beneath them is not built with
      stones,
   Not Art but Nature traced these lovely lines,
And carved this graceful arabesque of vines;
   No organ but the wind here sighs and
      moans,

No sepulchre conceals a martyr's bones,
   No marble bishop on his tomb reclines.
Enter ! the pavement, carpeted with leaves,
   Gives back a softened echo to thy tread !
   Listen ! the choir is singing ; all the birds,
In leafy galleries beneath the eaves,
   Are singing ! listen, ere the sound be fled,
   And learn there may be worship without
      words.

THE BURIAL OF THE POET.

RICHARD HENRY DANA.

IN the old churchyard of his native town,
   And in the ancestral tomb beside the wall,
   We laid him in the sleep that comes to all,
   And left him to his rest and his renown.
The snow was falling, as if Heaven dropped
      down
   White flowers of Paradise to strew his
      pall ; —
   The dead around him seemed to wake, and
      call
   His name, as worthy of so white a crown.
And now the moon is shining on the scene,
   And the broad sheet of snow is written o'er
   With shadows cruciform of leafless trees,
As once the winding-sheet of Saladin
   With chapters of the Koran ; but, ah !
      more
   Mysterious and triumphant signs are these.

NIGHT.

INTO the darkness and the hush of night
  Slowly the landscape sinks, and fades away,
  And with it fade the phantoms of the day,
  The ghosts of men and things, that haunt
    the light.
The crowd, the clamor, the pursuit, the flight,
  The unprofitable splendor and display,
  The agitations, and the cares that prey
Upon our hearts, all vanish out of sight.
The better life begins; the world no more
  Molests us; all its records we erase
  From the dull common-place book of our
    lives,
That like a palimpsest is written o'er
  With trivial incidents of time and place,
  And lo! the ideal, hidden beneath, revives.

·:·L'EΠVOI·:·

THE POET AND HIS SONGS.

As the birds come in the Spring,
  We know not from where;
As the stars come at evening
  From depths of the air;

As the rain comes from the cloud,
  And the brook from the ground;
As suddenly, low or loud,
  Out of silence a sound;

As the grape comes to the vine,
  The fruit to the tree;
As the wind comes to the pine,
  And the tide to the sea;

As come the white sails of ships
  O'er the ocean's verge;

As comes the smile to the lips,
  The foam to the surge;

So come to the Poet his songs,
  All hitherward blown
From the misty realm, that belongs
  To the vast Unknown.

His, and not his, are the lays
  He sings; and their fame
Is his, and not his; and the praise
  And the pride of a name.

For voices pursue him by day,
  And haunt him by night,
And he listens, and needs must obey,
  When the Angel says: "Write!"

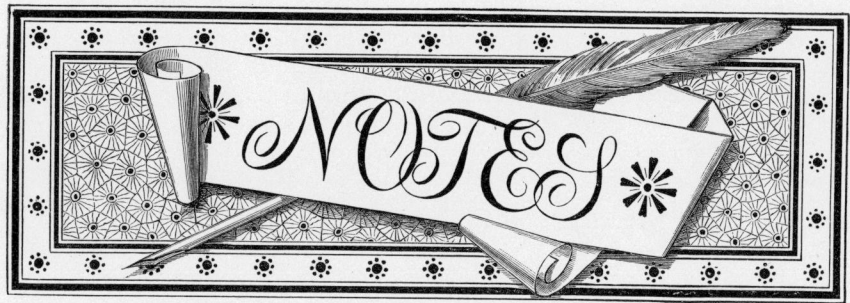

ON THE ILLUSTRATIONS.

IN the Lists of Illustrations giving the subjects treated and the names of artists and engravers, the attentive reader will have observed that the designs are, as far as possible, notes to the poems. Wherever a poem has been suggested by objects or scenes of which a faithful picture could be given, the artist most familiar with the original suggestion of the poem has reproduced it, and the designs thus do not merely repeat in line what the poet has already said in verse, but throw light upon the poem and serve to interpret it. The faithfulness with which this has been done will be apparent to those acquainted like the artists with the subjects treated, and in many instances the reader will require no other hint than the picture itself gives, but there are a few cases where it seems desirable to add information.

Frontispiece. The portrait is from a photograph taken in 1869, in the poet's sixty-third year.

Page 10. The view is of the bridge over the Moldau, at Prague.

Page 14. Bethlehem and Nazareth in Pennsylvania were formerly, more than now, occupied by Moravians; the buildings seen in the sketch are the ancient houses belonging to the Moravian sisterhood in Bethlehem. The central one contains the chapel.

Page 31. The portrait of King Christian is from a painting in the Royal Museum of Copenhagen.

Page 32. In the same gallery is a painting of King Christian's ship, and it has furnished accurate details for the picture here given of the contest.

Page 41. The view of the old tower at Newport is given in accordance with the author's note to the poem.

Page 45. A sketch from nature of Norman's Woe, as seen off the Essex coast, Massachusetts, midway between Gloucester and Magnolia.

Page 58. From a water-color painting, in Mr. Longfellow's possession, of the blacksmith shop and chestnut tree, which stood for many years on Brattle Street, in Cambridge, not far from the poet's house. The smithy was subsequently removed to make place for a dwelling-house, and the tree has since been cut down upon the plea that its low-hanging branches rendered passage dangerous.

Page 62. Upon the opposite side of Brattle Street, where Mr. Longfellow lives, there is an open field belonging to him which gives him an unobstructed view of the river Charles and of the country beyond. The view here given is taken from the front of the poet's house.

Pages 77–116. The rich dress represented in the figure subjects illustrative of "The Spanish Student" is from actual Spanish costumes of the period covered by the poem. The landscapes are from studies made at the places indicated.

Page 121. Mr. Longfellow pointed out to the artist the place which suggested the poem, and the illustration is a view taken from the point where the poet might have let his horse rest.

Page 128. The staircase with the clock is from a drawing made in Mr. Longfellow's house. As he has intimated in the poem, the house was the headquarters of Washington when in camp at Cambridge, and the features of the house are much the same now as then. The staircase is that leading from the main hall, which one sees on entering. The tiled fire-place sketched in the corner of the picture is from that in the nursery of the poet's children.

Page 129. A glimpse of one of the walks in the poet's garden: —

> "Along the garden walks,
> The tracks of thy small carriage-wheels I trace."

Page 137. The antique pitcher represented is in Mr. Longfellow's possession.

Page 138. A view of the old Gold house, known now as the Plunkett mansion, in Pittsfield, Mass.

Page 148. From a painting belonging to Mr. Longfellow; the village of Grand Pré is seen, in the distance, with Blomidon rising in the north. In the Nova Scotia of the present, the features of the landscape remain as in the old Acadia; it is the village scenes which have changed.

Page 170. As in other cases, the sketch on this page is taken from nature, the scene being the lakes of the Atchafalaya in Louisiana.

Page 177. This also is from a study on the spot by Thomas Moran.

Page 200. The sketch at the left is of the farm-house of the Devereux family, where the scene of the poem is laid. In filling the interior the artist restored the old furniture which once stood there but now is found in the city home of one of the descendants of General Devereux.

Page 223. From studies by the painter among the Rocky Mountains.

Facing page 232. From the prairie looking toward the Rocky Mountains, drawn from studies made there by the artist.

Facing page 253. The landscapes illustrating Hiawatha are from sketches made in the localities by the several artists. In this instance the subject has been idealized by the painter from the actual scene.

Page 307. The engraving of Standish Hall is from a sketch taken in 1879. The exterior of the hall, in Duxbury, England, remains as originally built ; the interior was burned about ten years before, but has since been restored exactly in accordance with the original plan.

Page 328. This sketch of the old Standish spring is from a drawing made thirty years ago, when the spring was still to be seen. It has since been destroyed.

Page 343. From a recent photographic view taken in Deering's Oaks, near Portland, Maine.

Page 347. A sketch of a vineyard on the Ohio River.

Page 353. A view of Mr. Longfellow's study, where a great part of his work has been done. On the table is seen his writing-desk, and near the window his standing desk. The carved chair at the left is made from the chestnut tree of which he sang in " The Village Blacksmith." The wood of the tree, after it was cut down, was preserved, and the school-children of Cambridge had the chair made from it and gave it to Mr. Longfellow on his birthday. His answer to the gift will be found on page 891.

Page 355. The artist sketched the *Cumberland* as she lay in Hampton Roads just before her engagement with the *Merrimac*, and it was from the sketch that he made this picture.

Facing page 373. The old Wayside Inn of Sudbury, Mass., generally known as Howe's Tavern. It is still standing, but is no longer used as a tavern.

Page 379. The North or Christ Church, still standing in Salem Street, Boston. The authorities of Boston have placed a tablet upon the face of the tower, commemorating Revere's signal service. There has been a controversy among antiquarians as to the locality, whether the church where the lanterns were hung, was Christ Church, familiarly known as the North, or the Old North (Congregational) with its low tower, torn down for firewood during the siege of Boston.

Page 426. Sketched from nature in 1879; the overhanging second stories are rarely seen now except in the oldest New England houses. Killingworth in Connecticut, the scene of the poem, was one of the earliest settlements of the New Haven colony.

Page 428. The details of this interior are from the old town hall of Killingworth.

Page 445. From a view on the coast of Denmark. The rocks in the foreground indicate graves.

Page 476. A recent view of the town of Haddonsfield.

Page 500. The sea from Nahant Head. For many years Mr. Longfellow spent his summers in his cottage at Nahant.

Page 503. The upper picture gives a sketch of Hawthorne's home, the Old Manse, still standing in Concord, Mass., and the lower shows his grave beneath the pines on the hill-side in the Concord grave-yard.

Page 506. Another view of Nahant with the Spouting Horn, and Egg Rock with its light-house.

Page 519. From a photograph taken in 1878.

Pages 585–670. The costumes in the illustrations of " The Golden Legend " were studied in the localities of the drama by Mr. Dielman, as were also architectural details, with special reference to designs in connection with " The Golden Legend," so that the pictures serve as authentic and valuable notes to the poem.

Facing page 629. The interior of the monk's cell is a careful study in all its details of a cell in a monastery of the period of the drama.

Page 678. The face of Governor Endicott here and in other pictures is from an authentic portrait.

Page 683. The house at the left is from the old building recently standing in Dock Square.

Facing page 737. From a sketch taken by the artist in 1879.

Page 822. View of the Charles near Mr. Lowell's house, not far from Mr. Longfellow's. The accompanying picture shows Mount Auburn cemetery, with its tower.

Page 827. From a sketch made during the war, at Newport News.

Page 829. The churchyard at Tarrytown commands a wide view of the Hudson River. Here is the grave of Washington Irving, designated by a larger stone.

Page 851. James Russell Lowell's house on Elmwood Avenue, Cambridge. The house was known as the Oliver house in pre-revolutionary days. From a painting by Harry Fenn, in the possession of James R. Osgood.

Page 891. The chair is the same which was introduced into the picture of Mr. Longfellow's study, on page 353.

Page 893. From the pen given by a lady to Mr. Longfellow.

Page 896. A recent sketch made of the old church at Radnor, near Philadelphia.

Page 898. The weathercock upon the steeple of the Shepard Church, Cambridge, Dr. Alexander McKenzie, pastor, formerly stood on a church in Hanover Street, Boston, where it long served as a landmark, being one of the first points sighted by sailors on entering Boston harbor. When the church was taken down, the bird was removed to Cambridge.

Page 900. Mr. Dana's grave is in the old burial ground in Cambridge, lying between the First Church and Christ Church. Here also in the same place was buried Allston, Dana's friend and relative.

ON THE TEXT.

Page 18. *Coplas de Manrique.*

This poem of Manrique is a great favorite in Spain. No less than four poetic Glosses, or running commentaries, upon it have been published, no one of which, however, possesses great poetic merit. That of the Carthusian monk, Rodrigo de Valdepeñas, is the best. It is known as the "Glosa del Cartujo." There is also a prose Commentary by Luis de Aranda.

The following stanzas of the poem were found in the author's pocket, after his death on the field of battle.

"O World! so few the years we live,
Would that the life which thou dost give
Were life indeed!
Alas! thy sorrows fall so fast,
Our happiest hour is when at last
The soul is freed.

"Our days are covered o'er with grief,
And sorrows neither few nor brief
Veil all in gloom;
Left desolate of real good,
Within this cheerless solitude
No pleasures bloom.

"Thy pilgrimage begins in tears,
And ends in bitter doubts and fears,
Or dark despair;
Midway so many toils appear,
That he who lingers longest here
Knows most of care.

"Thy goods are bought with many a groan,
By the hot sweat of toil alone,
And weary hearts;
Fleet-footed is the approach of woe,
But with a lingering step and slow
Its form departs."

Page 31. *King Christian.*

Nils Juel was a celebrated Danish Admiral, and Peder Wessel, a Vice-Admiral, who for his great prowess received the popular title of Tordenskiold, or Thundershield. In childhood he was a tailor's apprentice, and rose to his high rank before the age of twenty-eight, when he was killed in a duel.

Page 41. *The Skeleton in Armor.*

This ballad was suggested to me while riding on the sea-shore at Newport. A year or two previous a skeleton had been dug up at Fall River, clad in broken and corroded armor; and the idea occurred to me of connecting it with the Round Tower at Newport, generally known hitherto as the Old Windmill,

114

though now claimed by the Danes as a work of their early ancestors. Professor Rafn, in the "Mémoires de la Société Royale des Antiquaires du Nord," for 1838–1839, says: —

"There is no mistaking in this instance the style in which the more ancient stone edifices of the North were constructed, — the style which belongs to the Roman or Ante-Gothic architecture, and which, especially after the time of Charlemagne, diffused itself from Italy over the whole of the West and North of Europe, where it continued to predominate until the close of the twelfth century, — that style which some authors have, from one of its most striking characteristics, called the round arch style, the same which in England is denominated Saxon and sometimes Norman architecture.

"On the ancient structure in Newport there are no ornaments remaining, which might possibly have served to guide us in assigning the probable date of its erection. That no vestige whatever is found of the pointed arch, nor any approximation to it, is indicative of an earlier rather than of a later period. From such characteristics as remain, however, we can scarcely form any other inference than one, in which I am persuaded that all who are familiar with Old-Northern architecture will concur, THAT THIS BUILDING WAS ERECTED AT A PERIOD DECIDEDLY NOT LATER THAN THE TWELFTH CENTURY. This remark applies, of course, to the original building only, and not to the alterations that it subsequently received; for there are several such alterations in the upper part of the building, which cannot be mistaken, and which were most likely occasioned by its being adapted in modern times to various uses; for example, as the substructure of a windmill, and latterly as a hay magazine. To the same times may be referred the windows, the fireplace, and the apertures made above the columns. That this building could not have been erected for a windmill is what an architect will easily discern."

I will not enter into a discussion of the point. It is sufficiently well established for the purpose of a ballad; though doubtless many a citizen of Newport who has passed his days within sight of the Round Tower will be ready to exclaim, with Sancho: "God bless me! did I not warn you to have a care of what you were doing, for that it was nothing but a windmill; and nobody could mistake it, but one who had the like in his head."

Page 44. *Skoal!*

In Scandinavia, this is the customary salutation when drinking a health. I have slightly changed the orthography of the word, in order to preserve the correct pronunciation.

Page 46. *The Luck of Edenhall.*

The tradition upon which this ballad is founded, and the "shards of the Luck of Edenhall," still exist in England. The goblet is in the possession of Sir Christopher Musgrave, Bart., of Eden Hall, Cumberland; and is not so entirely shattered as the ballad leaves it.

Page 46. *The Elected Knight.*

This strange and somewhat mystical ballad is from Nyerup and Rahbek's "Danske Viser" of the Middle Ages. It seems to refer to the first preaching of Christianity in the North, and to the institution of Knight-Errantry. The three maidens I suppose to be Faith, Hope, and Charity. The irregularities of the original have been carefully preserved in the translation.

Page 48. *The Children of the Lord's Supper.*

There is something patriarchal still lingering about rural life in Sweden, which renders it a fit theme for song. Almost primeval simplicity reigns over that Northern land, — almost primeval solitude and stillness. You pass out from the gate of the city, and as if by magic the scene changes to a wild, woodland landscape. Around you are forests of fir. Overhead hang the long, fan-like branches, trailing with moss, and heavy with red and blue cones. Under foot is a carpet of yellow leaves; and the air is warm and balmy. On a wooden bridge you cross a little silver stream; and anon come forth into a pleasant and sunny land of farms. Wooden fences divide the adjoining fields. Across the road are gates, which are opened by troops of children. The peasants take off their hats as you pass; you sneeze, and they cry, "God bless you!" The houses in the villages and smaller towns are all built of hewn timber, and for the most part painted red. The floors of the taverns are strewn with the fragrant tips of fir boughs. In many villages there are no taverns, and the peasants take turns in receiving travellers. The thrifty housewife shows you into the best chamber, the walls of which are hung round with rude pictures from the Bible; and brings you her heavy silver spoons, — an heirloom, — to dip the curdled milk from the pan. You have oaten cakes baked some months before, or bread with anise-seed and coriander in it, or perhaps a little pine bark.

Meanwhile the sturdy husband has brought his horses from the plough, and harnessed them to your carriage. Solitary travellers come and go in uncouth one-horse chaises. Most of them have pipes in their mouths, and, hanging around their necks in front, a leather wallet, in which they carry tobacco, and the great banknotes of the country, as large as your two hands. You meet, also, groups of Dalekarlian peasant-women, travelling homeward or townward in pursuit of work. They walk barefoot, carrying in their hands their shoes, which have high heels under the hollow of the foot, and soles of birch bark.

Frequent, too, are the village churches, standing by the roadside, each in its own little Garden of Gethsemane. In the parish register great events are doubtless recorded. Some old king was christened or buried in that church; and a little sexton, with a rusty key, shows you the baptismal font, or the coffin. In the churchyard are a few flowers, and much green grass; and daily the shadow of the church spire, with its long, tapering finger, counts the tombs, representing a dial-plate of human life, on which the hours and minutes are the graves of men. The stones are flat, and large, and low, and perhaps sunken, like the roofs of old houses. On some are armorial bearings; on others only the initials of the poor tenants, with a date, as on the roofs of Dutch cottages. They all sleep with their heads to the westward. Each held a lighted taper in his hand when he died; and in his coffin were placed his little heart-treasures, and a piece of money for his last journey. Babes that came lifeless into the world were carried in the arms of gray-haired old men to the only cradle they ever slept in; and in the shroud of the dead mother were laid the little garments of the child that lived and died in her bosom. And over this scene the village pastor looks from his window in the stillness of midnight, and says in his heart, "How quietly they rest, all the departed!"

Near the churchyard gate stands a poorbox, fastened to a post by iron bands, and secured by a padlock, with a sloping wooden roof to keep off the rain. If it be Sunday, the peasants sit on the church steps and con their psalm-books. Others are coming down the road with their beloved pastor, who talks to them of holy things from beneath his broad-brimmed hat. He speaks of fields and harvests, and of the parable of the sower that went forth to sow. He leads them to the Good Shepherd, and to the pleasant pastures of the spirit-land. He is their patriarch, and, like Melchizedek, both priest and king, though he has no other throne than the church pulpit. The women carry psalm-books in their hands, wrapped in silk handkerchiefs, and listen devoutly to the good man's words. But the young men, like Gallio, care for none of these things. They are busy counting the plaits in the kirtles of the peasant-girls, their number being an indication of the wearer's wealth. It may end in a wedding.

I will endeavor to describe a village wedding in Sweden. It shall be in summer-time, that there may be flowers, and in a southern province, that the bride may be fair. The early song of the lark and of chanticleer are mingling in the clear morning air, and the sun, the heavenly bridegroom with golden locks, arises in the east, just as our earthly bridegroom with yellow hair arises in the south. In the yard there is a sound of voices and trampling of hoofs, and horses are led forth and saddled. The steed that is to bear the bridegroom has a bunch of flowers upon his forehead, and a garland of corn-flowers around his neck. Friends from the neighboring farms come riding in, their blue cloaks streaming to the wind; and finally the happy bridegroom, with a whip in his hand, and a monstrous nosegay in the breast of his black jacket, comes forth from his chamber; and then to horse and away, towards the village where the bride already sits and waits.

Foremost rides the spokesman, followed by some half-dozen village musicians. Next comes the bridegroom between his two groomsmen, and then forty or fifty friends and wedding guests, half of them perhaps with pistols and guns in their hands. A kind of baggage-wagon brings up the rear, laden with food and drink for these merry pilgrims. At the entrance of every village stands a triumphal arch, adorned with flowers and ribbons and evergreens; and as they pass beneath it the wedding guests fire a salute, and the whole procession stops. And straight from every pocket flies a black-jack, filled with punch or brandy. It is passed from hand to hand among the crowd; provisions are brought from the wagon, and after eating and drinking and hurrahing the procession moves forward again, and at length draws near the house of the bride. Four heralds ride forward to announce that a knight and his attendants are in the neighboring forest, and pray for hospitality. "How many are you?" asks the bride's father. "At least three hundred," is the answer; and to this the host replies, "Yes; were you seven times as many, you should all be welcome; and in token thereof receive this cup." Whereupon each herald receives a can of ale; and soon after the whole jovial company comes storming into the farmer's yard, and, riding round the May-pole, which stands in the centre, alights amid a grand salute and flourish of music.

In the hall sits the bride, with a crown upon her head and a tear in her eye, like the Virgin Mary in old church paintings. She is dressed in a red bodice and kirtle with loose linen sleeves. There is a gilded belt around her waist; and around her neck strings of golden beads, and a golden chain. On the crown rests a wreath of wild roses, and below it another of cypress. Loose over her shoulders falls her flaxen hair; and her blue innocent eyes are fixed upon the ground. O thou good soul! thou hast hard hands, but a soft heart! Thou art poor. The very ornaments thou wearest are not thine. They have been hired for this great day. Yet art thou rich; rich in health, rich in hope, rich in thy first, young, fervent love. The blessing of Heaven be upon thee! So thinks the parish priest, as he joins together the hands of bride and bridegroom, saying in deep, solemn tones, "I give thee in marriage this damsel, to be thy wedded wife in all honor, and to share the half of thy bed, thy lock and key, and every third penny which you two may possess, or may inherit, and all the rights which Upland's laws provide, and the holy King Erik gave."

The dinner is now served, and the bride sits between the bridegroom and the priest. The spokesman delivers an oration after the ancient custom of his fathers. He interlards it well with quotations from the Bible; and invites the Saviour to be present at this marriage feast, as he was at the marriage feast in Cana of Galilee. The table is not sparingly set forth. Each makes a long arm and the feast goes cheerly on. Punch and brandy pass round between the courses, and here and there a pipe is smoked while waiting for the next dish. They sit long at table; but, as all things must have an end, so must a Swedish dinner. Then the dance begins. It is led off by the bride and the priest, who perform a solemn minuet together. Not till after midnight comes the last dance. The girls form a ring around the bride, to keep her from the hands of the married women, who endeavor to break through the magic circle, and seize their new sister. After long struggling they succeed; and the crown is taken from her head and the jewels from her neck, and her bodice is unlaced and her kirtle taken off; and like a vestal virgin clad all in white she goes, but it is to her marriage chamber, not to her grave; and the wedding guests follow her with lighted candles in their hands. And this is a village bridal.

Nor must I forget the suddenly changing seasons of the Northern clime. There is no long and lingering spring, unfolding leaf and blossom one by one; no long and lingering autumn, pompous with many-colored leaves and the glow of Indian summers. But winter and summer are wonderful, and pass into each other. The quail has hardly ceased piping in the corn, when winter from the folds of trailing clouds sows broadcast over the land snow, icicles, and rat-

tling hail. The days wane apace. Erelong the sun
hardly rises above the horizon, or does not rise at all.
The moon and the stars shine through the day; only,
at noon, they are pale and wan, and in the southern
sky a red, fiery glow, as of sunset, burns along the
horizon, and then goes out. And pleasantly under
the silver moon, and under the silent, solemn stars,
ring the steel-shoes of the skaters on the frozen sea,
and voices, and the sound of bells.

And now the Northern Lights begin to burn,
faintly at first, like sunbeams playing in the waters
of the blue sea. Then a soft crimson glow tinges the
heavens. There is a blush on the cheek of night.
The colors come and go, and change from crimson to gold, from gold to crimson. The snow is
stained with rosy light. Two-fold from the zenith,
east and west, flames a fiery sword; and a broad
band passes athwart the heavens like a summer sunset. Soft purple clouds come sailing over the sky,
and through their vapory folds the winking stars
shine white as silver. With such pomp as this is
Merry Christmas ushered in, though only a single
star heralded the first Christmas. And in memory of
that day the Swedish peasants dance on straw; and
the peasant-girls throw straws at the timbered roof
of the hall, and for every one that sticks in a crack
shall a groomsman come to their wedding. Merry
Christmas indeed! For pious souls there shall be
church songs and sermons, but for Swedish peasants,
brandy and nut-brown ale in wooden bowls; and the
great Yule-cake crowned with a cheese, and garlanded
with apples, and upholding a three-armed candlestick
over the Christmas feast. They may tell tales, too,
of Jöns Lundsbracka, and Lunkenfus, and the great
Riddar Finke of Pingsdaga.[1]

And now the glad, leafy midsummer, full of blossoms and the song of nightingales, is come! Saint
John has taken the flowers and festival of heathen
Balder; and in every village there is a May-pole
fifty feet high, with wreaths and roses and ribbons
streaming in the wind, and a noisy weather-cock on
top, to tell the village whence the wind cometh and
whither it goeth. The sun does not set till ten o'clock
at night; and the children are at play in the streets
an hour later. The windows and doors are all open,
and you may sit and read till midnight without a candle. Oh, how beautiful is the summer night, which
is not night, but a sunless yet unclouded day, descending upon earth with dews and shadows and refreshing
coolness! How beautiful the long, mild twilight,
which like a silver clasp unites to-day with yesterday! How beautiful the silent hour, when Morning
and Evening thus sit together, hand in hand, beneath

[1] Titles of Swedish popular tales.

the starless sky of midnight! From the church-
tower in the public square the bell tolls the hour,
with a soft, musical chime; and the watchman, whose
watch-tower is the belfry, blows a blast in his horn,
for each stroke of the hammer, and four times, to the
four corners of the heavens, in a sonorous voice he
chants, —

> "Ho! watchman, ho!
> Twelve is the clock!
> God keep our town
> From fire and brand
> And hostile hand!
> Twelve is the clock!"

From his swallow's nest in the belfry he can see the
sun all night long; and further north the priest stands
at his door in the warm midnight, and lights his pipe
with a common burning-glass.

Page 49. *The Feast of the Leafy Pavilions.*
In Swedish, *Löfhyddohögtiden*, the Leafhuts'-high-
tide.

Page 49. *Hörberg.*
The peasant-painter of Sweden. He is known
chiefly by his altar-pieces in the village churches.

Page 49. *Wallín.*
A distinguished pulpit-orator and poet. He is
particularly remarkable for the beauty and sublimity
of his psalms.

Page 77. *As Lope says.*

> "La cólera
> De un Español sentado no se templa,
> Sino le representan en dos horas
> Hasta el final juicio desde el Génesis."
> *Lope de Vega.*

Page 79. *Abrenuncio Satanas!*
"Digo, Señora, respondió Sancho, lo que tengo
dicho, que de los azotes abernuncio. Abrenuncio,
habeis de decir, Sancho, y no como decis, dijo el Du-
que." — *Don Quixote*, Part II., ch. 35.

Page 85. *Fray Carrillo.*
The allusion here is to a Spanish Epigram.

> "Siempre Fray Carrillo estás
> Cansándonos acá fuera;
> Quien en tu celda estuviera
> Para no verte jamas!"
> *Böhl de Faber. Floresta*, No. 611.

Page 85. *Padre Francisco.*
This is from an Italian popular song.

> "'Padre Francesco,
> Padre Francesco!'
> — Cosa volete del Padre Francesco? —
> 'V'è una bella ragazzina
> Che si vuole confessar!'
> Fatte l' entrare, fatte l' entrare!
> Che la voglio confessare."
> *Kopisch. Volksthümliche Poesien aus allen Mundarten*
> *Italiens und seiner Inseln*, p. 194.

Page 86. *Ave! cujus calcem clare.*

From a monkish hymn of the twelfth century, in Sir Alexander Croke's " Essay on the Origin, Progress, and Decline of Rhyming Latin Verse," p. 109.

Page 89. *The gold of the Busné.*

Busné is the name given by the Gypsies to all who are not of their race.

Page 90. *Count of the Calés.*

The Gypsies call themselves Calés. See Borrow's valuable and extremely interesting work, " The Zincali; or an Account of the Gypsies in Spain." London, 1841.

Page 92. *Asks if his money-bags would rise.*

" ¿ Y volviéndome á un lado, ví á un Avariento, que estaba preguntando á otro, (que por haber sido embalsamado, y estar léxos sus tripas no hablaba, porque no habian llegado si habian de resucitar aquel dia todos los enterrados) si resucitarian unos bolsones suyos ? " — *El Sueño de las Calaveras.*

Page 92. *And amen! said my Cid the Campeador.*

A line from the ancient " Poema del Cid."

> " Amen, dixo Mio Cid el Campeador."
>
> Line 3044.

Page 92. *The river of his thoughts.*

This expression is from Dante : —

> " Si che chiaro
> Per essa scenda della mente il fiume."

Byron has likewise used the expression ; though I do not recollect in which of his poems.

Page 92. *Mari Franca.*

A common Spanish proverb, used to turn aside a question one does not wish to answer : —

> " Porque casó Mari Franca
> Quatro leguas de Salamanca."

Page 93. *Ay, soft, emerald eyes.*

The Spaniards, with good reason, consider this color of the eye as beautiful, and celebrate it in song; as, for example, in the well-known " Villancico : " —

> " Ay ojuelos verdes,
> Ay los mis ojuelos,
> Ay hagan los cielos
> Que de mí te acuerdes!
>
> .   .   .   .
>
> Tengo confianza
> De mis verdes ojos."
>
> *Böhl de Faber. Floresta*, No. 255.

Dante speaks of Beatrice's eyes as emeralds. " Purgatorio," xxxi. 116. Lami says, in his " Annotazioni," " Erano i suoi occhi d' un turchino verdiccio, simile a quel del mare."

Page 94. *The Avenging Child.*

See the ancient Ballads of " El Infante Vengador," and " Calaynos."

Page 94. *All are sleeping.*

From the Spanish. Böhl de Faber. " Floresta," No. 282.

Page 100. *Good night.*

From the Spanish ; as are likewise the songs immediately following, and that which commences the first scene of Act. III.

Page 109. *The evil eye.*

" In the Gitano language, casting the evil eye is called *Querelar nasula*, which simply means making sick, and which, according to the common superstition, is accomplished by casting an evil look at people, especially children, who, from the tenderness of their constitution, are supposed to be more easily blighted than those of a more mature age. After receiving the evil glance, they fall sick, and die in a few hours.

" The Spaniards have very little to say respecting the evil eye, though the belief in it is very prevalent, especially in Andalusia, amongst the lower orders. A stag's horn is considered a good safeguard, and on that account a small horn, tipped with silver, is frequently attached to the children's necks by means of a cord braided from the hair of a black mare's tail. Should the evil glance be cast, it is imagined that the horn receives it, and instantly snaps asunder. Such horns may be purchased in some of the silversmiths' shops at Seville." — BORROW's *Zincali*, vol. i., ch. 9.

Page 109. *On the top of a mountain I stand.*

This and the following scraps of song are from Borrow's " Zincali ; or an Account of the Gypsies in Spain."

The Gypsy words in the same scene may be thus interpreted : —

John-Dorados, pieces of gold.

Pigeon, a simpleton.

In your morocco, stripped.

Doves, sheets.

Moon, a shirt.

Chirelin, a thief.

Murcigalleros, those who steal at nightfall.

Rastilleros, footpads.

Hermit, highway-robber.

Planets, candles.

Commandments, the fingers.

Saint Martin asleep, to rob a person asleep.

Lanterns, eyes.

Goblin, police officer.

Papagayo, a spy.

Vineyards and Dancing John, to take flight.

Page 114. *If thou art sleeping, maiden.*

From the Spanish ; as is likewise the song of the Contrabandista on page 115.

Page 120. *All the Foresters of Flanders.*

The title of Foresters was given to the early governors of Flanders, appointed by the kings of France. Lyderick du Bucq, in the days of Clotaire the Second, was the first of them; and Beaudoin Bras-de-Fer, who stole away the fair Judith, daughter of Charles the Bald, from the French court, and married her in Bruges, was the last. After him the title of Forester was changed to that of Count. Philippe d'Alsace, Guy de Dampierre, and Louis de Crécy, coming later in the order of time, were therefore rather Counts than Foresters. Philippe went twice to the Holy Land as a Crusader, and died of the plague at St. Jean-d'Acre, shortly after the capture of the city by the Christians. Guy de Dampierre died in the prison of Compiégne. Louis de Crécy was son and successor of Robert de Béthune, who strangled his wife, Yolande de Bourgogne, with the bridle of his horse, for having poisoned, at the age of eleven years, Charles, his son by his first wife, Blanche d'Anjou.

Page 120. *Stately dames, like queens attended.*

When Philippe-le-Bel, king of France, visited Flanders with his queen, she was so astonished at the magnificence of the dames of Bruges, that she exclaimed: "Je croyais être seule reine ici, mais il paraît que ceux de Flandre qui se trouvent dans nos prisons sont tous des princes, car leurs femmes sont habillées comme des princesses et des reines."

When the burgomasters of Ghent, Bruges, and Ypres went to Paris to pay homage to King John, in 1351, they were received with great pomp and distinction; but, being invited to a festival, they observed that their seats at table were not furnished with cushions; whereupon, to make known their displeasure at this want of regard to their dignity, they folded their richly embroidered cloaks and seated themselves upon them. On rising from table, they left their cloaks behind them, and, being informed of their apparent forgetfulness, Simon van Eertrycke, burgomaster of Bruges, replied, "We Flemings are not in the habit of carrying away our cushions after dinner."

Page 120. *Knights who bore the Fleece of Gold.*

Philippe de Bourgogne, surnamed Le Bon, espoused Isabella of Portugal on the 10th of January, 1430; and on the same day instituted the famous order of the Fleece of Gold.

Page 121. *I beheld the gentle Mary.*

Marie de Valois, Duchess of Burgundy, was left by the death of her father, Charles le Téméraire, at the age of twenty, the richest heiress of Europe. She came to Bruges, as Countess of Flanders, in 1477, and in the same year was married by proxy to the Archduke Maximilian. According to the custom of the time, the Duke of Bavaria, Maximilian's substitute, slept with the princess. They were both in complete dress, separated by a naked sword, and attended by four armed guards. Marie was adored by her subjects for her gentleness and her many other virtues.

Maximilian was son of the Emperor Frederick the Third, and is the same person mentioned afterwards in the poem of "Nuremberg" as the Kaiser Maximilian, and the hero of Pfinzing's poem of "Teuerdank." Having been imprisoned by the revolted burghers of Bruges, they refused to release him, till he consented to kneel in the public square, and to swear on the Holy Evangelists and the body of Saint Donatus that he would not take vengeance upon them for their rebellion.

Page 121. *The bloody battle of the Spurs of Gold.*

This battle, the most memorable in Flemish history, was fought under the walls of Courtray, on the 11th of July, 1302, between the French and the Flemings, the former commanded by Robert, Comte d'Artois, and the latter by Guillaume de Juliers, and Jean, Comte de Namur. The French army was completely routed, with a loss of twenty thousand infantry and seven thousand cavalry; among whom were sixty-three princes, dukes, and counts, seven hundred lords-banneret, and eleven hundred noblemen. The flower of the French nobility perished on that day; to which history has given the name of the *Journee des Eperons d'Or*, from the great number of golden spurs found on the field of battle. Seven hundred of them were hung up as a trophy in the church of Notre Dame de Courtray; and, as the cavaliers of that day wore but a single spur each, these vouched to God for the violent and bloody death of seven hundred of his creatures.

Page 121. *Saw the fight at Minnewater.*

When the inhabitants of Bruges were digging a canal at Minnewater, to bring the waters of the Lys from Deynze to their city, they were attacked and routed by the citizens of Ghent, whose commerce would have been much injured by the canal. They were led by Jean Lyons, captain of a military company at Ghent, called the *Chaperons Blancs.* He had great sway over the turbulent populace, who, in those prosperous times of the city, gained an easy livelihood by laboring two or three days in the week, and had the remaining four or five to devote to public affairs. The fight at Minnewater was followed by open rebellion against Louis de Maele, the Count of Flanders and Protector of Bruges. His superb château of Wondelghem was pillaged and burnt; and the insurgents forced the gates of Bruges, and entered in triumph, with Lyons mounted at their head. A few days afterwards he died suddenly, perhaps by poison.

Meanwhile the insurgents received a check at the village of Nevèle; and two hundred of them perished in the church, which was burned by the Count's orders. One of the chiefs, Jean de Lannoy, took refuge in the belfry. From the summit of the tower he held forth his purse filled with gold, and begged for deliverance. It was in vain. His enemies cried to him from below to save himself as best he might; and, half suffocated with smoke and flame, he threw himself from the tower and perished at their feet. Peace was soon afterwards established, and the Count retired to faithful Bruges.

Page 121. *The Golden Dragon's nest.*

The Golden Dragon, taken from the church of St. Sophia, at Constantinople, in one of the Crusades, and placed on the belfry of Bruges, was afterwards transported to Ghent by Philip van Artevelde, and still adorns the belfry of that city.

The inscription on the alarm-bell at Ghent is, "*Mynen naem is Roland; als ik klep is er brand, and als ik luy is er victorie in het land.*" My name is Roland; when I toll there is fire, and when I ring there is victory in the land.

Page 123. *That their great imperial city stretched its hand through every clime.*

An old popular proverb of the town runs thus:—

> "*Nürnberg's Hand*
> *Geht durch alle Land.*"

> Nuremberg's hand
> Goes through every land.

Page 124. *Sat the poet Melchior singing Kaiser Maximilian's praise.*

Melchior Pfinzing was one of the most celebrated German poets of the sixteenth century. The hero of his "Teuerdank" was the reigning emperor, Maximilian; and the poem was to the Germans of that day what the "Orlando Furioso" was to the Italians. Maximilian is mentioned before, in the "Belfry of Bruges." See page 121.

Page 124. *In the church of sainted Sebald sleeps enshrined his holy dust.*

The tomb of Saint Sebald, in the church which bears his name, is one of the richest works of art in Nuremberg. It is of bronze, and was cast by Peter Vischer and his sons, who labored upon it thirteen years. It is adorned with nearly one hundred figures, among which those of the Twelve Apostles are conspicuous for size and beauty.

Page 124. *In the church of sainted Lawrence stands a pix of sculpture rare.*

This pix, or tabernacle for the vessels of the sacra-

ment, is by the hand of Adam Kraft. It is an exquisite piece of sculpture in white stone, and rises to the height of sixty-four feet. It stands in the choir, whose richly painted windows cover it with varied colors.

Page 124. *Wisest of the Twelve Wise Masters.*

The Twelve Wise Masters was the title of the original corporation of the Mastersingers. Hans Sachs, the cobbler of Nuremberg, though not one of the original Twelve, was the most renowned of the Mastersingers, as well as the most voluminous. He flourished in the sixteenth century; and left behind him thirty-four folio volumes of manuscript, containing two hundred and eight plays, one thousand and seven hundred comic tales, and between four and five thousand lyric poems.

Page 125. *As in Adam Puschman's song.*

Adam Puschman, in his poem on the death of Hans Sachs, describes him as he appeared in a vision:—

> "An old man,
> Gray and white, and dove-like,
> Who had, in sooth, a great beard,
> And read in a fair, great book,
> Beautiful with golden clasps."

Page 131. *The Occultation of Orion.*

Astronomically speaking, this title is incorrect; as I apply to a constellation what can properly be applied to some of its stars only. But my observation is made from the hill of song, and not from that of science; and will, I trust, be found sufficiently accurate for the present purpose.

Page 133. *Who, unharmed, on his tusks once caught the bolts of the thunder.*

"A delegation of warriors from the Delaware tribe having visited the governor of Virginia, during the Revolution, on matters of business, after these had been discussed and settled in council, the governor asked them some questions relative to their country, and among others, what they knew or had heard of the animal whose bones were found at the Saltlicks on the Ohio. Their chief speaker immediately put himself into an attitude of oratory, and, with a pomp suited to what he conceived the elevation of his subject, informed him that it was a tradition handed down from their fathers, 'that in ancient times a herd of these tremendous animals came to the Big-bone licks, and began an universal destruction of the bear, deer, elks, buffaloes, and other animals which had been created for the use of the Indians: that the Great Man above, looking down and seeing this, was so enraged that he seized his lightning, descended on the earth, seated himself on a neighboring mountain, on a rock of which his seat and the print of his feet are still to be seen, and hurled his bolts among them till the whole were slaughtered, except the big bull, who, presenting his forehead to the shafts, shook them off as they fell; but missing one at length, it wounded him in the side; whereon, springing round, he bounded over the Ohio, over the Wabash, the Illinois, and finally over the great lakes, where he is living at this day.'" — JEFFERSON'S *Notes on Virginia*, Query VI.

Page 136. *Walter von der Vogelweid.*

Walter von der Vogelweid, or Bird-Meadow, was one of the principal Minnesingers of the thirteenth century. He triumphed over Heinrich von Ofterdingen in that poetic contest at Wartburg Castle, known in literary history as the War of Wartburg.

Page 140. *Like imperial Charlemagne.*

Charlemagne may be called by preëminence the monarch of farmers. According to the German tradition, in seasons of great abundance, his spirit crosses the Rhine on a golden bridge at Bingen, and blesses the cornfields and the vineyards. During his lifetime, he did not disdain, says Montesquieu, "to sell the eggs from the farmyards of his domains, and the superfluous vegetables of his gardens; while he distributed among his people the wealth of the Lombards and the immense treasures of the Huns."

Page 193.

> *Behold, at last,*
> *Each tall and tapering mast*
> *Is swung into its place.*

I wish to anticipate a criticism on this passage, by stating that sometimes, though not usually, vessels are launched fully sparred and rigged. I have availed myself of the exception as better suited to my purposes than the general rule; but the reader will see that it is neither a blunder nor a poetic license. On this subject a friend in Portland, Maine, writes me thus: —

"In this State, and also, I am told, in New York, ships are sometimes rigged upon the stocks, in order to save time, or to make a show. There was a fine, large ship launched last summer at Ellsworth, fully sparred and rigged. Some years ago a ship was launched here, with her rigging, spars, sails, and cargo aboard. She sailed the next day and — was never heard of again! I hope this will not be the fate of your poem!"

Page 198. *Sir Humphrey Gilbert.*

"When the wind abated and the vessels were near enough, the Admiral was seen constantly sitting in the stern, with a book in his hand. On the 9th of September he was seen for the last time, and was heard by the people of the *Hind* to say, 'We are as near heaven by sea as by land.' In the following night, the lights of the ship suddenly disappeared. The people in the other vessel kept a good lookout for him during the remainder of the voyage. On the 22d of September they arrived, through much tempest and peril, at Falmouth. But nothing more was seen or heard of the Admiral." — BELKNAP'S *American Biography*, i. 203.

Page 211. *The Blind Girl of Castèl-Cuillè.*

Jasmin, the author of this beautiful poem, is to the South of France what Burns is to the South of Scotland, — the representative of the heart of the people, — one of those happy bards who are born with their mouths full of birds (*la bouco pleno d' aouzelous*). He has written his own biography in a poetic form, and the simple narrative of his poverty, his struggles, and his triumphs is very touching. He still lives at Agen, on the Garonne; and long may he live there to delight his native land with native songs!

The following description of his person and way of life is taken from the graphic pages of "Béarn and the Pyrenees," by Louisa Stuart Costello, whose charming pen has done so much to illustrate the French provinces and their literature.

"At the entrance of the promenade, Du Gravier, is a row of small houses, — some *cafés*, others shops, the indication of which is a painted cloth placed across the way, with the owner's name in bright gold letters, in the manner of the arcades in the streets, and their announcements. One of the most glaring of these was, we observed, a bright blue flag, bordered with gold; on which, in large gold letters, appeared the name of 'Jasmin, Coiffeur.' We entered, and were welcomed by a smiling, dark-eyed woman, who informed us that her husband was busy at that moment dressing a customer's hair, but he was desirous to receive us, and begged we would walk into his parlor at the back of the shop.

. . . .

"She exhibited to us a laurel crown of gold, of delicate workmanship, sent from the city of Clemence Isaure, Toulouse, to the poet; who will probably one day take his place in the *capitoul*. Next came a golden cup, with an inscription in his honor, given by the citizens of Auch; a gold watch, chain, and seals, sent by the king, Louis Philippe; an emerald ring worn and presented by the lamented Duke of Orleans; a pearl pin, by the graceful Duchess, who, on the poet's visit to Paris accompanied by his son, received him in the words he puts into the mouth of Henri Quatre: —

> 'Brabes Gascous!
> A moun amou per bous aou dibes creyre:
> Benès! benès! ey plazé de bous beyre:
> Aproucha bous!'

A fine service of linen, the offering of the town of Pau, after its citizens had given fétes in his honor, and loaded him with caresses and praises; and knick-knacks and jewels of all descriptions, offered to him by lady-ambassadresses and great lords; English 'misses'; and 'miladis' and French, and foreigners of all nations who did or did not understand Gascon.

"All this, though startling, was not convincing; Jasmin, the barber, might only be a fashion, a *furore*, a caprice, after all; and it was evident that he knew how to get up a scene well. When we had become nearly tired of looking over these tributes to his genius, the door opened, and the poet himself appeared, His manner was free and unembarrassed, well-bred, and lively; he received our compliments naturally, and like one accustomed to homage; said he was ill, and unfortunately too hoarse to read anything to us, or should have been delighted to do so. He spoke with a broad Gascon accent, and very rapidly and eloquently; ran over the story of his successes; told us that his grandfather had been a beggar, and all his family very poor; that he was now as rich as he wished to be; his son placed in a good position at Nantes; then showed us his son's picture, and spoke of his disposition; to which his brisk little wife added, that, though no fool, he had not his father's genius, to which truth Jasmin assented as a matter of course. I told him of having seen mention made of him in an English review; which he said had been sent him by Lord Durham, who had paid him a visit; and I then spoke of 'Me cal mouri' as known to me. This was enough to make him forget his hoarseness and every other evil; it would never do for me to imagine that that little song was his best composition; it was merely his first; he must try to read to me a little of 'L'Abuglo,' — a few verses of 'Francouneto.' 'You will be charmed,' said he; 'but if I were well, and you would give me the pleasure of your company for some time, if you were not merely running through Agen, I would kill you with weeping, — I would make you die with distress for my poor Margarido, — my pretty Francouneto!'

"He caught up two copies of his book, from a pile lying on the table, and making us sit close to him he pointed out the French translation on one side, which he told us to follow while he read in Gascon. He began in a rich, soft voice, and as he advanced, the surprise of Hamlet on hearing the player-king recite the disasters of Hecuba was but a type of ours, to find ourselves carried away by the spell of his enthusiasm. His eyes swam in tears; he became pale and red; he trembled; he recovered himself; his face was now joyous, now exulting, gay, jocose; in fact, he was twenty actors in one; he rang the changes from Rachel to Bouffé; and he finished by delighting

us, besides beguiling us of our tears, and overwhelming us with astonishment.

"He would have been a treasure on the stage; for he is still, though his first youth is past, remarkably good-looking and striking; with black, sparkling, eyes, of intense expression; a fine, ruddy complexion; a countenance of wondrous mobility; a good figure; and action full of fire and grace; he has handsome hands, which he uses with infinite effect; and, on the whole, he is the best actor of the kind I ever saw. I could now quite understand what a troubadour or *jongleur* might be, and I look upon Jasmin as a revived specimen of that extinct race. Such as he is might have been Gaucelm Faidit, of Avignon, the friend of Cœur de Lion, who lamented the death of the hero in such moving strains; such might have been Bernard de Ventadour, who sang the praises of Queen Elinore's beauty; such Geoffrey Rudel, of Blaye, on his own Garonne; such the wild Vidal; certain it is, that none of these troubadours of old could more move, by their singing or reciting, than Jasmin, in whom all their long-smothered fire and traditional magic seems re-illumined.

"We found we had stayed hours instead of minutes with the poet; but he would not hear of any apology, — only regretted that his voice was so out of tune, in consequence of a violent cold, under which he was really laboring, and hoped to see us again. He told us our countrywomen of Pau had laden him with kindness and attention, and spoke with such enthusiasm of the beauty of certain 'misses,' that I feared his little wife would feel somewhat piqued; but, on the contrary, she stood by, smiling and happy and enjoying the stories of his triumphs. I remarked that he had restored the poetry of the troubadours; asked him if he knew their songs; and said he was worthy to stand at their head. 'I am, indeed, a troubadour,' said he, with energy; 'but I am far beyond them all: they were but beginners; they never composed a poem like my Francouneto! there are no poets in France now, — there cannot be; the language does not admit of it; where is the fire, the spirit, the expression, the tenderness, the force of the Gascon? French is but the ladder to reach to the first floor of Gascon, — how can you get up to a height except by a ladder!'

.   .   .   .

"I returned by Agen, after an absence in the Pyrenees of some months, and renewed my acquaintance with Jasmin and his dark-eyed wife. I did not expect that I should be recognized; but the moment I entered the little shop I was hailed as an old friend. 'Ah!' cried Jasmin, 'enfin la voilà encore!' I could not but be flattered by this recollection, but soon found it was less on my own account that I was thus welcomed, than because a circumstance had occurred to the poet which he thought I could perhaps explain. He produced several French newspapers, in which he pointed out to me an article headed ' Jasmin à Londres ;' being a translation of certain notices of himself, which had appeared in a leading English literary journal. He had, he said, been informed of the honor done him by numerous friends, and assured me his fame had been much spread by this means; and he was so delighted on the occasion, that he had resolved to learn English, in order that he might judge of the translations from his works, which, he had been told, were well done. I enjoyed his surprise while I informed him that I knew who was the reviewer and translator ; and explained the reason for the verses giving pleasure in an English dress to be the superior simplicity of the English language over Modern French, for which he has a great contempt, as unfitted for lyrical composition. He inquired of me respecting Burns, to whom he had been likened ; and begged me to tell him something of Moore. The delight of himself and his wife was amusing, at having discovered a secret which had puzzled them so long.

" He had a thousand things to tell me ; in particular, that he had only the day before received a letter from the Duchess of Orleans, informing him that she had ordered a medal of her late husband to be struck, the first of which would be sent to him : she also announced to him the agreeable news of the king having granted him a pension of a thousand francs. He smiled and wept by turns, as he told us all this ; and declared, much as he was elated at the possession of a sum which made him a rich man for life, the kindness of the Duchess gratified him even more.

" He then made us sit down while he read us two new poems ; both charming, and full of grace and *naïveté ;* and one very affecting, being an address to the king, alluding to the death of his son. As he read, his wife stood by, and fearing we did not quite comprehend his language, she made a remark to that effect : to which he answered impatiently, ' Nonsense, — don't you see they are in tears ? ' This was unanswerable ; and we were allowed to hear the poem to the end ; and I certainly never listened to anything more feelingly and energetically delivered.

" We had much conversation, for he was anxious to detain us, and in the course of it he told me he had been by some accused of vanity. ' Oh,' he rejoined, ' what would you have ! I am a child of nature, and cannot conceal my feelings ; the only difference between me and a man of refinement is, that he knows how to conceal his vanity and exultation at

success, which I let everybody see.' " — *Béarn and the Pyrenees,* i. 369, *et seq.*

Page 218. *A Christmas Carol.*

The following description of Christmas in Burgundy is from M. Fertiault's " Coup d' Œil sur les Noels en Bourgogne," to the Paris edition of " Les Noels Bourguignons de Bernard de la Mennoye (Gui Barôzai)," 1842.

" Every year at the approach of Advent, people refresh their memories, clear their throats, and begin preluding, in the long evenings by the fireside, those carols whose invariable and eternal theme is the coming of the Messiah. They take from old closets pamphlets, little collections begrimed with dust and smoke, to which the press, and sometimes the pen, has consigned these songs ; and as soon as the first Sunday of Advent sounds, they gossip, they gad about, they sit together by the fireside, sometimes at one house, sometimes at another, taking turns in paying for the chestnuts and white wine, but singing with one common voice the grotesque praises of the *Little Jesus.* There are very few villages even, which, during all the evenings of Advent, do not hear some of these curious canticles shouted in their streets, to the nasal drone of bagpipes. In this case the minstrel comes as a reënforcement to the singers at the fireside ; he brings and adds his dose of joy (spontaneous or mercenary, it matters little which) to the joy which breathes around the hearth-stone ; and when the voices vibrate and resound, one voice more is always welcome. There, it is not the purity of the notes which makes the concert, but the quantity, — *non qualitas, sed quantitas ;* then (to finish at once with the minstrel), when the Saviour has at length been born in the manger, and the beautiful Christmas Eve is passed, the rustic piper makes his round among the houses, where every one compliments and thanks him, and, moreover, gives him in small coin the price of the shrill notes with which he has enlivened the evening entertainments.

" More or less until Christmas Eve, all goes on in this way among our devout singers, with the difference of some gallons of wine or some hundreds of chestnuts. But this famous eve once come, the scale is pitched upon a higher key ; the closing evening must be a memorable one. The toilet is begun at nightfall ; then comes the hour of supper, admonishing divers appetites ; and groups, as numerous as possible, are formed to take together this comfortable evening repast. The supper finished, a circle gathers around the hearth, which is arranged and set in order this evening after a particular fashion, and which at a later hour of the night is to become the object of special interest to the children. On the burning brands an enormous log has been placed. This log assuredly does not change its nature, but it changes its name during this evening: it is called the *Suche* (the Yule-log). 'Look you,' say they to the children, 'if you are good this evening, Noel' (for with children one must always personify) 'will rain down sugar-plums in the night.' And the children sit demurely, keeping as quiet as their turbulent little natures will permit. The groups of older persons, not always as orderly as the children, seize this good opportunity to surrender themselves with merry hearts and boisterous voices to the chanted worship of the miraculous Noel. For this final solemnity, they have kept the most powerful, the most enthusiastic, the most electrifying carols. Noel! Noel! Noel! This magic word resounds on all sides: it seasons every sauce, it is served up with every course. Of the thousands of canticles which are heard on this famous eve, ninety-nine in a hundred begin and end with this word; which is, one may say, their Alpha and Omega, their crown and footstool. This last evening, the merry-making is prolonged. Instead of retiring at ten or eleven o'clock, as is generally done on all the preceding evenings, they wait for the stroke of midnight: this word sufficiently proclaims to what ceremony they are going to repair. For ten minutes or a quarter of an hour, the bells have been calling the faithful with a triple-bob-major; and each one, furnished with a little taper streaked with various colors (the Christmas Candle), goes through the crowded streets, where the lanterns are dancing like Will-o'-the-Wisps, at the impatient summons of the multitudinous chimes. It is the Midnight Mass. Once inside the church, they hear with more or less piety the Mass, emblematic of the coming of the Messiah. Then in tumult and great haste they return homeward, always in numerous groups; they salute the Yule-log; they pay homage to the hearth; they sit down at table; and, amid songs which reverberate louder than ever, make this meal of after-Christmas, so long looked for, so cherished, so joyous, so noisy, and which it has been thought fit to call, we hardly know why, *Rossignon*. The supper eaten at nightfall is no impediment, as you may imagine, to the appetite's returning; above all, if the going to and from church has made the devout eaters feel some little shafts of the sharp and biting north-wind. *Rossignon* then goes on merrily, — sometimes far into the morning hours; but, nevertheless, gradually throats grow hoarse, stomachs are filled, the Yule-log burns out, and at last the hour arrives when each one, as best he may, regains his domicile and his bed, and puts with himself between the sheets the material for a good sore-throat, or a good indigestion, for the morrow. Previous to this, care has been taken to place in the slippers, or wooden shoes of the children, the sugar-plums, which shall be for them, on their waking, the welcome fruits of the Christmas log."

In the Glossary, the *Suche*, or Yule-log, is thus defined: —

"This is a huge log, which is placed on the fire on Christmas Eve, and which in Burgundy is called, on this account, *lai Suche de Noei*. Then the father of the family, particularly among the middle classes, sings solemnly Christmas carols with his wife and children, the smallest of whom he sends into the corner to pray that the Yule-log may bear him some sugar-plums. Meanwhile, little parcels of them are placed under each end of the log, and the children come and pick them up, believing, in good faith, that the great log has borne them."

Page 221. THE SONG OF HIAWATHA. This Indian Edda — if I may so call it — is founded on a tradition, prevalent among the North American Indians, of a personage of miraculous birth, who was sent among them to clear their rivers, forests, and fishing-grounds, and to teach them the arts of peace. He was known among different tribes by the several names of Michabou, Chiabo, Manabozo, Tarenyawagon, and Hiawatha. Mr. Schoolcraft gives an account of him in his "Algic Researches," vol. i., p. 134; and in his "History, Condition, and Prospects of the Indian Tribes of the United States," Part III., p. 314, may be found the Iroquois form of the tradition, derived from the verbal narrations of an Onondaga chief.

Into this old tradition I have woven other curious Indian legends, drawn chiefly from the various and valuable writings of Mr. Schoolcraft, to whom the literary world is greatly indebted for his indefatigable zeal in rescuing from oblivion so much of the legendary lore of the Indians.

The scene of the poem is among the Ojibways on the southern shore of Lake Superior, in the region between the Pictured Rocks and the Grand Sable.

VOCABULARY.

Adjidau′mo, *the red squirrel.*
Ahdeek′, *the reindeer.*
Ahkose′win, *fever.*
Ahmeek′, *the beaver.*
Algon′quin, *Ojibway.*
Annemee′kee, *the thunder.*
Apuk′wa, *a bulrush.*
Baim-wa′wa, *the sound of the thunder.*
Bemah′gut, *the grapevine.*
Be′na, *the pheasant.*
Big-Sea-Water, *Lake Superior.*
Bukada′win, *famine.*
Cheemaun′, *a birch canoe.*

Chetowaik', *the plover.*

Chibia'bos, *a musician; friend of Hiawatha; ruler in the Land of Spirits.*

Dahin'da, *the bull-frog.*

Dush-kwo-ne'she, *or* Kwo-ne'she, *the dragon-fly.*

Esa, *shame upon you.*

Ewa-yea', *lullaby.*

Ghee'zis, *the sun.*

Gitche Gu'mee, *the Big-Sea-Water, Lake Superior.*

Gitche Man'ito, *the Great Spirit, the Master of Life.*

Gushkewau', *the darkness.*

Hiawa'tha, *the Wise Man, the Teacher; son of Mudjekeewis, the West-Wind, and Wenonah, daughter of Nokomis.*

Ia'goo, *a great boaster and story-teller.*

Inin'ewug, *men, or pawns in the Game of the Bowl.*

Ishkoodah', *fire; a comet.*

Jee'bi, *a ghost, a spirit.*

Joss'akeed, *a prophet.*

Kabibonok'ka, *the North-Wind.*

Kagh, *the hedgehog.*

Ka'go, *do not.*

Kahgahgee', *the raven.*

Kaw, *no.*

Kaween', *no indeed.*

Kayoshk', *the sea-gull.*

Kee'go, *a fish.*

Keeway'din, *the Northwest Wind, the home-wind.*

Kena'beek, *a, serpent.*

Keneu', *the great war-eagle.*

Keno'zha, *the pickerel.*

Ko'ko-ko'ho, *the owl.*

Kuntasoo', *the Game of Plum-stones.*

Kwa'sind, *the Strong Man.*

Kwo-ne'she, *or* Dush-kwo-ne'she, *the dragon-fly.*

Mahnahbe'zee, *the swan.*

Mahng, *the loon.*

Mahn-go-tay'see, *loon-hearted brave.*

Mahnomo'nee, *wild rice.*

Ma'ma, *the woodpecker.*

Maskeno'zha, *the pike.*

Me'da, *a medicine-man.*

Meenah'ga, *the blueberry.*

Megissog'won, *the great Pearl-Feather, a magician and the Manito of Wealth.*

Meshinau'wa, *a pipe-bearer.*

Minjekah'wun, *Hiawatha's mittens.*

Minneha'ha, *Laughing Water; a water-fall on a stream running into the Mississippi, between Fort Snelling and the Falls of St. Anthony.*

Minneha'ha, *Laughing Water; wife of Hiawatha.*

Minne-wa'wa, *a pleasant sound, as of the wind in the trees.*

Mishe-Mo'kwa, *the Great Bear.*

Mishe-Nah'ma, *the Great Sturgeon.*

Miskodeed', *the Spring Beauty, the Claytonia Virginica.*

Monda'min, *Indian corn.*

Moon of Bright Nights, *April.*

Moon of Leaves, *May.*

Moon of Strawberries, *June.*

Moon of the Falling Leaves, *September.*

Moon of Snow-Shoes, *November.*

Mudjekee'wis, *the West-Wind; father of Hiawatha.*

Mudway-aush'ka, *sound of waves on a shore.*

Mushkoda'sa, *the grouse.*

Na'gow Wudj'oo, *the Sand Dunes of Lake Superior.*

Nah'ma, *the sturgeon.*

Nah'ma-wusk, *spearmint.*

Nee-ba-naw'baigs, *water spirits.*

Nenemoo'sha, *sweetheart.*

Nepah'win, *sleep.*

Noko'mis, *a grandmother; mother of Wenonah.*

No'sa, *my father.*

Nush'ka, *look! look!*

Odah'min, *the strawberry.*

Okahah'wis, *the fresh-water herring.*

Ome'me, *the pigeon.*

Ona'gon, *a bowl.*

Onaway', *awake.*

Ope'chee, *the robin.*

Osse'o, *Son of the Evening Star.*

Owais'sa, *the bluebird.*

Oweenee', *wife of Osseo.*

Ozawa'beek, *a round piece of brass or copper in the Game of the Bowl.*

Pah-puk-kee'na, *the grasshopper.*

Pau'guk, *death.*

Pau-Puk-Kee'wis, *the handsome Yenadizze, the Storm-Fool.*

Pauwa'ting, *Sault Sainte Marie.*

Pe'boan, *Winter.*

Pem'ican, *meat of the deer or buffalo dried and pounded.*

Pezhekee', *the bison.*

Pishnekuh', *the brant.*

Pone'mah, *hereafter.*

Pugasaing', *Game of the Bowl.*

Puggawau'gun, *a war-club.*

Puk-Wudj'ies, *little wild men of the woods; pygmies.*

Sah-sah-je'wun, *rapids.*

Sah'wa, *the perch.*

Segwun', *Spring.*

Sha'da, *the pelican.*

Shahbo'min, *the gooseberry.*

Shah-shah, *long ago.*

Shaugoda'ya, *a coward.*

Shawgashee', *the craw-fish.*

Shawonda'see, *the South-Wind.*

Shaw-shaw, *the swallow.*

Shesh'ebwug, *ducks; pieces in the Game of the Bowl.*

Shin'gebis, *the diver or grebe.*

Showain' neme'shin, *pity me.*

Shuh-shuh'gah, *the blue heron.*

Soan-ge-ta'ha, *strong hearted.*

Subbeka'she, *the spider.*

Sugge'ma, *the mosquito.*

To'tem, *family coat of arms.*

Ugh, *yes.*

Ugudwash', *the sun-fish.*

Unktahee', *the God of Water.*

Wabas'so, *the rabbit; the North.*

Wabe'no, *a magician, a juggler.*

Wabe'no-wusk, *yarrow.*

Wa'bun, *the East-Wind.*

Wa'bun An'nung, *the Star of the East, the Morning Star.*

Wahono'win, *a cry of lamentation.*

Wah-wah-tay'see, *the fire-fly.*

Wam'pum, *beads of shell.*

Waubewy'on, *a white skin wrapper.*

Wa'wa, *the wild goose.*

Waw'beek, *a rock.*

Waw-be-wa'wa, *the white goose.*

Wawonais'sa, *the whippoorwill.*

Way-muk-kwa'na, *the caterpillar.*

Wen'digoes, *giants.*

Weno'nah, *Hiawatha's mother, daughter of Nokomis.*

Yenadiz'ze, *an idler and gambler; an Indian dandy.*

Page 221. *In the Vale of Tawasentha.*

This valley, now called Norman's Kill, is in Albany County, New York.

Page 222. *On the Mountains of the Prairie.*

Mr. Catlin, in his "Letters and Notes on the Manners, Customs, and Condition of the North American Indians," vol. ii., p. 160, gives an interesting account of the *Côteau des Prairies,* and the Red Pipestone Quarry. He says : —

"Here (according to their traditions) happened the mysterious birth of the red pipe, which has blown its fumes of peace and war to the remotest corners of the continent; which has visited every warrior, and passed through its reddened stem the irrevocable oath of war and desolation. And here, also, the peace-breathing calumet was born, and fringed with the eagle's quills, which has shed its thrilling fumes over the land, and soothed the fury of the relentless savage.

"The Great Spirit at an ancient period here called the Indian nations together, and, standing on the precipice of the red pipe-stone rock, broke from its wall a piece, and made a huge pipe by turning it in his hand, which he smoked over them, and to the North, the South, the East, and the West, and told them that this stone was red, — that it was their flesh, — that they must use it for their pipes of peace, — that it belonged to them all, and that the war-club and scalping-knife must not be raised on its ground. At the last whiff of his pipe his head went into a great cloud, and the whole surface of the rock for several miles was melted and glazed; two great ovens were opened beneath, and two women (guardian spirits of the place) entered them in a blaze of fire; and they are heard there yet (Tso-mec-cos-tee and Tso-me-cos-te-won-dee), answering to the invocations of the high-priests or medicine-men, who consult them when they are visitors to this sacred place."

Page 226. *Hark you, Bear! you are a coward.*

This anecdote is from Heckewelder. In his account of the Indian Nations, he describes an Indian hunter as addressing a bear in nearly these words. "I was present," he says, "at the delivery of this curious invective; when the hunter had despatched the bear, I asked him how he thought that poor animal could understand what he said to it. 'Oh,' said he in answer, 'the bear understood me very well; did you not observe how *ashamed* he looked while I was upbraiding him?'" — *Transactions of the American Philosophical Society,* vol. i., p. 240

Page 230. *Hush! the Naked Bear will hear thee!*

Heckewelder, in a letter published in the "Transactions of the American Philosophical Society," vol. iv., p. 260, speaks of this tradition as prevalent among the Mohicans and Delawares.

"Their reports," he says, "run thus : that among all animals that had been formerly in this country, this was the most ferocious; that it was much larger than the largest of the common bears, and remarkably long-bodied; all over (except a spot of hair on its back of a white color) naked. . . . .

"The history of this animal used to be a subject of conversation among the Indians, especially when in the woods a hunting. I have also heard them say to their children when crying : 'Hush! the naked bear will hear you, be upon you, and devour you.'"

Page 235. *Where the Falls of Minnehaha,* etc.

"The scenery about Fort Snelling is rich in beauty. The Falls of St. Anthony are familiar to travellers, and to readers of Indian sketches. Between the fort and these falls are the 'Little Falls,' forty feet in height, on a stream that empties into the Mississippi. The Indians called them Mine-hah-hah, or 'laughing waters.'" — Mrs. EASTMAN'S *Dacotah, or Legends of the Sioux,* Introd., p. ii.

Page 257. *Sand Hills of the Nagow Wudjoo.*

A description of the *Grand Sable,* or great sand-dunes of Lake Superior, is given in Foster and Whitney's "Report on the Geology of the Lake Superior Land District," Part II., p. 131.

"The Grand Sable possesses a scenic interest little inferior to that of the Pictured Rocks. The explorer passes abruptly from a coast of consolidated sand to one of loose materials; and although in the one case the cliffs are less precipitous, yet in the other they attain a higher altitude. He sees before him a long reach of coast, resembling a vast sand-bank, more than three hundred and fifty feet in height, without a trace of vegetation. Ascending to the top, rounded hillocks of blown sand are observed, with occasional clumps of trees, standing out like oases in the desert."

Page 258. *Onaway! Awake, beloved!*

The original of this song may be found in "Littell's Living Age," vol. xxv., p. 45.

Page 259. *Or the Red Swan floating, flying.*

The fanciful tradition of the Red Swan may be found in Schoolcraft's "Algic Researches," vol. ii., p. 9. Three brothers were hunting on a wager to see who would bring home the first game.

"They were to shoot no other animal," so the legend says, "but such as each was in the habit of killing. They set out different ways; Odjibwa, the youngest, had not gone far before he saw a bear, an animal he was not to kill, by the agreement. He followed him close, and drove an arrow through him, which brought him to the ground. Although contrary to the bet, he immediately commenced skinning him, when suddenly something red tinged all the air around him. He rubbed his eyes, thinking he was perhaps deceived; but without effect, for the red hue continued. At length he heard a strange noise at a distance. It first appeared like a human voice, but after following the sound for some distance, he reached the shores of a lake, and soon saw the object he was looking for. At a distance out in the lake sat a most beautiful Red Swan, whose plumage glittered in the sun, and who would now and then make the same noise he had heard. He was within long bow-shot, and, pulling the arrow from the bowstring up to his ear, took deliberate aim and shot. The arrow took no effect; and he shot and shot again till his quiver was empty. Still the swan remained, moving round and round, stretching its long neck and dipping its bill into the water, as if heedless of the arrows shot at it. Odjibwa ran home and got all his own and his brothers' arrows, and shot them all away. He then stood and gazed at the beautiful bird. While standing, he remembered his brothers' saying that in their deceased father's medicine-sack were three magic arrows. Off he started, his anxiety to kill the swan overcoming all scruples. At any other time, he would have deemed it sacrilege to open his father's medicine-sack; but now he hastily seized the three arrows and ran back, leaving the other contents of the sack scattered over the lodge. The swan was still there. He shot the first arrow with great precision, and came very near to it. The second came still closer; as he took the last arrow, he felt his arm firmer, and, drawing it up with vigor, saw it pass through the neck of the swan a little above the breast. Still it did not prevent the bird from flying off, which it did, however, at first slowly, flapping its wings and rising gradually into the air, and then flying off toward the sinking of the sun." — Pages 10–12.

Page 263.   *When I think of my beloved.*

The original of this song may be found in "Oneóta," p. 15.

Page 264.   *Sing the mysteries of Mondamin.*

The Indians hold the maize, or Indian corn, in great veneration. "They esteem it so important and divine a grain," says Schoolcraft, "that their story-tellers invented various tales, in which this idea is symbolized under the form of a special gift from the Great Spirit. The Odjibwa-Algonquins, who call it Mon-da-min, that is, this Spirit's grain or berry, have a pretty story of the kind, in which the stalk in full

tassel is represented as descending from the sky, under the guise of a handsome youth, in answer to the prayers of a young man at his fast of virility, or coming to manhood.

"It is well known that corn-planting and corn-gathering, at least among all the still *uncolonized* tribes, are left entirely to the females and children, and a few superannuated old men. It is not generally known, perhaps, that this labor is not compulsory, and that it is assumed by the females as a just equivalent, in their view, for the onerous and continuous labor of the other sex, in providing meats, and skins for clothing, by the chase, and in defending their villages against their enemies, and keeping intruders off their territories. A good Indian housewife deems this a part of her prerogative, and prides herself to have a store of corn to exercise her hospitality, or duly honor her husband's hospitality in the entertainment of the lodge guests." — *Oneóta*, p. 82.

Page 264.   *Thus the fields shall be more fruitful.*

"A singular proof of this belief, in both sexes, of the mysterious influence of the steps of a woman on the vegetable and insect creation, is found in an ancient custom, which was related to me, respecting corn-planting. It was the practice of the hunter's wife, when the field of corn had been planted, to choose the first dark or overclouded evening to perform a secret circuit, *sans habillement*, around the field. For this purpose she slipped out of the lodge in the evening, unobserved, to some obscure nook, where she completely disrobed. Then, taking her matchecota, or principal garment, in one hand, she dragged it around the field. This was thought to insure a prolific crop, and to prevent the assaults of insects and worms upon the grain. It was supposed they could not creep over the charmed line." — *Oneóta*, p. 83.

Page 266.   *With his prisoner-string he bound him.*

"These cords," says Mr. Tanner, "are made of the bark of the elm tree, by boiling and then immersing it in cold water. . . . . The leader of a war party commonly carries several fastened about his waist, and if, in the course of the fight, any one of his young men takes a prisoner, it is his duty to bring him immediately to the chief, to be tied, and the latter is responsible for his safe keeping." — *Narrative of Captivity and Adventures*, p. 412.

Page 267.

Wagemin, the thief of cornfields,
Paimosaid, who steals the maize-ear.

"If one of the young female huskers finds a *red* ear of corn, it is typical of a brave admirer, and is regarded as a fitting present to some young warrior. But if the ear be *crooked*, and tapering to a point, no matter what color, the whole circle is set in a roar, and *wa-ge-min* is the word shouted aloud. It is the symbol of a thief in the cornfield. It is considered as the image of an old man stooping as he enters the lot. Had the chisel of Praxiteles been employed to produce this image, it could not more vividly bring to the minds of the merry group the idea of a pilferer of their favorite mondámin. . . . .

"The literal meaning of the term is, a mass, or crooked ear of grain; but the ear of corn so called is a conventional type of a little old man pilfering ears of corn in a cornfield. It is in this manner that a single word or term, in these curious languages, becomes the fruitful parent of many ideas. And we can thus perceive why it is that the word *wagemin* is alone competent to excite merriment in the husking circle.

"This term is taken as a basis of the cereal chorus, or corn song, as sung by the Northern Algonquin tribes. It is coupled with the phrase *Paimosaid*, — a permutative form of the Indian substantive, made from the verb *pim-o-sa*, to walk. Its literal meaning is, *he who walks*, or *the walker*; but the ideas conveyed by it are, he who walks by night to pilfer corn. It offers, therefore, a kind of parallelism in expression to the preceding term." — *Oneóta*, p. 254.

Page 273. *Pugasaing, with thirteen pieces.*

This Game of the Bowl is the principal game of hazard among the Northern tribes of Indians. Mr. Schoolcraft gives a particular account of it in "Oneóta," p. 85." "This game," he says, "is very fascinating to some portions of the Indians. They stake at it their ornaments, weapons, clothing, canoes, horses, everything in fact they possess; and have been known, it is said, to set up their wives and children, and even to forfeit their own liberty. Of such desperate stakes I have seen no examples, nor do I think the game itself in common use. It is rather confined to certain persons, who hold the relative rank of gamblers in Indian society, — men who are not noted as hunters or warriors, or steady providers for their families. Among these are persons who bear the term of *Ienadizze-wug*, that is, wanderers about the country, braggadocios, or fops. It can hardly be classed with the popular games of amusement, by which skill and dexterity are acquired. I have generally found the chiefs and graver men of the tribes, who encouraged the young men to play ball, and are sure to be present at the customary sports, to witness, and sanction, and applaud them, speak lightly and disparagingly of this game of hazard. Yet it cannot be denied that some of the chiefs, distinguished in war and the chase, at the West, can be referred to as lending their example to its fascinating power."

See also his "History, Conditions, and Prospects of the Indian Tribes," Part II., p. 72.

Page 280. *To the Pictured Rocks of sandstone.*

The reader will find a long description of the Pictured Rocks in Foster and Whitney's "Report on the Geology of the Lake Superior Land District," Part II., p. 124. From this I make the following extract: —

"The Pictured Rocks may be described, in general terms, as a series of sandstone bluffs extending along the shore of Lake Superior for about five miles, and rising, in most places, vertically from the water, without any beach at the base, to a height varying from fifty to nearly two hundred feet. Were they simply a line of cliffs, they might not, so far as relates to height or extent, be worthy of a rank among great natural curiosities, although such an assemblage of rocky strata, washed by the waves of the great lake, would not, under any circumstances, be destitute of grandeur. To the voyager, coasting along their base in his frail canoe, they would, at all times, be an object of dread; the recoil of the surf, the rock-bound coast, affording for miles no place of refuge, — the lowering sky, the rising wind, — all these would excite his apprehension, and induce him to ply a vigorous oar until the dreaded wall was passed. But in the Pictured Rocks there are two features which communicate to the scenery a wonderful and almost unique character. These are, first, the curious manner in which the cliffs have been excavated and worn away by the action of the lake, which, for centuries, has dashed an ocean-like surf against their base; and, second the equally curious manner in which large portions of the surface have been colored by bands of brilliant hues.

"It is from the latter circumstance that the name, by which these cliffs are known to the American traveller, is derived; while that applied to them by the French voyageurs ('Les Portails') is derived from the former, and by far the most striking peculiarity.

"The term *Pictured Rocks* has been in use for a great length of time; but when it was first applied, we have been unable to discover. It would seem that the first travellers were more impressed with the novel and striking distribution of colors on the surface than with the astonishing variety of form into which the cliffs themselves have been worn. . . . .

"Our voyageurs had many legends to relate of the pranks of the *Menni-bojou* in these caverns, and, in answer to our inquiries, seemed disposed to fabricate stories, without end, of the achievements of this Indian deity."

Page 291. *Toward the sun his hands were lifted.*

In this manner, and with such salutations, was

Father Marquette received by the Illinois. See his "Voyages et Découvertes," Section V.

Page 333.

> *That of our vices we can frame*
> *A ladder.*

The words of St. Augustine are, "De vitiis nostris scalam nobis facimus, si vitia ipsa calcamus."

Sermon III., *De Ascensione.*

Page 334. *The Phantom Ship.*

A detailed account of this "apparition of a Ship in the Air" is given by Cotton Mather in his "Magnalia Christi," Book I., ch. 6. It is contained in a letter from the Rev. James Pierpont, Pastor of New Haven. To this account Mather adds these words : —

"Reader, there being yet living so many credible gentlemen that were eyewitnesses of this wonderful thing, I venture to publish it for a thing as undoubted as 't is wonderful."

Page 338. *And the Emperor but a Macho.*

Macho, in Spanish, signifies a mule. *Golondrina* is the feminine form of *Golondrino*, a swallow, and also a cant name for a deserter.

Page 341. *Oliver Basselin.*

Oliver Basselin, the "*Père joyeux du Vaudeville*," flourished in the fifteenth century, and gave to his convivial songs the name of his native valleys, in which he sang them, Vaux-de-Vire. This name was afterwards corrupted into the modern *Vaudeville.*

Page 342. *Victor Galbraith.*

This poem is founded on fact. Victor Galbraith was a bugler in a company of volunteer cavalry, and was shot in Mexico for some breach of discipline. It is a common superstition among soldiers, that no balls will kill them unless their names are written on them. The old proverb says, "Every bullet has its billet."

Page 343. *I remember the sea-fight far away.*

This was the engagement between the Enterprise and Boxer, off the harbor of Portland, in which both captains were slain. They were buried side by side, in the cemetery on Mountjoy.

Page 347. *Santa Filomena.*

"At Pisa the church of San Francisco contains a chapel dedicated lately to Santa Filomena; over the altar is a picture, by Sabatelli, representing the Saint as a beautiful, nymph-like figure, floating down from heaven, attended by two angels bearing the lily, palm, and javelin, and beneath, in the foreground, the sick and maimed, who are healed by her intercession." — MRS. JAMESON, *Sacred and Legendary Art*, ii., 298.

Page 585. THE GOLDEN LEGEND. The old *Legenda Aurea*, or Golden Legend, was originally written in Latin, in the thirteenth century, by Jacobus de Voragine, a Dominican friar, who afterwards became Archbishop of Genoa, and died in 1292.

He called his book simply "Legends of the Saints." The epithet of Golden was given it by his admirers; for, as Wynkin de Worde says, "Like as passeth gold in value all other metals, so this Legend exceedeth all other books." But Edward Leigh, in much distress of mind, calls it "a book written by a man of a leaden heart for the basenesse of the errours, that are without wit or reason, and of a brazen forehead, for his impudent boldnesse in reporting things so fabulous and incredible."

This work, the great text-book of the legendary lore of the Middle Ages, was translated into French in the fourteenth century by Jean de Vignay, and in the fifteenth into English by William Caxton. It has lately been made more accessible by a new French translation: "La Legende Dorée, traduite du Latin, par M. G. B." Paris, 1850. There is a copy of the original, with the "Gesta Longobardorum" appended, in the Harvard College Library, Cambridge, printed at Strasburg, 1496. The title-page is wanting; and the volume begins with the *Tabula Legendorum.*

I have called this poem the Golden Legend, because the story upon which it is founded seems to me to surpass all other legends in beauty and significance. It exhibits, amid the corruptions of the Middle Ages, the virtue of disinterestedness and self-sacrifice, and the power of Faith, Hope, and Charity, sufficient for all the exigencies of life and death. The story is told, and perhaps invented, by Hartmann von der Aue, a Minnesinger of the twelfth century. The original may be found in Mailáth's "Altdeutsche Gedichte," with a modern German version. There is another in Marbach's "Volksbücher," No. 32.

Page 585.

> *For these bells have been anointed,*
> *And baptized with holy water!*

The consecration and baptism of bells is one of the most curious ceremonies of the Church in the Middle Ages. The Council of Cologne ordained as follows : —

"Let the bells be blessed, as the trumpets of the Church militant, by which the people are assembled to hear the word of God; the clergy to announce his mercy by day, and his truth in their nocturnal vigils: that by their sound the faithful may be invited to prayers, and that the spirit of devotion in them may be increased. The fathers have also maintained that demons, affrighted by the sound of bells calling Christians to prayers, would flee away; and when they fled, the persons of the faithful would be secure: that the destruction of lightnings and whirlwinds would be averted, and the spirits of the storm defeated." — *Edinburgh Encyclopædia*, Art. "Bells."

See also Scheible's " Kloster," vi., 776.

Page 603. *It is the malediction of Eve!*

"Nec esses plus quam femina, quæ nunc etiam viros transcendis, et quæ maledictionem Evæ in benedictionem vertisti Mariæ." — *Epistola Abælardi Heloissæ.*

Page 615. *To come back to my text!*

In giving this sermon of Friar Cuthbert as a specimen of the *Risus Paschales*, or street-preaching of the monks at Easter, I have exaggerated nothing. This very anecdote, offensive as it is, comes from a discourse of Father Barletta, a Dominican friar of the fifteenth century, whose fame as a popular preacher was so great that it gave rise to the proverb, —

Nescit predicare
Qui nescit Barlettare.

"Among the abuses introduced in this century," says Tiraboschi, " was that of exciting from the pulpit the laughter of the hearers; as if that were the same thing as converting them. We have examples of this, not only in Italy, but also in France, where the sermons of Menot and Maillard, and of others, who would make a better appearance on the stage than in the pulpit, are still celebrated for such follies."

If the reader is curious to see how far the freedom of speech was carried in these popular sermons, he is referred to Scheible's " Kloster," vol. i., where he will find extracts from Abraham a Sancta Clara, Sebastian Frank, and others; and in particular an anonymous discourse called " Der Gräuel der Verwüstung," The Abomination of Desolation, preached at Ottakring, a village west of Vienna, November 25, 1782, in which the license of language is carried to its utmost limit.

See also " Prédicatoriana, ou Révélations singulières et amusantes sur les Prédicateurs; par G. P. Philomneste." (Menin.) This work contains extract from the popular sermons of St. Vincent Ferrier, Barletta, Menot, Maillard, Marini, Raulin, Valladier, De Besse, Camus, Père André, Bening, and the most eloquent of all, Jacques Brydaine.

My authority for the spiritual interpretation of bell-ringing, which follows, is Durandus, " Ration Divin. Offic.," Lib. I., cap. 4.

Page 618. THE NATIVITY: a Miracle-Play.

A singular chapter in the history of the Middle Ages is that which gives account of the early Christian Drama, the Mysteries, Moralities, and Miracle-Plays, which were at first performed in churches, and afterwards in the streets, on fixed or movable stages. For the most part, the Mysteries were founded on the historic portions of the Old and New Testaments, and the Miracle-Plays on the lives of Saints; a distinction not always observed, however, for in Mr. Wright's " Early Mysteries and other Latin Poems of the Twelfth and Thirteenth Centuries," the Resurrection of Lazarus is called a Miracle, and not a Mystery. The Moralities were plays in which the Virtues and Vices were personified.

The earliest religious play which has been preserved is the " Christos Paschon " of Gregory Nazianzen, written in Greek, in the fourth century. Next to this come the remarkable Latin plays of Roswitha, the Nun of Gandersheim, in the tenth century, which, though crude and wanting in artistic construction, are marked by a good deal of dramatic power and interest. A handsome edition of these plays, with a French translation, has been lately published, entitled " Théâtre de Rotsvitha, Religieuse allemande du Xe Siècle. Par Charles Magnin." Paris, 1845.

The most important collections of English Mysteries and Miracle-Plays are those known as the Townley, the Chester, and the Coventry Plays. The first of these collections has been published by the Surtees Society, and the other two by the Shakespeare Society. In his Introduction to the Coventry Mysteries, the editor, Mr. Halliwell, quotes the following passage from Dugdale's " Antiquities of Warwickshire " : —

" Before the suppression of the monasteries, this city was very famous for the pageants, that were played therein, upon Corpus-Christi day; which, occasioning very great confluence of people thither, from far and near, was of no small benefit thereto; which pageants being acted with mighty state and reverence by the friars of this house, had theaters for the severall scenes, very large and high, placed upon wheels, and drawn to all the eminent parts of the city, for the better advantage of spectators : and contain'd the story of the New Testament, composed into old English Rithme, as appeareth by an ancient MS. intituled *Ludus Corporis Christi*, or *Ludus Conventriæ.* I have been told by some old people, who in their younger years were eyewitnesses of these pageants so acted, that the yearly confluence of people to see that shew was extraordinary great, and yielded no small advantage to this city."

The representation of religious plays has not yet been wholly discontinued by the Roman Church. At Ober-Ammergau, in the Tyrol, a grand spectacle of this kind is exhibited once in ten years. A very graphic description of that which took place in the year 1850 is given by Miss Anna Mary Howitt, in her " Art-Student in Munich," vol. i., chap. 4. She says : —

" We had come expecting to feel our souls revolt

at so material a representation of Christ, as any representation of him we naturally imagined must be in a peasant's Miracle-Play. Yet so far, strange to confess, neither horror, disgust, nor contempt was excited in our minds. Such an earnest solemnity and simplicity breathed throughout the whole of the performance, that to me, at least, anything like anger, or a perception of the ludicrous, would have seemed more irreverent on my part than was this simple, childlike rendering of the sublime Christian tragedy. We felt at times as though the figures of Cimabue's, Giotto's, and Perugino's pictures had become animated, and were moving before us; there was the same simple arrangement and brilliant color of drapery, — the same earnest, quiet dignity about the heads, whilst the entire absence of all theatrical effect wonderfully increased the illusion. There were scenes and groups so extraordinarily like the early Italian pictures, that you could have declared they were the works of Giotto and Perugino, and not living men and women, had not the figures moved and spoken, and the breeze stirred their richly colored drapery, and the sun cast long, moving shadows behind them on the stage. These effects of sunshine and shadow, and of drapery fluttered by the wind, were very striking and beautiful; one could imagine how the Greeks must have availed themselves of such striking effects in their theatres open to the sky."

Mr. Bayard Taylor, in his "Eldorado," gives a description of a Mystery he saw performed at San Lionel, in Mexico. See vol. ii., chap. 11.

" Against the wing-wall of the Hacienda del Mayo, which occupied one end of the plaza, was raised a platform, on which stood a table covered with scarlet cloth. A rude bower of cane-leaves, on one end of the platform, represented the manger of Bethlehem; while a cord, stretched from its top across the plaza to a hole in the front of the church, bore a large tinsel star, suspended by a hole in its centre. There was quite a crowd in the plaza, and very soon a procession appeared, coming up from the lower part of the village. The three kings took the lead; the Virgin, mounted on an ass that gloried in a gilded saddle and rose-besprinkled mane and tail, followed them, led by the angel; and several women, with curious masks of paper, brought up the rear. Two characters of the harlequin sort — one with a dog's head on his shoulders, and the other a bald-headed friar, with a huge hat hanging on his back — played all sorts of antics for the diversion of the crowd. After making the circuit of the plaza, the Virgin was taken to the platform, and entered the manger. King Herod took his seat at the scarlet table, with an attendant in blue coat and red sash, whom I took to be

his Prime Minister. The three kings remained on their horses in front of the church; but between them and the platform, under the string on which the star was to slide, walked two men in long white robes and blue hoods, with parchment folios in their hands. These were the Wise Men of the East, as one might readily know from their solemn air, and the mysterious glances which they cast towards all quarters of the heavens.

" In a little while, a company of women on the platform, concealed behind a curtain, sang an angelic chorus to the tune of ' O pescator dell'onda.' At the proper moment, the Magi turned towards the platform, followed by the star, to which a string was conveniently attached, that it might be slid along the line. The three kings followed the star till it reached the manger, when they dismounted, and inquired for the sovereign whom it had led them to visit. They were invited upon the platform, and introduced to Herod, as the only king; this did not seem to satisfy them, and, after some conversation, they retired. By this time the star had receded to the other end of the line, and commenced moving forward again, they following. The angel called them into the manger, where, upon their knees, they were shown a small wooden box, supposed to contain the sacred infant; they then retired, and the star brought them back no more. After this departure, King Herod declared himself greatly confused by what he had witnessed, and was very much afraid this newly found king would weaken his power. Upon consultation with his Prime Minister, the Massacre of the Innocents was decided upon, as the only means of security.

" The angel, on hearing this, gave warning to the Virgin, who quickly got down from the platform, mounted her bespangled donkey, and hurried off. Herod's Prime Minister directed all the children to be handed up for execution. A boy, in a ragged sarape, was caught and thrust forward; the Minister took him by the heels in spite of his kicking, and held his head on the table. The little brother and sister of the boy, thinking he was really to be decapitated, yelled at the top of their voices, in an agony of terror, which threw the crowd into a roar of laughter. King Herod brought down his sword with a whack on the table, and the Prime Minister, dipping his brush into a pot of white paint which stood before him, made a flaring cross on the boy's face. Several other boys were caught and served likewise; and finally the two harlequins, whose kicks and struggles nearly shook down the platform. The procession then went off up the hill, followed by the whole population of the village. All the evening there were fandangoes in the méson, bonfires and rockets on the plaza, ringing of bells, and high mass in the church, with the accompaniment of two guitars, tinkling to lively polkas."

In 1852 there was a representation of this kind by Germans in Boston: and I have now before me the copy of a play-bill, announcing the performance, on June 10, 1852, in Cincinnati, of the "Great Biblico-Historical Drama, the Life of Jesus Christ," with the characters and the names of the performers.

Page 629. *The Scriptorium.*

A most interesting volume might be written on the Calligraphers and Chrysographers, the transcribers and illuminators of manuscripts in the Middle Ages. These men were for the most part monks, who labored, sometimes for pleasure and sometimes for penance, in multiplying copies of the classics and the Scriptures.

"Of all bodily labors which are proper for us," says Cassiodorus, the old Calabrian monk, "that of copying books has always been more to my taste than any other. The more so, as in this exercise the mind is instructed by the reading of the Holy Scriptures, and it is a kind of homily to the others, whom these books may reach. It is preaching with the hand, by converting the fingers into tongues; it is publishing to men in silence the words of salvation; in fine, it is fighting against the demon with pen and ink. As many words as a transcriber writes, so many wounds the demon receives. In a word, a recluse, seated in his chair to copy books, travels into different provinces without moving from the spot, and the labor of his hands is felt even where he is not."

Nearly every monastery was provided with its Scriptorium. Nicolas de Clairvaux, St. Bernard's secretary, in one of his letters describes his cell, which he calls Scriptoriolum, where he copied books. And Mabillon, in his "Études Monastiques," says that in his time were still to be seen at Citeaux "many of those little cells, where the transcribers and bookbinders worked."

Silvestre's "Paléographie Universelle" contains a vast number of fac-similes of the most beautiful illuminated manuscripts of all ages and all countries; and Montfaucon in his "Palæographia Græca" gives the names of over three hundred calligraphers. He also gives an account of the books they copied, and the colophons with which, as with a satisfactory flourish of the pen, they closed their long-continued labors. Many of these are very curious; expressing joy, humility, remorse; entreating the reader's prayers and pardon for the writer's sins; and sometimes pronouncing a malediction on any one who should steal the book. A few of these I subjoin: —

"As pilgrims rejoice, beholding their native land, so are transcribers made glad, beholding the end of a book."

"Sweet is it to write the end of any book."

"Ye who read, pray for me, who have written this book, the humble and sinful Theodulus."

"As many therefore as shall read this book, pardon me, I beseech you, if aught I have erred in accent acute and grave, in apostrophe, in breathing soft or aspirate; and may God save you all! Amen."

"If anything is well, praise the transcriber; if ill, pardon his unskilfulness."

"Ye who read, pray for me, the most sinful of all men, for the Lord's sake."

"The hand that has written this book shall decay, alas! and become dust, and go down to the grave, the corrupter of all bodies. But all ye who are of the portion of Christ, pray that I may obtain the pardon of my sins. Again and again I beseech you with tears, brothers and fathers, accept my miserable supplication, O holy choir! I am called John, woe is me! I am called Hiereus, or Sacerdos, in name only, not in unction."

"Whoever shall carry away this book, without permission of the Pope, may he incur the malediction of the Holy Trinity, of the Holy Mother of God, of Saint John the Baptist, of the one hundred and eighteen holy Nicene Fathers, and of all the Saints; the fate of Sodom and Gomorrah; and the halter of Judas! Anathema, amen."

"Keep safe, O Trinity, Father, Son, and Holy Ghost, my three fingers, with which I have written this book."

"Mathusalas Machir transcribed this divinest book in toil, infirmity, and dangers many."

"Bacchius Barbardorius and Michael Sophianus wrote this book in sport and laughter, being the guests of their noble and common friend Vincentius Pinellus, and Petrus Nunnius, a most learned man."

This last colophon Montfaucon does not suffer to pass without reproof. "Other calligraphers," he remarks, "demand only the prayers of their readers, and the pardon of their sins; but these glory in their wantonness."

Page 635. *Drink down to your peg!*

One of the canons of Archbishop Anselm, promulgated at the beginning of the twelfth century, ordains "that priests go not to drinking-bouts, nor drink to pegs." In the times of the hard-drinking Danes, King Edgar ordained that "pins or nails should be fastened into the drinking-cups or horns at stated distances, and whosoever should drink beyond those marks at one draught should be obnoxious to a severe punishment."

Sharpe, in his "History of the Kings of England,"

says : " Our ancestors were formerly famous for com-potation ; their liquor was ale, and one method of amusing themselves in this way was with the peg-tankard. I had lately one of them in my hand. It had on the inside a row of eight pins, one above another, from top to bottom. It held two quarts, and was a noble piece of plate, so that there was a gill of ale, half a pint Winchester measure, between each peg. The law was, that every person that drank was to empty the space between pin and pin, so that the pins were so many measures to make the company all drink alike, and to swallow the same quantity of liquor. This was a pretty sure method of making all the company drunk, especially if it be considered that the rule was, that whoever drank short of his pin, or beyond it, was obliged to drink again, and even as deep as to the next pin."

Page 636. *The convent of St. Gildas de Rhuys.*

Abelard, in a letter to his friend Philintus, gives a sad picture of this monastery. " I live," he says, " in a barbarous country, the language of which I do not understand ; I have no conversation but with the rudest people. my walks are on the inaccessible shore of a sea, which is perpetually stormy. my monks are only known by their dissoluteness, and liv-ing without any rule or order. could you see the abby, Philintus, you would not call it one. the doors and walls are without any ornament, except the heads of wild boars and hinds feet, which are nailed up against them, and the hides of frightful animals. the cells are hung with the skins of deer. the monks have not so much as a bell to wake them, the cocks and dogs supply that defect. in short, they pass their whole days in hunting ; would to heaven that were their greatest fault ! or that their pleasure terminated there ! I endeavor in vain to recall them to their duty ; they all combine against me, and I only ex-pose myself to continual vexations and dangers. I imagine I see every moment a naked sword hang over my head. sometimes they surround me, and load me with infinite abuses ; sometimes they abandon me, and I am left alone to my own tormenting thoughts. I make it my endeavor to merit by my sufferings, and to appease an angry God. sometimes I grieve for the loss of the house of the Paraclete, and wish to see it again. ah Philintus, does not the love of Heloise still burn in my heart ? I have not yet triumphed over that unhappy passion. in the midst of my retirement I sigh, I weep, I pine, I speak the dear name Heloise, and am pleased to hear the sound." — *Letters of the Celebrated Abelard and Heloise. Translated by Mr. John Hughes.* Glasgow, 1751.

Page 648. *Were it not for my magic garters and staff.*

The method of making the Magic Garters and the Magic Staff is thus laid down in " Les Secrets Mer-veilleux du Petit Albert," a French translation of " Alberti Parvi Lucii Libellus de Mirabilibus Naturæ Arcanis " : —

" Gather some of the herb called motherwort, when the sun is entering the first degree of the sign of Capricorn ; let it dry a little in the shade, and make some garters of the skin of a young hare ; that is to say, having cut the skin of the hare into strips two inches wide, double them, sew the before-men-tioned herb between, and wear them on your legs. No horse can long keep up with a man on foot, who is furnished with these garters." — Page 128.

" Gather, on the morrow of All-Saints, a strong branch of willow, of which you will make a staff, fashioned to your liking. Hollow it out, by remov-ing the pith from within, after having furnished the lower end with an iron ferule. Put into the bottom of the staff the two eyes of a young wolf, the tongue and heart of a dog, three green lizards, and the hearts of three swallows. These must all be dried in the sun, between two papers, having been first sprinkled with finely pulverized saltpetre. Besides all these, put into the staff seven leaves of vervain, gathered on the eve of St. John the Baptist, with a stone of divers colors, which you will find in the nest of the lapwing, and stop the end of the staff with a pomel of box, or of any other material you please, and be as-sured that this staff will guarantee you from the perils and mishaps which too often befall travellers, either from robbers, wild beasts, mad dogs, or ven-omous animals. It will also procure you the good-will of those with whom you lodge." — Page 130.

Page 652. *Saint Elmo's stars.*

So the Italian sailors call the phosphorescent gleams that sometimes play about the masts and rig-ging of ships.

Page 653. *The School of Salerno.*

For a history of the celebrated schools of Salerno and Monte-Cassino, the reader is referred to Sir Alexander Croke's Introduction to the " Regimen Sanitatis Salernitanum ; " and to Kurt Sprengel's " Geschichte der Arzneikunde," i. 463, or Jourdan's French translation of it, " Histoire de la Medecine," ii. 354.

INDEX

[The titles in small capital letters are those of the principal divisions of the work, those in lower-case are single poems, or the sub-divisions of long poems.]

The arrangement of this work and the drawing and engraving have been under the supervision of
A V. S. ANTHONY.

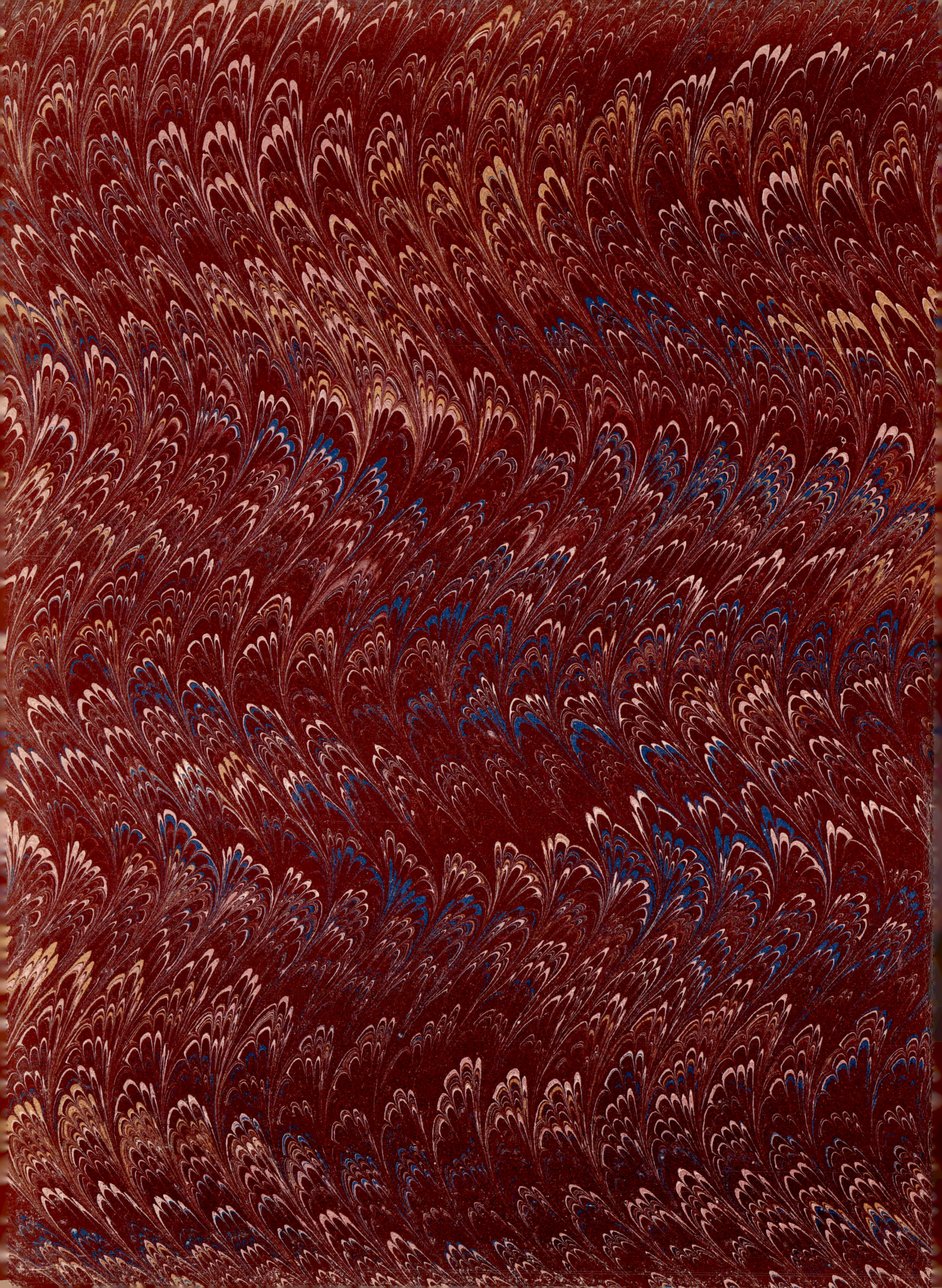